Take a Tip *from the*
Experts *who praise*
## SPORTS BETTING FOR WINNERS

"Miech gives us the skinny on a billion-dollar business, particularly pertinent now that Vegas is no longer a forbidden city for pro sports but rather welcomed by teams and leagues with open arms (and wallets). I'll lay you 9-to-5 you'll feel richer for reading *Sports Betting for Winners*."
—**Mike Downey,** award-winning sports columnist, *Chicago Tribune* and *Los Angeles Times*

"Las Vegas sports bettors, like Las Vegas magicians, aren't supposed to reveal their secrets. But Miech has managed a heist worthy of his adopted hometown. He's broken into the vault, sneaked off with the goods, and is eager to share the spoils. The result is this entertaining, informative, anecdote-filled book."
—**Steve Rushin,** author of *Sting-Ray Afternoons* and *Nights in White Castle*

"Miech has outdone himself with this poignant behind-the-curtains revelation of a world of parlays and money-line wagers, of mob-ruled games, and characters named Lem and Lefty. The brilliant storyteller walks us through the fascinating world of numbers and tips, of Pros and Joes, of how those on both sides of a betting counter try and massacre each other. Miech weaves insight from some of the world's most prominent names in sports betting into a historic, entertaining, and informative journey."
—**Ed Graney,** sportswriter,
*Las Vegas Review-Journal*

## Also by Rob Miech

*Phenom: The Making of Bryce Harper*

*The Last Natural: Bryce Harper's
Big Gamble in Sin City and
the Greatest Amateur Season Ever*

*Eleventh Heaven: Ed O'Bannon and the 1995 National
Basketball Champion UCLA Bruins*

*Of Cowards and True Men: Irrepressible, Unabashed Boxing
Trainer Kenny Adams and a Bittersweet Science*

# SPORTS BETTING
## ——— for ———
# WINNERS

### TIPS AND TALES FROM THE
### NEW WORLD OF SPORTS BETTING

## ROB MIECH

CITADEL PRESS
Kensington Publishing Corp.
www.kensingtonbooks.com

CITADEL PRESS BOOKS are published by

Kensington Publishing Corp.
119 West 40th Street
New York, NY 10018

All Kensington titles, imprints, and distributed lines are available at special quantity discounts for bulk purchases for sales promotions, premiums, fund-raising, educational, or institutional use.

Special book excerpts or customized printings can also be created to fit specific needs. For details, write or phone the office of the Kensington sales manager: Kensington Publishing Corp., 119 West 40th Street, New York, NY 10018, attn: Sales Department; phone 1-800-221-2647.

ISBN-13: 978-0-8065-4030-6
ISBN-10: 0-8065-4030-3

First Citadel trade paperback printing: November 2019

10 9 8 7 6 5 4 3 2

Printed in the United States of America


Electronic edition:

ISBN-13: 978-0-8065-4031-3 (e-book)
ISBN-10: 0-8065-4031-1 (e-book)

*For Big Bro, Brockster,*
*& the Cal Delta lads*

# CONTENTS

# AUTHOR'S NOTE

This project is the culmination of hundreds of interview and correspondence hours, noted in the present-tense "says." Information and elements culled from widespread research and the review of many books, articles, and related material are noted via the past-tense "said," or the like. Any and all errors are mine, and mine alone.

The subject matter is of an extremely fluid nature: the vagaries of attempting to select winners, against an expert line, of athletic contests. What worked for one bettor yesterday will not exactly be duplicated today, or tomorrow, and should not be construed with certainty. Sure things do not exist, no matter the aggressive or persistent bark of that blow-hard tout. Mind the advice of Jimmy Vaccaro, the veteran of the Las Vegas gambling scene, who says, "You never, *ever* know when it comes to athletes and sports." Truer words have never been spoken regarding the industry.

Should anyone even slightly question what they're doing, or why they're doing it, and seek help, the National Council on Problem Gambling provides a Helpline—at 1 (800) 522-4700. Other resources, like Gamblers Anonymous, have many branches and can be found online.

# Introduction

LEGALIZED SPORTS GAMBLING is expanding into fresh nooks of the U.S., becoming more mainstream by the day, since a federal bill that had prevented each state from deciding its own sports-betting fate was eliminated in May 2018. The art continues to be "dragged from the shadows, into the harsh light of respectability." That's how Graham Sharpe depicted the actions of William Hill, the blossoming bookmaker who zipped around Birmingham, England, on a battered motorbike to collect tuppence and tanner bets nearly one hundred years ago. That line, however, is more pertinent than ever today about the industry on this side of the pond.

Today, fans can make wagers—for far more than two or six pence—from inside a National Football League stadium, an act whose likelihood would have drawn guffaws not so long ago due to that league's rancor toward anything half hinting at gambling or Las Vegas. Now, that league is re-planting one of its franchises in Las Vegas, a city as synonymous with betting as Monte Carlo. In 2020, fans of the Las Vegas Raiders will be able to sit in a shiny new domed stadium and make in-game bets on the action taking place before their very eyes. As recently as the first few months of 2016, such a statement would have been ridiculed and dismissed by anyone of sound and rational mind.

Not now. Toward the end of 2018, NFL commissioner–mouthpiece Roger Goodell, who had never hidden his venom toward Las Vegas, was downright giddy as he hailed the city's many attractions and offerings in announcing that the 2020 NFL draft would be staged here. The Goodell Pirouette.

Another English bookshop was even trying to finagle title sponsorship of that new Las Vegas sporting palace, although a major southwest cable company appeared best poised to utilize the building as a billboard for ten or twenty years. With sports-betting taboos disintegrating daily, anything now seems possible, nothing off the table. In moves that many would have considered to be outlandish ideas as recently as when the calendar flipped to 2018, professional teams and leagues have cozied up to casinos and bookmakers as sponsorship partners. And in October 2018, a watershed Las Vegas television broadcast of a soccer match focused entirely on shifting odds supplied by William Hill, on whose current empire the sun never sets. The play on the pitch seemed secondary to the mobile action. The betting, and all of its angles, was the point of the revolutionary "BetCast."

"It shows you how much the USA has changed," says Nigel Seeley, a veteran England-based journalist connected to his country's gambling industry who was flown to Las Vegas to partake in that BetCast. "This is the kind of thing that will happen in the future in American sports, and not only with Las Vegas football teams. It could happen in New York. It could happen with the NFL. A whole channel could be devoted to BetCasts. Because, at the end of the day, sports betting is going to be massive over here."

At this writing, Rhode Island—and its exorbitant fifty-one per-cent tax that gets siphoned directly to the state—had become the eighth state to engage in the business of legalized sports wager-ing. Arkansas, New York, and Washington, D.C., were on deck, and Illinois, Maryland, Michigan, Missouri, South Dakota, and Virginia, among others, were in the hole, trying to figure it all out. *Forbes* estimates that more than thirty states will have sanctioned single-event sports betting by the early 2020s.

Punters, and their appetite for information and action, will feed each other, perhaps voraciously, with sports gambling's new-found liberation. *Sports Business Journal* took note, naming "the

American Sports Gambler" as its Person of the Year in its issue dated December 17, 2018. For one hundred years, it wrote, the U.S. sports industry had worked "relentlessly" to keep gambling at an "arm's length." Not anymore.

"For a lot of us working in this space, we've been laying the groundwork for this opportunity," says industry veteran Quinton Singleton, a couple of months into a post as chief operating officer of Bet.Works, which provides all facets of sports-book operations—technology, regulation, compliance, and risk-management—to entities, like tribal casinos, seeking to expand their business into this arena. "And now it's a whirlwind of activity moving faster than I would have expected."

This book will make some sense of that whirlwind, serving as a main course of that meal, an indispensable guide to deliver context and perspective, to clarify, educate, and entertain. And, hopefully, to win a tuppence or tanner. Tips and lessons will accompany opinions and anecdotes—laced with caveats and cautionary tales—from the country's gaming capital, where legalized sports wagering started, blossomed, and continues to flourish.

It will surprise some, for example, and shock others that a new sports book in an East Coast casino doesn't just pilfer odds from an offshore site in the Caribbean and transpose them onto its big board, as its own—it swipes those numbers from a resource in *Eastern Europe*. What's more, an official for that New Jersey company admitted that, when its action on games becomes too lopsided, it will "lay off" that liability at said shop in Sofia, Bulgaria.

"Which is insane!" says professional handicapper Tom Barton. "Admitting that they're using an offshore is beyond . . ." Barton does admit that the ubiquity of William Hill is impressive and a double-edged sword. "The name that everybody knows right now. What's funny is, in the handicapping community they're sort of hated; if you start winning, they pull the plug on you. They're so big, it doesn't matter to them."

Other insights from some of the industry's formidable figures—from casino owners Michael Gaughan and Derek Stevens, to veteran sports-book director Jay Kornegay, iconic gambler Lem Banker, and the right honorable and worldly Michael (Roxy) Roxborough, including a raft of handicappers, oddsmakers, and bettors, and the acclaimed broadcaster Brent Musburger—will shed light on sports gambling's many allures, intrigues, and pitfalls. Roxborough uncovered a fine angle that goes against the conventional wisdom of many professional bettors but has proven to be fertile, rare action that gives the player an edge.

Methods and tactics are as varied as the personalities seeking to profit from the venture. Some might clash. Redundancies and contradictions are inevitable. Remember, too, that past success does not guarantee future results. It's all offered up as a buffet menu, to be picked and plucked to accommodate circumstance, preference, and situation.

Lem Banker binged at the buffet, but even he required an occasional helping hand. He once needed the services of the notorious Frank (Lefty) Rosenthal to influence a Minneapolis bookie into paying Banker the thirty grand owed to him. Banker also reveals Rosenthal's escapades in the kitchen of a popular Chicago nightclub, possibly solving a notorious decades-old mystery involving the poisoning of the University of Oklahoma football team in 1959.

A Las Vegas resident since 1957 who has been barred from, among other joints, Jackie Gaughan's Union Plaza, the ninety-one-year-old Banker has some steadfast rules, like not chasing a bad bet with an immediate wager while frothing to get even, and passing on games rather than betting just to have action. Recent years have not been kind to him, troubling family issues bubbling quite publicly, but he retains pachyderm-like epidermis and a sharp sense of humor. And in my first meeting with him, he had just won all three NFL games on which he had wagered. Banker says, "God's in my corner."

After a long meeting at the other end of the city, way too long by the ever-shortening length of South Point owner Michael Gaughan's answers and the rows of lighted buttons on the base of his telephone (he was very eager to learn the up-to-the-minute house ledger), the son of Jackie Gaughan pauses, leans forward, our eyes lock, and he says. "The American public roots for the underdog but bets favorites. You can put that in your [book]."

The greatest intellectual challenge, Matt Youmans says of sports betting, is "in terms of trying to win, to come out ahead." An authoritative figure who speaks and writes about the games, teams, and odds for the Vegas Stats & Information Network (VSiN) satellite radio channel, his entire life had been on course for such a gig at that pioneering network.

"I mean, when you lose, it fucks with your head, right? You have to be able to win the mental game, not only with yourself but with the games you're betting. It's a great challenge, a constant challenge. I love the challenge of it. Obviously, sometimes you get so agitated you feel like, 'Why the fuck do I do this?' But it's in your blood. You're never going to quit."

Roxy Roxborough, who has accomplished the rare industry grand slam by having bet, made book, set odds, and participated in casino ownership, puts it succinctly. "If you spend your whole life in sports gambling, you are always having fun or never having fun. It is a fine line."

Now hailed as possibly the most successful sports bettor in the world, Tony (The Lizard) Bloom did not start out that way. He owns his boyhood-favorite Brighton & Hove Albion Football Club and is a world-class poker player, and his Starlizard company annually earns many millions of pounds, in information fees and wagers, on English football action in Asia. He began, however, when he was fifteen, betting in British shops with a fake ID that showed he was eighteen.

"Early on, I was a hopeless gambler, really," Bloom said in former England cricket captain Mike Atherton's book *Gambling* (2006). "I liked to think that I understood the form and had a strategy, but I was just guessing, really." More on the secretive Bloom later.

Sports betting is a burgeoning field whose noise, disinformation, and disingenuousness can be deafening, at best, daunting, at worst. Arrogance and ignorance abound in the business. A longtime national sports-broadcasting figure, who should have known better, since he purports to have once been so knee-deep in sports gambling, wonders aloud—on more than three hundred radio stations, coast-to-coast—about being able to bet on Nevada and Nevada–Las Vegas basketball and football games at Silver State sports books. In January of *2001* it became legal to wager on the Wolf Pack and Rebels. I run that snippet by professional handicapper Ted Sevransky, who writes, "It's only been seventeen and a half years!"

Only twenty-six years ago, three-term New Jersey senator Bill Bradley, the former Princeton University and New York Knicks basketball player, authored that federal decree restricting states from deciding the sports-gambling issue for themselves. He was agitated about the U.S. Supreme Court circular-filing his beloved bill. Unfortunate, he said in May 2018. "A ruling that had no basis in what sport really is." He talked about people having been able to bet on high-school games and summer-circuit, or travel-ball, hoops tournaments involving fourteen-year-olds.

That sounded fishy. I contacted Westgate Las Vegas SuperBook vice president Jay Kornegay, then, to confirm that neither he nor anyone under him—or anyone, by his reckoning, at a rival book in Las Vegas—had ever posted odds or point spreads on a high school game. Of course not, he said. So what gives when such fodder comes from someone like Bill Bradley, a supposed expert on the topic who, nonetheless, spews forth such fiction, with zero basis in reality?

Moreover, a few weeks after the demise of that bill, former major-league pitcher Al Leiter went before a state legislature subcommittee hearing in New Jersey and spoke about the possibility of a rookie pitcher, making minimum salary, being tempted to indulge a friend into betting half a million dollars on the first pitch of a game being called a ball or a strike. A nonsensical posit, since such a proposition wager would have a very low limit even if it were offered, which, in Las Vegas, it would never appear on any book's menu.

I followed up with Kornegay in his office.

"People write things that just aren't accurate," he says. "People that don't even know the business are speaking on behalf of the business, and they don't know anything about our business. They just heard from *somebody* that they could take five hundred thousand on the first pitch of a baseball game." He laughs. "It's like, 'What?' When they spend time with us, whether it's me or any of the respected operators in town, it's relieving for them because it isn't just the big Wild West desert out here.

"And I can tell you right now, none of that was high school sports. Okay? All right."

The proliferation of sports gambling has been inevitable because economic lures are irresistible. In the thirty-six states, including Nevada, that allow some form of commercial gambling or tribal-casino gaming, gross revenues topped seventy billion dollars, for the first time, in 2016.

Those new to sports betting seek a chunk of an illicit market tabbed to be worth approximately one hundred and fifty billion dollars; some say it's much higher, closer to half a trillion, while an Ohio State economist pegs it at about seventy billion dollars. Whatever the true figure, it is prodigious. That is the carrot enticing officials of states that do not have sports gambling as they struggle with budget deficits. One observer believes New Jersey, due to immense interest and ample disposable income in the heavily populated region, might soon surpass Nevada in handle.

In Nevada, a record $4.87 billion was wagered on sporting events in 2017, more than doubling the handle—or gross—from just seven years earlier. People always want more, iconic oddsmaker Jimmy Vaccaro famously said. The hold, or net revenue, was two hundred and forty-nine million dollars, representing an average of not even a million and a half for each of the state's hundred and ninety-two race and sports books. In 2018, the state's handle and hold, respectively, blossomed to $5.01 billion and $301 million.

Virgin sports-betting jurisdictions ogling those figures had best adjust their sights, at that per-shop net, out of which salaries and operating expenses are extracted. The South Point, for example, pays two hundred and fifty thousand dollars every two years for the right to show NFL games in its sports book. High taxes, surcharges, and fees will dissuade investment, bolstering illegal bookies with deep clientele lists and/or offshore entities.

On the consumer side, attempting to solve sports gambling's many riddles, the biases and irrationalities of the game behind the game is not—with respect to what Jimmy Vaccaro will say—such an easy endeavor. The South Point's humongous electronic board displaying all of its betting offerings, the sides and totals, first-half and five-inning lines, can be enough of a challenge to decipher. Misdiagnosing fluctuations in the numbers and undisciplined wagering can transform a Pro into a Joe in the whiff of a bat or drop of a ball, decimating a bankroll. This will serve as an anti-chump tutorial, from the nation's gambling capital.

Las Vegas.

Where the former three-term mayor and lawyer (and director emeritus of The Mob Museum) Oscar Goodman, who earned major stripes representing mafia figures like Lefty Rosenthal and Anthony (the Ant) Spilotro, admits to being a lifetime degenerate gambler, eager to wager on anything, anytime. He wrote that in his *Being Oscar* autobiography, and he knew that over the long haul he would not win. "I know that going in, but I still love to bet. Maybe I'll figure out a winning system; it's every gambler's hope."

Where former pro basketball player Jalen Rose throws the bones at the Palms while donning a white New Orleans Jazz uniform, MARAVICH on the back. Pete Rose, after an afternoon and evening on the periphery of the Palms race book, briefcase at his side, unwittingly inks, in the former N9NE restaurant, his autograph on the back of a Mandalay Bay sports-book drink coupon. It currently resides beside its face-up brother at the bottom of an eleven-by-fourteen glass frame, Charlie Hustle, frozen in black-and-white eternity, Superman-diving toward home plate.

Where a penultimate NFL gambling day evolves, from start to finish, sitting next to the actor James Carter Walker Jr. at the Stardust, capped in the final minute by everything that needed to unfold a certain way actually unfolding a certain way. Field goal made, field goal missed. A touchdown, a fumble. The wallet is ten times thicker. Better known as the actor-comedian Jimmie J.J. Walker, he never hears the signature *Dy-no-mite!* line that brought him sit-com fame in the seventies. At least, he never hears it from his left side.

Where a dining experience at the famous Piero's—onetime neighbor of Michael Gaughan's Royal Inn, which has royal significance in the city's sports-betting lore—includes overhearing a morose group of older gentlemen, a Last Supper tribute for the one reporting to prison the next morning, at a neighboring table. Steve Lawrence, having risen from his usual corner booth, appears grateful upon hearing that a fellow patron's favorite tune from Lawrence's vast songbook is "I Take It On Home," and that, hopefully, it's of some solace knowing Eydie, at that very moment, is singing with the angels.

Where, at an off-strip establishment, two proprietor-toughs rest on elbows at the end of a bar. When it seems as if they'll discuss the boys back east, or bark at a lackey to fetch his shine box, they instead match stomach issues and order milk.

Where the late famed boxing scribe Bert Sugar, crowned by customary fedora, corner-mouth stogie emitting smoke whispers, buys drinks at the Foundation Room, atop the Mandalay Bay, for two new friends. He regales with tales of Ali, Frazier, Norton, and Foreman, and having played poker in upstate New York with a certain statesman. "That JFK," Sugar says, "what a shitty bluffer."

Where every trip to the grocery store includes, upon checkout, gamboling by banks of video-poker machines. Customers who sign up for a Players Reward card and earn a hundred points—at a buck a point, or one hundred dollars of machine activity—receive twenty bucks in free play and three months of gratis Terrible Herbst car washes, the seventeen-dollar Outlaw variety; at a wash a week, over ninety days, that's more than twice the value of money played, not including winnings. "This is so strong that even avowed you-can't-beat-those-damned-machines non-gamblers almost have to do it," writes Anthony Curtis, who for years has highlighted city bargains in his monthly *Las Vegas Advisor* newsletter.

(Jerry Herbst, whose Southern Nevada empire consisted of more than one hundred and sixty convenience stores and car washes, many of which were marked by giant American flags on tall poles, died in November 2018. He had said that every time his father, Ed, opened another filling station in Chicago—pony rides for kids, free orchids for women, roller-skating pump girls in short-shorts for, uh, the guys, complimentary bubble gum for all—in the late thirties and forties, the competition would say, "Here comes that terrible Herbst.")

All have been witnessed during a residency of more than seventeen years, including Vegas vows, serving as sole witness, inside the Little Chapel of the West. A redwood A-frame complemented by a small spire, it belongs nestled among tall pines in Tahoe. It was built here, at the south end of the Strip, in 1942, a short walk from where the WELCOME TO FABULOUS LAS VEGAS sign would be erected in 1959. Designer Betty Willis declined to copyright the vibrant and well-known horizontal-diamond landmark, altruism that cost her millions over the decades.

The nuptials. I stroll in early on a Sunday morning, greet the beaming couple—the son of my mom's friend, his bride—and stand in place, wondering who will inform me of my duties, when . . . *Do you take?* It's over. During breakfast at the Peppermill, a Strip mainstay, I suppress the trivia nugget that widespread gambling and the quickie six-week divorce were both signed into state law on the same day in 1931.

Las Vegas, where I would not suppress surprise upon learning that every NFL bet I've made, since December 2011, has constituted an illegal act, illicit behavior I have repeated with impunity and will continue to do so, in 2020, inside that slick new domed stadium up the street.

# ONE
# The Predictable Unpredictability

Up here, twenty-three stories above the center cut of one of the world's famous thoroughfares, Van Smith embodies every sports gambler's fantasy. He has been supporting a comfortable retirement lifestyle solely by betting money on the outcome of sporting events—the "predictable unpredictability of athletic contests," wrote Michael Vernetti.

Doing so in the soul, the heart—"the hub," says Las Vegas hotel-casino mogul Derek Stevens—of the sports-betting world adds panache to Van's pursuit. He had grown weary of dealing with "Uncle Nate," making book around the corner in back of the warehouse, and the murky offshore outlets. For twenty-five years, the golden goal had been beating the master-bookmakers in their own backyard, where he has marked his territory.

The cherished Ashton VSGs are well stocked in the richly lacquered humidor, two clutches of Cohibas, *de la Habana,* reserved for confidants. Two waist-high metallic wine racks cradle dozens of bottles, a rotation of four modest Cabernet Sauvignons—nothing Château de *Whomever*—share top-row status. The wardrobe might be the weakness. In a compact bedroom, rows of shoes are stacked against a wall, tailored dress shirts and suits draped on a moveable rack. Duru's, on North La Salle, is his sartorial specialist. He dangles the exquisite dark model with chalk pinstripes.

Wearing crisp-pleated denim pants and an orange short-sleeve silk shirt fresh from the dry cleaner, the fifty-nine-year-old Chicago native eases back in his cozy tan recliner. Mug clean-shaven, dark mane—Brylcreemed, maybe—combed straight back; the blocky visage and deep-dish twang are dead ringers for the actor Jim Belushi. He says "Duke 'im" when referring to tipping someone, "Depends what's in your kick" in reference to the size of a wager. Van's blue suede shoes, no socks, nestle on the footrest.

His dream defined. As legalized sports wagering spreads into new domains, in the wake of the U.S. Supreme Court's May 2018 quashing of the *Professional and Amateur Sports Protection Act of 1992* (also known as PASPA, or the Bradley Act), those able to actually profit from the endeavor—and profit well, like Van—will serve as exemplars from whom there is much to glean.

I had met Van—his chosen alias, for reasons that will become obvious—at a pool party, thrown by mutual friends in southwestern Las Vegas, in the summer of 2017. He had prospered in the food and beverage industry, and other businesses, in the Midwest and South. With no fanfare, he added that he bets on sports. A line, in Vegas, as common as, *This heat!* Van, however, appeared composed and cool. Coaxed to continue, he imparted how he aimed to make at least thirty thousand dollars, in each of five specialty arenas, over the ensuing twelve months; to earn a hundred and fifty grand and maintain his life of leisure if not luxury.

Those absolutes lingered. I had reason to check in with him in the summer of 2018.

He had made two hundred thousand dollars.

"I don't think I'll ever own a house again," says Van, who rents this simple one-bedroom domicile in the sky for about two grand a month. "I'll tell you why: I would rather put my money into me, on the betting. Every year, my goal is to be able to increase my bet size by, oh, twenty or twenty-five percent. Plus, I like the flexibility; if I want to get outta Dodge, I get outta Dodge. What I'm getting at is, I'd rather have my money working for me."

Strict principles keep the lifelong bachelor in blue suede, with twenty-four-hour concierge access, a valet that whisks his new black Cadillac XTS to him at a finger snap. He manages an expanding bankroll by adhering to exceptional discipline, following prescribed patterns and tactics, a chartered course. He tinkers daily with his college-lined notebooks, filled with hand-written game results and abbreviations, weekly and seasonal records. Maybe a hundred notebooks, chronicling fifteen years or so of action—one for each season of the six sports he charts—are stored in two states. "That kind of discipline? Rare," says professional bettor–handicapper Tom Barton. Roxy Roxborough says, "I'm glad for him, but this is a moving target."

The most-recent notebooks lay in a TV-stand drawer. Van fetches them. That a successful professional gambler will reveal some of his tricks of the trade is as uncommon an act as it is gracious, akin to grandma unveiling the secret generations-old lasagna recipe from the old country.

From up here, Van can see for miles along the Las Vegas Strip, south to the South Point, north to a downtown area that was an eyesore not so long ago. It has undergone a magnificent makeover, thanks in large part to Derek Stevens, whose indicators have compelled him to continue upgrading Fremont Street. Best of all, because Van seldom bets high-rent figures—of at least five digits—he believes he is operating "below the radar," out of the microscopic attention of sports-book directors and casino executives, and revenuers. Roxy Roxborough agrees with that assessment. "If you're not betting enough to move the lines, people can live under the radar for a long, long time."

Down here, however, where the core of the Westgate Las Vegas trident, were it to be wedged free, just might spear through the opening of the U-shaped desk in his office, Jay Kornegay sees more, much more. The executive vice president of operations for the property's SuperBook, the finest sports book in the land, has stellar vantage points from this windowless bunker. On the far wall, twelve television screens each feature a different college football game. They're all business, he says, except for this one. He points to Colorado State, his alma mater. "That one's personal." He grins.

Computer screens on his desk display figures in various colors, where every dollar is flowing, that constantly change. The nerve center. Through Kornegay's office doors are other desks. Out that jamb, to the right, is a dark room, bodiless faces illuminated only by the green-glow of computer screens displaying the same minutiae as Kornegay's desktop. Corresponding point-spread countermoves, to dollar trickles that can turn into torrents within the beat of a heart, have been registered and are imminent, the money will change course, another counter-move: Kornegay's task is to keep that target moving within dictated parameters—tipped off by thresholds, colleagues, or his own well-honed senses—that will most benefit his superiors.

"Cat and mouse," he says. "We play with those educated bettors, too. There are false moves involved. People will bet [a game] early, and it isn't really the side they want. They come back [days later, to bet the other way]. You really have to look through all the clouds to see what they're doing. A lot of times, we do that correctly. Sometimes, we're wrong; [the initial wager] was actually a true move. We thought it was a false move, but it was a true move. So it goes, on and on and on."

Kornegay might master Go, the complicated and nuanced Japanese board game said to be a hundred times more difficult than chess.

Van and Jay represent the two sides of the industry's battlefield, although Van does tend to bet more than the hundred and thirty dollars that several book directors confirm as the size of the average customer's bet, but he rarely strays into five-digit territory that would draw undesired attention; in 1985, the Bank Secrecy Act forced patrons who make a wager of at least ten thousand dollars to file paperwork, Rule 6A to the Gaming Control Board of Nevada, notifying the Internal Revenue Service of such a transaction.

The two men appear Teflon-coated, especially immune, when it comes to odds and point spreads and money, to celebrating a recent windfall or wallowing over a setback. They have one eye on *right now*—not yesterday, not even that game that just ended—the other on tomorrow, the long game. Each is engaging, personally.

That Van does much of his shopping at Jay's place—and most of that via the Westgate mobile app—makes this a tidy tête-à-tête.

They are enemies, albeit gentleman adversaries. Their duel, the exchanged jabs and uppercuts, is metaphorical; they are a tad more than two miles from each other, and the challenger is a bit more than three hundred feet above the ground. Above the avarice, excitement, and maw, where wallets and heads, hearts and passions collide.

Veterans, experts, insiders, sharps, squares, beards, runners, poseurs, frauds, leeches, blowhards, rubes, stoops, and *Brussels sprouts*—that is, "touts," in ebullient Cockney rhyming slang—run the ground-floor gamut. Scum bags, ace bettor–handicapper Kelly Stewart calls many in that last species. Kornegay and his team monitor and classify each of their customers in eight distinctions, from the sharpest of the sharp "to your average Joe." These players are trying to get rich, finish in the black over the long haul, win more than they lose this week, end today's session with a few extra bucks to feel as if the next rib-eye will be on the house, not lose as much as yesterday or last weekend, or just add some entertainment value to something that might be otherwise unwatchable.

Some scoff at the battlefield corollary. Not veteran Las Vegas bookman Art Manteris. "I consider it combat," he wrote in his 1991 book *SuperBookie,* "and that's what makes it such a fascinating business."

Such skirmishes have been replicated in Atlantic City, New Jersey; Dover, Delaware; and Biloxi, Mississippi, and will be emulated in many other locales. It is no longer the sole domain of Las Vegas, but plenty can be learned about the art of sports gambling from where the business is rooted. That's why DraftKings, near the end of 2018, poached sports-book bosses Johnny Avello (Wynn Las Vegas), Frank Kunovic (Caesars Entertainment), and Ed Malinowski (Golden Entertainment) from Las Vegas properties.

The fifty-five-year-old Kornegay says he's sixty-five in bookie years, and when he welcomes a visitor into his bunker he makes for the tiny fridge in the corner. Water, diet soda, "or Jack Daniel's?" he says. A toast or two, on occasion, must be merited within these walls. Or, that's the perfect elixir to rinse the sourness of, say, a stunning Stanford football comeback against Oregon. Sharps and squares alike had piled onto the Cardinal, all week, so that one would sting the bottom line. In days of yore, that would have made for an unpleasant Saturday evening. Not today. "No, I don't sweat," Kornegay says. "The sweating days, I'm long past that."

He is rather affable—when lines lengthen at his windows, Kornegay often notices and mingles with customers, exchanging small talk about games, dinner arrangements, show times. He greets out-of-towners, especially those who reserve special seating in restricted SuperBook areas, like old friends. His responsibilities are growing, the latest being the expansion of the SuperBook brand—as SuperBook USA—across the country.

Las Vegas bookmakers have shown everyone that the odds are firmly in the house's favor. In September 2018, Battle Born State books registered an all-time monthly high in the amount of wagers they took in, or "handle," of $571 million. Their "hold," or amount they kept, was $56.3 million, a record monthly haul since those figures started being tracked in 1984. It gave the house the victory over the players for a sixty-second consecutive month. In twenty-six of the past twenty-eight Super Bowls, for another example, the books have finished in the black. Therein lies the charming challenge of trying to beat them.

Technology is fueling the business. In the action generated for Super Bowl LII, between New England and Philadelphia, the total amount of money wagered established a record of nearly $159 million in Nevada. An abundance of that action was generated via in-game, or live, betting courtesy of mobile apps. And in August 2018, for the first time, legal in-game wagering via the DraftKings Sportsbook app was available during an NFL game, to fans sitting in their MetLife Stadium seats to watch Cleveland play the Giants in East Rutherford, New Jersey. Wrote ESPN's Ben Fawkes, "What a time to be alive."

That such in-game NFL wagering will soon occur within another NFL stadium *in Las Vegas* qualifies this, most certainly, as an absurd time to be alive. Locals have fresh recall of that league, and commish Roger Goodell, barring Las Vegas from even buying ad time during its precious Super Bowl telecasts. Now, Goodell salivates over the trove of riches that awaits the NFL in Vegas. Camus, a maestro of the Theatre of the Absurd, would have reveled in the hypocritical about-face. "Purify gambling by conquering yourself—knowing such conquest to be absurd," he once wrote in a diary, the bulk of which have become a percipient three-volume set of notebooks. The Frenchman further enters our orbit with his idea that a critique of absurdity should weigh value judgment against factual judgment. That encapsulates sports betting.

At the start of 2016, the idea of a RaiderDome—my pseudonym for the nearly two-billion-dollar domed palace being built five miles from where this is being written—for the franchise relocating from Oakland would have been met, in Las Vegas, with extra tar and feathers. Two tight bill passages in the Nevada legislature, however, secured seven hundred and fifty million dollars via a tourist tax on hotel rooms, and the deal got done.

Look for sporting events to become even more bettor-friendly. Until that Las Vegas BetCast, games on American television had only received gambling attention in cutesy asides—Al Michaels coyly announcing after a late score in a blowout, "Now the game is *over!*" The BetCast match featured William Hill odds and Las Vegas Lights FC, in its inaugural-season finale at Sacramento. The broadcast booth, however, was the glass-walled studio, known as the Fish Bowl, of the Vegas Stats & Information Network—VSiN, or *Vee Sin*, at Channel 204 on the Sirius/XM satellite radio dial—in the center of the South Point casino.

VSiN included *#BetCast* in its live Tweets of the event. It hired Nigel Seeley, a forty-five-year-old journalist and regular VSiN contributor from Bromley, England, birthplace of H. G. Wells, to provide clever ("not even Burnley likes playing at Burnley") and colorful commentary. He did not disappoint. Had J. L. Baird (architect of the first accredited television transmission, in London in 1926), Lee Pete (a legend of Las Vegas sports-betting radio), and William Hill (one of eleven children who would use gambling as a post–Great War vehicle to escape rugged Birmingham, England) all occupied a Wells time machine, they might have conceived the BetCast.

William Hill, in particular, might be interested in witnessing how his own shop has emerged from the shadows. A sickly child, he would grow to six feet, with broad shoulders. At sixteen, he'd become adept at calculating probabilities and risk, and he'd shift from running betting slips and money, for co-workers at the Birmingham Small Arms factory, to making his own book. A rival said of Hill, "He played with numbers like a great pianist."

In 1933, he set up his own shingle at 97 Jermyn St., SW1, an avenue occupied three centuries earlier by Sir Isaac Newton. Gambling would be legalized in England in 1961—it would require another twenty-five years for such shops to be allowed to furnish television sets and coffee machines, and install toilets, for patrons.

At sixty-eight, Hill suffered a fatal heart attack in October 1971. His company has endured many iterations, through mergers and acquisitions, but his name and its famous marque—the midnight blue background, elegant yellow-cursive WILLIAM, and bold white-block HILL—have endured in august fashion.

The company has made a few forays into the FTSE 100 Index, England's blue-chip stock market. Worldwide, it has more than twenty-five hundred shops—including a hundred and seven clients in Nevada, where its midnight-blue hot-spot kiosks in many bars accept cash deposits to fuel mobile accounts—in which it employs nearly twenty thousand people, in nine countries. Those shingles are in nineteen time zones. The company whose roots are in the grime and grit of suburban Birmingham registered nearly two billion dollars in revenue in 2017.

What would Hill, the man himself, think today if he could observe how his midnight blue, yellow, and white tentacles have wrapped around the sports-betting world?

"I think he'd be absolutely staggered," says Nigel Seeley. "He wouldn't believe what a beast he's become and how the betting market has changed. He would be absolutely amazed."

Van did not catch the BetCast. Might be significant, he says, but he's too busy plotting with those notebooks to get involved with such fluctuating and uncertain variables, and rapid decision making, that define in-game, or live, betting. He is confounded why a state like Mississippi would not allow mobile apps—in the Magnolia State, sports wagers can only be executed in a casino, in person—out of the gate. He thinks sports gaming would "explode" if it were allowed across state lines. In fact, as Van stated that, in October 2018, Nevada's three-person Gaming Control Board was listening to industry representatives propose allowing Nevada casinos to accept sports wagers from states where such bets are legal.

Jimmy Vaccaro, an iconic figure in the Las Vegas sports-betting scene, furthered that idea audaciously when he fantasized, in the book *The Odds* (2001), about patrons being able to call in an out-of-state wager, from anywhere, to a Vegas casino, or execute a bet on its website, both of which are currently illegal. The masses would do it, he said, but lawmakers would always have their own agendas. "I mean, if Britain can do it why the fuck can't we?" Vaccaro noted in his characteristic blunt and direct manner. "I mean, *sports betting* ... are you fucking crazy? We could close up the off-shores in half an hour."

Van is cognizant of the masses inside Las Vegas casinos, heads tilted up at those gorgeous and inviting mammoth screens, or tapping at their mobile phones or punching at their computer keyboards in apartments or suburban homes, who flail miserably trying to make a buck betting on sports. Experts at the UNLV International Gaming Institute estimate that, at best, three people out of a hundred can win consistently at a rate of fifty-seven to fifty-eight percent; it's incumbent to clear 52.38 percent, factoring in the basic eleven-to-ten "vigorish" surcharge, just to break even on straight bets.

"Hit fifty-four to fifty-five percent in this business, over a period of time, and you're big time," says professional handicapper Paul Stone. Fifty percent is enough of an impediment for many bettors. "Because they don't have a plan," Van says. "I say that all the time."

In a perfect world, the mantra goes, the sports book seeks equal amounts bet on both sides. The vig on the losing side is the profit casinos reap. Complete folly, Kornegay will explain, especially that first part. The scale on any given game always tilts, sometimes dramatically, to a side. The house balances that as much as possible, making the other side more enticing via points or price adjustments, or both. That's gospel, the backbone of the industry—exposure, risk management, those thresholds—for the house. Vigorish, by the way, stems from *vyigrysh,* Russian for "winnings," linked to the juice, or take, of a shark's loan.

Van is prodded. Gently. Over the course of his first twenty-five adult years, he estimates he has lost more than a quarter of a million dollars betting on sports, mostly with bookies. "I used to be scattershot, an idiot," he says. "Betting stupidly, getting over my head." He would borrow money from his brother or mother to square his account with the man; his gainful employment made squaring with his relatives, and soon, a non-issue. The notebooks chronicle the turnaround. They detail every latter-day cycle, the tried and true angles, the plays that did not work out so well that required massaging—that still necessitate manipulating—that he began documenting since an epiphany of a phone conversation with a good friend around 2003.

He had been going about it all wrong, betting on whims, like a rookie. A schoolboy. He re-wired his synapses. He concentrated. He began playing chess, so to speak, having dumped the checkerboard. Now—for an hour or two every morning—he reviews those notebooks, inputs scores and other details, tracks records and units gained or lost, by hand, letters all caps, with a black ballpoint pen.

The notebooks are invaluable. Do you realize that this is not common? He squints. He pauses. He is pressed. He searches for, and settles on, the proper terms. No decibel-rise, no straightening of his recliner.

"I'm a machine."

Jimmy Vaccaro strolls into his shop early one afternoon. He stands in the aisle in the front row of columns of red-leather chairs and glares up at the green, yellow, red, and white numbers and letters on the giant board. It's a Monday in the middle of the summer, so baseball is about the only game in Las Vegas. Typically, that sport does not attract much action. Still, it is Vaccaro's business to note line movements. Blips will raise a seventy-three-year-old bushy gray eyebrow, and those of significance will warrant his further attention and involvement.

Short with a thick-gray mop and a grandfatherly countenance, his uniform is white short-sleeve SOUTH POINT T-shirt over a white long-sleeve SOUTH POINT T-shirt, jeans, black slip-ons that almost look like bathroom slippers. Sometimes he'll don a white SOUTH POINT sweatshirt. It will smash triple digits outside, again, today. The typical Las Vegas sports book, however, is frigid, requiring layers if not long sleeves—both, for veterans. The greenhorn, betrayed by shorts and tank top, can be seen occasionally blowing into his or her cupped hands, maybe even sipping coffee, when it hovers in the one-teens outside.

The South Point is Vaccaro's latest gig, as senior lines-maker. It's a gilded 2,163-room property about three miles south of the Strip—"the tip of the Strip," says a radio ad. Require a tonsorial touch-up? See John (the Barber) Taddio for a trim or a straight-razor shave, and—during the fall and winter—a keen play or two in the National Hockey League. He's so good at puck prognostications, he contributes to those picks on VSiN on occasion.

This place and this arrangement are noteworthy, because Vaccaro works for Michael Gaughan, son of a Las Vegas pillar. The late Jackie Gaughan helped build the first legal sports book in a casino, downtown at the Union Plaza. He and his son would establish an imposing precedent, a record nine hotel-casinos owned by a father-son team, that some industry insiders believe will never be broken.

Michael built the Royal Inn, opening it in 1970. Five years later, he hired a newcomer to the city named Jimmy Vaccaro to deal blackjack. Shortly afterward, Gaughan would ask Vaccaro if he knew anything about running a sports book. Vaccaro didn't. No matter, Gaughan said, we'll learn together. Vaccaro supervised a nook of the Royal to begin a new phase of his career. At the Barbary Coast, a few years later, they would rule some of the prime sports-betting real estate in the world.

Being the city's lone bookmaker—then at the Mirage's new sports book, whose layout he designed—to post odds on Mike Tyson's fight against Buster Douglas in Tokyo in 1990 contributes to Vaccaro's deserved recognition as a paragon of the business. Tyson opened as the heavy favorite, with thirty-one-to-one odds on a Douglas upset. Money poured in on Iron Mike; someone laid sixty-two grand to win two thousand, another patron plopped seventy thousand down to win two grand. Another ninety-eight grand came in on Tyson. Wall Street in the Desert, Vaccaro calls those seemingly sure-thing scenarios in which punters seek to win a quick nominal amount at the risk of a bundle.

Douglas's knockout victory was an upset for the ages. The professional bettor Lem Banker had wagered on Buster Douglas. The Mirage did very well, not so much in its coffers—where Vaccaro estimated the take to be about a hundred and fifty thousand—as in publicity, where he gauged that the world-wide attention to his new operation might have been worth nine figures.

Vaccaro has long espoused, regarding a bet involving humans, *You can never, ever know.* That Tyson fight is proof, and other evidence is as regular as sunrise. In Art Manteris's book, Vaccaro said he "got lucky" the way he made book on Tyson in Tokyo. "I was trying to get some publicity and a little money on Douglas. I've had people say, 'If you've got sixty thousand dollars, why would you want two thousand dollars more?' And my answer is, 'People always want more.' "

He also posted the first NFL season victory total, on Dallas, in 1989. When a woman could not locate that figure on the Mirage board, she asked Vaccaro where it was; at that time, he says, such an offering did not exist. She asked him what number he'd post. She dumped thirty thousand five hundred dollars out of her purse, catching the attention of Vaccaro and associate Russ Culver. They said five and a half, and she put the cash on Over. That was Troy Aikman's first season, and the Cowboys won only one game. Randy Galloway, the fine sportswriter for the *Dallas Morning News,* wrote a few paragraphs about it, which the Associated Press picked up. Jimmy Vaccaro once again garnered national headlines and made money for his bosses.

Michael Gaughan reunited with Jimmy Vaccaro, at the South Point, in 2015. Gaughan, seventy-five, also employs Chris Andrews (as director) and Vinnie Magliulo (as oddsmaker) in his sports book. Combined with Vaccaro, that gives the property more than a hundred and twenty combined years of odds-setting and bookmaking experience, a triumvirate of talent unmatched by any other casino in the state.

It's a savvy arrangement for Gaughan Gaming, making the South Point a destination for locals and visitors alike. Among all the betting options in town, for instance, that trio is renowned for posting money-line odds on big underdogs in both college and pro football. Other book directors—or, more likely, their bosses, or *their* bosses at corporate headquarters—are too timid to do likewise. Michael Gaughan, more than many, is attuned to offering value and variety. He has made a nice living from making shrewd business moves.

At McCarran International Airport, it would be difficult to miss his video-poker machines near every gate. There are almost fifteen hundred of them. He has owned the McCarran concession—Michael Gaughan Airport Slots—for years. In a sweet deal for the airport, about eighty-seven percent of that revenue ($25.7 million in a recent fiscal year) remains on the property that is named for the former U.S. senator, Pat McCarran, who unabashedly protected the gaming industry.

Michael Gaughan always enjoyed being behind his own counter, working beside people he hired, especially on a busy fall Sunday morning.

"You ever been here at quarter to ten on a Sunday?" he says. "We're taking bets after games start, which we're not supposed to do . . . [but] I'm in there and I'm old school." For a customer who has just forked over a few hundred dollars, and the ticket writer is about to tap at his screen, and at that very moment Jacksonville kicks off in Houston . . . well, perhaps Gaughan has erred on the side of his customer, once or twice, in that vacuum of a millisecond.

So it's 2014, a quarter to ten on a fall Sunday. Gaughan has a female visitor before him. She has him in time on this planet. She has made her request. Gaughan mishits keys. People behind her grumble. Tick. Tock. He fumbles with the computer screen.

"You're not very fast," she said.

"Ma'am," he said, "I'm one of the trainees." He has a propensity to stutter, which does not go unnoticed to this devil-dowager standing across from him.

"How come," she says, "they put a dumb shit like *you* in the window on a Sunday morning?"

"Yes, ma'am, you're right. Ray! Take this station! I'm done!"

He becomes flustered all over again as he relives the scene from behind a large desk in his large office on the ground floor in the back of the South Point. "I yelled for backup. I haven't written a ticket since."

For his guile and experience, Jimmy Vaccaro is hailed by Michael Gaughan. Gaughan himself isn't so hip to the next technological advancements, but it isn't an industry secret that Vaccaro especially rues the gadgets and quants and algorithms, the British computers that spit out the key numbers of a game or match. With a grin and a sigh, Gaughan leans forward and almost whispers, "We're bringing Jimmy into the twenty-first century."

Vaccaro carries a Styrofoam container, leftovers from another lunch with the boys at the Greek joint, in his left arm like a football as he scans the big board. "Chop suey," he says of how that splash of colors, numbers, and letters—a Christmas tree splattered against a big black canvas—must appear to a first-timer, a rookie. "But when you explain it to them one time, they seem to get it. During football season, I tell them, 'Don't be nervous. Come up and ask questions. It's easy.'"

## THE SKINNY

451   Lions   51   +200
452   Vikings   –5½   –250

This is an example of the "chop suey" to which Jimmy Vaccaro refers. It is a typical football "line," the odds, or spread, on the game showing that the Minnesota Vikings are the favored team, by five and a half points. A wager on the Vikings, giving those points, or on the Detroit Lions taking the points, is called a "side" bet. It comes with the aforementioned "vigorish," or "vig," also termed "juice," of ten percent. That means to win $20 on, say, the Vikings covering that spread will require a wager of $22; a winning ticket, meaning the Viking defeat the Lions by six or more points, will yield $42. It is obtained at the window by asking the writer, "Four fifty-two side bet for twenty-two bucks." To win $100, a $110 bet would have to be made; a winning ticket would return $210. Like the Lions plus the points? It will be a winner if the Lions flat-out win or lose by no more than five points. It's another "side" bet, so it involves those same eleven-to-ten odds

The "51" designates the projected "total," or "over-under," the combined final scores of both teams, which also comes with the eleven-to-ten price tag. Like the Under? It can be had by using either team number, 451 or 452, "to the Under, for twenty-two bucks."

The numbers to the far right of each team's line are the money lines. No points are involved here, and neither is the vig. This is a bet on the outright winner, so since the Lions are the underdogs, by 5½ points, their money-line number will be greater because that 5½-point padding is being disregarded. That ticket can be had by saying, "Four fifty-one money line, for twenty bucks." That wager will pay plus-200, or two-to-one odds, so a $20 winning wager will return $60; the winning $40 plus the outlay of $20. Since the Vikings are the favored team, expected to win by at least six points, the cost of them to simply win the game is steep; a wager of $25, at minus-250 odds, will return $10. To win $100, a $250 bet must be made.

Another common wager from this line is a parlay, whose return odds are sweeter since it requires winning two bets, at least, to pay off. Like the Vikings to beat the spread and both teams' points to total higher than fifty-one? "Four fifty-two to the Over parlay, for twenty bucks." If Minnesota wins by at least six points and both teams combine to score at least fifty-two points, the payoff will be about $52, so the ticket will return $72, the winning amount plus the original bet. That's a two-way, or two-leg, parlay. The return odds increase with the more legs that are played.

Parlays, and parlay cards, are very popular in the books during football season. They are big money makers for the house because they are difficult to hit and, even if a patron does win one, the return odds always fall short of the true odds, so the book saves money even when it loses. It's good to be the house.

To make sense of all that chop suey, it will behoove many to learn from Las Vegas luminaries. Consumers, corporate entities, and state officials can cull important lessons and learn about every facet of the industry where it all originated. Based on issues—sloppy algorithms, poor thresholds, messy lines—that have plagued some newcomers, they would be very wise to take heed.

During several visits to the nation's capitol, to inform politicos about his lifetime's work in the gaming industry, its various moving parts and how it operates, Vaccaro has doled out countless invitations for them to visit Las Vegas. To his vocal dismay, his offers have been unrequited. Yet other Las Vegas sports-betting figures have had success, and lasting relationships have paid dividends for both parties, dealing with international legal authorities, executives from various sports leagues, and officials from governing bodies of collegiate sports.

Gambling has made the Gaughan family wealthy. Michael Gaughan is at once the personification of another era and a symbol, a voice, of its future. He knows how to market his brand. His son, racecar driver (and former Georgetown University hoops bench-warmer) Brendan, has worn a SOUTH POINT fire suit since his first NASCAR truck race, in 1997. In the NASCAR series, in 2018, his pop partnered the South Point marque with Richard Childress Racing for a seventh consecutive season—Daniel Hemric behind the wheel of the number twenty-one Chevrolet, bearing the hotel logo on the hood, trunk, and rear quarter panels.

When the racing association awarded a second race, to be staged in September 2018, to the Las Vegas Motor Speedway, site of a spring race since 1998, Michael secured sponsorship. Brad Keselowski won the inaugural South Point 400 on September 16, 2018.

Michael Gaughan hires people who match his boldness and ingenuity, and that describes Steve Stallworth, the former UNLV quarterback who backed up Randall Cunningham and once led the Rebels to an upset victory over Wisconsin. He runs the South Point's equestrian center and arena, where he once booked a famous Mexican matador in the city's first bullfights, albeit PETA-friendly "duels" with Velcro-crowned animals and Velcro-tipped "swords."

When Gaughan owned the Orleans, Stallworth managed its arena. He earned a notch in the chronology of events that helped further nudge sports betting out of the shadows and into the mainstream when he booked the University of Florida and Kansas University basketball teams in that barn in 2006. Until then, such a collegiate sporting event had never been staged on the same premises as a casino. Five years earlier, Cincinnati promoter Chris Spencer had arranged three tournaments on casino grounds, but subsequent political fury forced him to shift the games to area high schools.

Stallworth needed about ten passes by Michael Gaughan before getting the green light, and the private plane, to pursue Gators and Jayhawks officials. If he convinced one, he knew he'd get the other. There was no explicit NCAA rule forbidding such games, so he went to work. "As soon as [Kansas athletic director] Lew Perkins blessed it, the rest was history," Stallworth tells me. That ignited a wave in which, these days, four springtime conference basketball tournaments are sometimes held in Las Vegas, as are several holiday events. The advent of RaiderDome, in conjunction with such widespread acceptance of sports betting, is expected to eventually land a Final Four.

A short stroll from Stallworth's second-floor office is VSiN, the slick, modern-day version of the Stardust Line, which first sent sports-betting chatter into the airwaves in 1982. The avuncular Lee Pete and squeaky-voiced sidekick Donnie Bader ran the festivities, which included Jim Brown on several occasions and, once, a tipsy Joe Namath. On clear evenings, its signal blanketed the west, even leaked across both national borders, with reports of reception in some Pacific islands.

Exotic disseminations about "the spread," how much the sharps might move it and how the squares might react, instead of who will be batting cleanup for the Yankees tomorrow, seemed taboo to ears not within the legal confines of Nevada.

Ron Futrell, a longtime Las Vegas TV personality and UNLV instructor, first heard the show's siren call after signing off at a television studio in Yakima, Washington. He set a push button on the radio of his Toyota truck to KDWN 720-AM, from somewhere out in the big Wild West desert. "Fifty thousand watts, clear channel," he says. "You could pick it up in Yakima like it was next door. The Stardust Line had to be the first regular sports-talk radio show *ever*. It absolutely piqued my interest in trying to find a job in Las Vegas."

Today, in the Fish Bowl, VSiN is the Stardust Line on steroids. It caters to a world-wide audience, and its video feed is available via the FuboTV Internet service, with eminent broadcaster Brent Musburger as its flagship personality. On a carriage being pulled by the Budweiser Clydesdales, Musburger was ushered into the prodigious South Point canopied entryway for a studio unveiling and press conference in February 2017.

After a late-afternoon show nearly two years later, Musburger laughs. "It's been great. Working with these guys is fun, because of all the anecdotes and all the stories surrounding gambling, all the characters that come in and out. I always sort of *knew*. I hung around out here enough to know that, Hey, wait a minute, there's stuff going on."

Jimmy (the Greek) Snyder gave Musburger his first tours of Las Vegas back in the sixties, at the Rose Bowl turf club, so Musburger has been interested in, and familiar with, odds and point spreads for a long time. Lefty Rosenthal, who arrived in 1968, ran the sawdust-floored Rose Bowl. "Handwritten tickets," Musburger says. "They climbed ladders to write the results, even the horses, on the boards."

VSiN represented a natural and smooth, maybe inevitable, transition for Musburger. Stay interested, he told Steve Lavin when the former coach was embarking on a broadcasting career and inquired for a single nugget of advice. At seventy-nine, Musburger's combination of experience, polish, professionalism—and interest—is unmatched in the business. As he speaks, he is a half-point out of the money in the Westgate SuperBook's 2018 NFL SuperContest, which lured more than three thousand entrants, at a grand a pop. He will finish in a tie for fifty-sixth, grossing Musburger thirty-eight hundred dollars.

## THE SKINNY

A self-described streak bettor, in his two years living in Las Vegas the eminent broadcaster Brent Musburger's claim to wagering fame arrived during the 2017 baseball season. Once a team wins three consecutive games, Musburger, whom many veterans in the television business call "Big Dog," jumps on that team to win a fourth in a row. He rides the wave till it ends.

In '17, the Los Angeles Dodgers had winning streaks of five, six (three times), nine, ten, and eleven games. Those two longest skeins paid very nice dividends to Musburger. "I'm a streak bettor. If you win three in a row, I'll bet you the next day. You take your profit out as you go along when you do that, but streaks are the way to go in baseball."

Although he's a full-time resident, Musburger has gone days without making a wager. It's different, he says, when you live here, as opposed to flying in for a weekend. "Being in the middle of it, it's not as exotic as it was when I used to travel in for those weekends. When you travel in, you tend to force action because you're only going to be here for a couple of days."

Musburger reinforces that he bets what he will not miss, nothing of significance that had been earmarked for bills or other important living expenses.

"That's good advice for everybody," he says. "Keep your real money in your left pocket and what you're going to have fun with over in your right pocket. And don't force bets. Don't try to double-down on things, be smart about it. What you realize, here in the middle of it, is how hard it is to beat the numbers on a regular basis. Youngsters, in particular, should be really careful. The books don't get any smaller. The hotels don't get any smaller. Now there are some professionals who do well, let's be honest about it. But they work the numbers."

In October 2018, VSiN established an East Coast presence when it unveiled a studio at the Ocean Resort Casino in Atlantic City, New Jersey. In the not-so-distant future, VSiN—for whom South Point oddsmaker Vinny Magliulo also serves as a vice president of strategic partnerships and marketing—will also send its signal from a state-of-the-art studio in Derek Stevens's project at 18 Fremont, the former downtown site of the Las Vegas Club.

In 1959, Jackie Gaughan bought the Las Vegas Club. Decades later, Stevens would purchase it and tear it down; renderings of his proposed 777-room edifice are chic and slick, ultra-modern, with a theater-setting sports book that, Stevens vows, will trump the extravagant Westgate SuperBook. (There are rumors of a third Las Vegas VSiN studio, to be constructed high above the

SuperBook's eastern entry.) Eighteen Fremont will join The D and Golden Gate in the Stevens stable.

He also bought the former Clark County Courthouse, for three million dollars, and turned it into a venue for concerts and viewing parties. Its popularity has paralleled the incredible splash made by the city's first major sports team, the Vegas Golden Knights of the NHL, which advanced all the way to the Stanley Cup Final to cap their inaugural 2017–18 season.

That thirteen people had made preseason bets on the Knights to win it all, at five hundred-to-one odds, at the SuperBook did not rankle Jay Kornegay as much as the constant attention that that proposition received; at three hundred-to-one, money kept pouring in on it, and at a hundred-to-one, at eighty-to-one, fifty-to-one, twenty-to-one, and it just kept coming. So when the Washington Capitals ousted Vegas in five games to lift the towering bowl-capped silver trophy, there was considerable relief in the Westgate executive offices, and other corporate suites in Las Vegas. In an odd twist, however, Kornegay and his staff, and many ticket writers and book directors around town, were all rooting for the home team till the bitter end.

When Vegas beat Winnipeg to advance to the Final, the sports book at Green Valley Ranch erupted—on both sides of the counter, an unusual confluence in which every employee also clapped, whooping and hollering, for several seconds. Old-timers say such civic camaraderie was last experienced in Las Vegas in the spring of 1990, when UNLV smash-and-grabbed its way to the NCAA basketball championship. Its thirty-point crushing of Duke in the finale still stands as a record for title-game margin of victory.

None of those Rebels games appeared on sports-book betting boards, though, due to in-state amateur restrictions that would last ten more years—and whose eradication would be instigated by veteran bettor Lem Banker. The illegal line, in that championship game, had UNLV as the favorite by between two and four points. In his book, Art Manteris wrote that the Vegas books "would have been killed" had they been able to post a line.

Inside T-Mobile Arena, Knights fans could be seen tapping

their phones, and they weren't all checking in with the daughter or mother. In-game mobile apps were being employed, and a few book directors concurred that they lost approximately fifteen thousand dollars every time Vegas won a game in its début campaign.

Kornegay confirms that the SuperBook staff enjoyed the run. He and several of his employees own season tickets, as does Van Smith, the pro gambler in a constant numbers tug-of-war with Kornegay and his associates. Perhaps Van and Jay have even exchanged a high-five or two, in the moments after a big goal or convincing victory, at T-Mobile. Derek Stevens, a lifetime Red Wings supporter who covets his season ducats and is never above public displays of glee, might have yelled the mightiest inside that arena.

Three very different factions of the vibrant Las Vegas sports-gambling scene, all with the same common interest, if only for a few hours crammed together in an ice-cold barn. When the Golden Knights' games conclude, the real game—for each, against the others, sometimes in multiple ways—commences.

# TWO
# Like a West Point Cadet

THE UNIVERSITY OF OKLAHOMA football team rode into its 1959 season-opening game against Northwestern as a juggernaut. The Sooners had won a hundred and seven of their previous hundred and seventeen games, which included three national championships and a forty-seven-game winning streak that still stands as a record. On September 24, a Thursday, the point spread that favored Oklahoma by six points had been cut in half, a big move that meant waves of money had been coming in, at the thriving illicit book-making operations in the Chicago area and around the nation, on the host Wildcats.

The mysterious line movement—bookies would soon remove the game from their offerings—tipped off one of the more notorious episodes in college football, a cold case that would not be solved for almost sixty years. Until two trips were made to the home of Lester (Lem) Banker, on Campbell Avenue in Rancho Nevada Estates, a gated community protected by armed security personnel. Banker moved to Las Vegas in 1957, where he would fashion a sports-betting career that would make him famous.

"Let me tell you," Banker says with enthusiasm about that football game.

That Thursday evening, Oklahoma broke bread at the Chez Paree, a popular Chicago cabaret that, courtesy of certain mafia connections, could feature Frank Sinatra, Dean Martin, Jerry

Lewis, Joey Bishop, and a host of other celebrities, chorus lines, and elaborate dance numbers on any given occasion.

Dave (Dingy) Halper hired the talent but also posed as a Paree front man for The Outfit in Chicago, via part-owner Julius Caesar (Jules) Stein's close association with Al Capone and his first cousins, the Fischetti Brothers—Rocco, Charles, and Joseph. Among mafia business conducted inside the third-floor nightclub, at the corner of Ontario and Fairbanks, approval was granted to gun down bookmaker Willie Tarsch.

For five and a half dollars, patrons were served a seven-course meal and treated to top entertainment acts of the day. That night, Patrice Wymore—who in four months would begin shooting as Frank Sinatra's jilted girlfriend Adele Elkstrom in *Ocean's 11*—owned the stage. She had performed at an early age with a family of vaudeville performers. But by the time she sang and danced, some Sooners—feasting on a fruit cup, tossed salad, mashed potatoes, steak, rolls and butter, and ice cream—were not around to enjoy the show.

Lem Banker also inhabited the Chez Paree that night.

So did Lefty Rosenthal.

Twelve Oklahoma players and one assistant coach became sick. A cab arrived to hustle six Sooners back to the team's hotel, but so many of them became violently ill, during the trip, that the vehicle was re-routed to Louise Weiss Memorial Hospital in Evanston. Nine players would have their stomachs pumped, and seven would remain overnight for observation. One went into shock and was not released until the morning of the game, Saturday, September 26.

More than twenty players were affected. The fruit cocktail was widely pegged as the culprit. Remnants of it and contents of players' pumped stomachs that were saved—as evidence, to be examined—reportedly disappeared before they could be analyzed. Dr. W. G. Willard, the OU team physician, said he was certain the sick players had received "some kind of intoxication."

Northwestern routed Oklahoma, 45–13, at Dyche Stadium.

The Sooners fumbled twelve times. The Wildcats recovered five, turning each into a touchdown drive. The big victory, and others, would eventually land young Northwestern coach Ara Parseghian at Notre Dame.

Speculation about an underworld link to those events ran roughshod. *Look* magazine documented the timeline but failed to firmly connect the tainted food to gamblers and the mob. "Whatever the true story," said then-NCAA executive director Walter Byers, "of what happened at the Chez Paree, [*Look*] proves how such a plot can work and puts the colleges on guard."

In 1997, *Tulsa World* writer Bill Connors spoke with Eddie Crowder, a Sooner on that '59 squad, who recounted that coach Bud Wilkinson had discussed with him an investigation about the incident by noted sportswriter Tim Cohane. "[It] included information that [Cohane's] lawyers agreed was persuasive in backing up the contention that gamblers arranged the food poisoning, but they thought it was too risky to publish," Crowder told Connors. "I don't think we will ever know for sure what happened."

That Thursday night at the Chez Paree, Banker—who had in the previous two years befriended Rosenthal, a known mafia figure who would eventually matriculate to Las Vegas and earn immense notoriety, and on whose TV show Banker would appear—became very surprised upon seeing someone in the club's kitchen.

"Lefty Rosenthal!" says the ninety-one-year-old Banker. "The whole fucking [Oklahoma] team got dysentery, diarrhea . . . and Northwestern won the game straight up. Lefty was involved in the kitchen." Banker laughs. You saw him in there? "Yeah . . . Lefty was *doin' the cookin'*." Tampering with the fruit cocktail? "Whatever it was, he made sure . . . he paid attention to everything. The next day, a bunch of players were crapping in their pants." Some type of poison? "Yeah."

Before bookies had taken the game off their boards, Banker, Rosenthal—who in 1961 would take the fifth thirty-seven times in the bribery trial of a North Carolina basketball player, and in

1963 would plead no-contest in the alleged bribing of a New York University college basketball player—and many others had taken the points. "Yeah," says Banker, "I made a very big bet."

Banker grins. "When money's involved . . ."

Lem Banker is wrapped tight, dull-green Tartan pajama bottoms pulled up to his chest, long-sleeve white T-shirt bearing a Crayola-like kids' scene, gray knit skullcap, ailing back curving perfectly into the seat and back of his well-worn recliner. On another visit, on a colder day, a red blanket covers him to his neck. His breathing can be halting, voice sometimes a whisper, coughs interrupt thoughts, sentences stray and drift . . . the Godfather of Sports Betting is a shell of his former self.

Grandson Jonathan Ribaste, daughter Blaine, a maid, and two male caretakers tend to him in this thirty-six-hundred-square-foot single-story ranch-style home he bought, when it was built, in 1966. In 1973, the late Jerry Tarkanian bought a home one hundred yards to the east when he took the UNLV basketball coaching job. They'd run into each other on occasion but said little, "because of the gambling thing," says Banker of his profession. "May he rest in peace. He was a great coach, but the cheapest bastard. A great recruiter. He also had that excellent assistant, [Tim] Grgurich."

Banker possessed some vanity, relating to his appearance, always hitting the gym, and the heavy bag and weights in the backyard. He swam daily in his Olympic-size swimming pool. Tall, tan, notable muscles that drew eyes away from a receding hairline, he was the utter definition of beefcake, the virile, vogue term of his era coined by Hollywood gossip Sidney Skolsky. A man of no small presence and dignity, impressive to his subordinates and respected even by the underworld, *The Saint* author Leslie Charteris wrote of a chief inspector. He could have been describing Banker.

"A strapping gym guy," Chris Maathuis says of the somewhat imposing shadow that Banker once cast. The sports director for the local CBS television affiliate, Maathuis began, when he arrived in Las Vegas in 1997, taping weekly betting segments during football season with Banker, which they continued for about fifteen years. Maathuis has been saddened by Banker's health issues and very-public stories about maltreatment and filching by kin and caretakers. Lem thought they were poisoning him, says Maathuis.

Those issues will be addressed. Banker says the heart, on which he underwent a quadruple-bypass procedure in 2008, is as strong as that of an eighteen-year-old, according to his doctor. He adds, "The prostate is fine, too." An orthopedic surgeon could only go so far with a delicate back operation, in 2010. He glares at the walker and wheelchair by the kitchen table.

"I'm embarrassed," he says softly. "I used to walk around like a West Point cadet. I worked out all the time, had a lot of girlfriends."

One of who, he reveals, bore him a son in 1996. "I was back in New York," Banker says. "At Bloomingdale's department store, I met a model. Invited her to dinner. Went out. She had an apartment, we had an affair. That was it. I get letters; she had seen me on TV. I had to take a blood test. Sure enough . . . So, now, what can I do?" Banker proudly displays a framed photo of the young man, cropped hair and a caramel complexion, looking sharp. Just graduated from Yale with a degree in mechanical engineering, Banker beams.

Although his body is failing him, he's as unabashed, transparent, and straightforward as ever. Many labels have been conferred upon him by media outlets, contemporaries, and protégés. The world's most successful legal sports bettor, wrote the *Chicago Tribune*. When Banker talks, people listen, wrote *New York Newsday*. The top pro football selector in the country, wrote *The Wall Street Journal*.

Some veterans with deep knowledge of the city's sports-gambling past include Banker on an exclusive list of bona fide, ballsy bettors—who did their own handicapping, who did not rely mostly on scalping, or middling, who did not benefit from the bank-roll of a third party—that includes Billy Baxter and Tony Salinas.

## THE SKINNY

In the pantheon of the gambler's gambler, longtime veterans hailed for doing their own work and wagering their own money on those plays—largely straight plays as opposed to scalping, or middling—insiders say the list of luminaries is a short one. Lem Banker, Tony Salinas, and Billy Baxter are on it. "True 'cappers," one insider called them.

Baxter once lost a ten-grand wager when Major Riddle, who co-owned the Dunes and several other properties, did not live to eighty—he died, at seventy-three, in 1980. In his Southern drawl, Baxter said, "I thought he had more stamina than that." A Caesars pit boss claimed Baxter "pees ice cubes." Baxter parried praise. "If you can manage yourself," he told *Sports Illustrated,* "you can manage anything, and that's what good gamblers do best—manage themselves."

Art Manteris, in his book, paid Banker credit and respect for what the gambler has accomplished, but Manteris wrote that he'd be happier if Banker retired. Banker is not done yet, although he restricts his betting nowadays to four offshore sites. His maximum is far less than it used to be, but at a thousand dollars he's no piker.

He won all three NFL games he bet on a few days earlier, so the touch is still there. The Dallas Cowboys were getting three and a half points, but since they lost by three that was a winner. He had five hundred dollars on Dallas, and he followed a personal rule in which he bets on an underdog with the points, then puts a third of that wager on the money line. Maybe he'll get better than plus-200, or two-to-one odds, on that chance, so an outright underdog winner will pay fine dividends. Over many years, he knows NFL underdogs will win outright thirty-five to forty percent of the time. He lost the money-line play on the Cowboys, but it was a move that's been in his NFL regimen for decades.

Banker just won't be inching, with his walker, into a book to seek that action.

Jonathan Ribaste, the product of Blaine Banker's ill-fated marriage to Kansas City mob figure Peter Ribaste, often sits in the wheelchair, on the other side of the kitchen table, and taps at the computer to his right, scanning for point-spread changes, disparities, and inaccuracies at the Las Vegas casinos and offshore companies, via the website Vegas Insider. Jonathan enters Banker's bets, updates him on his bankroll.

Right now, though, Jonathan is not here. Banker's silver Mercedes-Benz E350—with the LEM license plates—is not in the semi-circular driveway because the grandson is out getting lunch. "I got robbed," Lem Banker says within two minutes of my taking a seat beside him. "My grandchild; he'll be here. There were nine hundred and seventy gold coins, a couple of million dollars' worth of jewelry. He was in jail for six months, but he's out now." Banker shrugs. "I made up with him because of my daughter."

Banker had met the woman who would become his bride in New York, just before moving to Nevada. Both relished their first date at Monmouth Park. She was a dancer, and he visited her in Havana, Cuba, when she was part of a troupe hired to celebrate the opening of the mob-run Riviera Hotel. They married upon landing in Las Vegas in 1957.

Debbie Banker, whom Ann-Margret is fortunate to have resembled, died in 2009. A year later, headlines would be written about how Lem Banker's daughter and grandson "robbed him blind" of three million dollars in assets. Going into that back surgery—"just in case," he says—he had signed over to them all of his possessions and valuables, which included bank accounts and access to safe-deposit boxes. It all disappeared. "My daughter was going through some tough times," says Banker, all but excusing whatever transpired in his very next breath. Authorities, it had been reported, could do nothing because Banker had signed the property over to his heirs.

Jonathan walks into the kitchen and slips a Styrofoam container out of a plastic bag. I shake his hand when Banker makes introductions. The grandson is sturdy, short curly dark hair receding a bit, thin smile, clear eyes, direct eye contact.

Later, Jonathan gives me a tour of the house that includes an ancient video-poker machine, presented to Lem by Si Redd, the grandfather of those contraptions, in the middle of the living room. In the den, posters and framed photographs clutter a couch and shelves, many trinkets on the bar. Jonathan plucks out a blow-up print of the entries, and odds, for the 2004 Kentucky Derby. Smarty Jones won it, paying $10.20, followed by Lion Heart ($8.20 to place) and Imperialism ($6.20 to show). A two-dollar trifecta (15–3–10) returned $987.60. "Paid pretty good," Jonathan says. "We had that winning ticket."

Ribaste smiles at the poster board of that fine first Saturday in May 2004. "This has been my whole life, being around this." *This* being point spreads, odds, money lines, leans, fades, rumors, and tips. "I remember trick-or-treating, but the NBA was on. So Halloween wasn't normal for me. It was, do trick-or-treat [fast] to come back and watch games."

When his grandfather feels up to it, Jonathan helps him into that big swimming pool, where Lem exercises as he hangs onto the concrete lip. The colder the water, Lem says, the better. He exhibits no self-pity for his plight. If not for that bad back, and the fact that he's in his tenth decade . . . "He's all 'there.' It's just, unfortunately, his back went out years ago and put him in this state," Jonathan says. "But as far as his wits, and pickin' games, that's all there."

What was publicized about the missing jewelry and gold coins and cash, Jonathan says, was misguided, inaccurate, or false. "Never should have hit the media the way it did," he says. His grandparents were all but surrogate parents to him, as influential in raising him as was his mother. He called Debbie Banker "mama." And he says he had properly inherited all of that cash and property from his grandmother, who left it to him in her will.

"Losing her was a big hit," says Jonathan. "I went through a bad stage. I had a bad time, losing money. One thing nobody knows is, it was casino play: blackjack, craps, roulette. It wasn't sports. Sports made me last longer. With casinos, you can't win, there's no other way to put it. I've never talked about it, never felt a need to."

Born in the Bronx, New York, Lem helped his father, Benjamin, in his confectionery store, assisting the old man with the tallying of the betting slips in the black-market side of the business. The father would take the son, an avid Lou Gehrig fan, to Yankee Stadium. Lem became more involved in gambling, and he came to running messages and packages for Ruby Stein, a mob-connected loan shark and bookmaker.

One day, at Stein's haberdashery business on the West Side of Manhattan, Banker was instructed to deliver a package of ten grand to someone. In his car, Banker counted the loot: there was twenty thousand. He went back inside to report the discrepancy, which indebted Stein to him for life.

Stein would be murdered, in May 1977, by James (Jimmy) Coonan, his former bodyguard who had risen in the hierarchy of the Westies, a diabolical Irish mob notorious for dismembering its murder victims. Coonan had owed fifty thousand dollars to Stein. With a jagged kitchen knife, Coonan had cut Stein's body into six pieces, but he had forgotten to puncture the stomach and lungs. In garbage bags, the body parts were plunked into the Hudson River, but the torso floated ashore as evidence. Coonan would complete the purchase of a house, for fifty grand, and say, "Thanks, Ruby."

Lem Banker makes no apologies for the characters he has encountered in his life. Just happened, he says. His bond with Rosenthal became cemented when Banker had made some bets with Dave (Bonie) Bone, the Minneapolis bookmaking kingpin who had been visiting Las Vegas and whom Banker calls "Bones." The city's turf clubs—for which Banker hired four or five runners, to keep him abreast of number discrepancies—had not yet opened that day for business, and Banker had an early-morning tip that three starters for the Memphis State basketball team would not play that day. He had to move fast.

"At that time, two thousand, to me, was a big bet," Banker says. "I call Bones, a big bookmaker, and he says, 'Bet whatever you want.' He was an arrogant bastard. I said, 'Can I bet ten thousand?' He said, 'Bet what you want.' I said, 'Ten thousand, three times.' Naturally, the game won . . . or I wouldn't be telling you the story."

Banker laughs.

"He didn't want to pay. I told Lefty. Remember, I had helped [Lefty] get his work card from Sheriff [Ralph] Lamb."

That was a sheriff's card, which enabled Rosenthal to be employed by a Clark County casino despite a sketchy criminal record. That past barred Rosenthal from obtaining a gaming license and, when Gaming Control Board agents frequently watched him operate in a managerial capacity, led to his ouster from casinos and the city.

"Lefty, at the Stardust, said, 'Lem, don't worry. It'll be in your bank account tomorrow morning.' And thirty grand was in my account the next morning," Banker says. "They would have killed Bones. Lefty knew everybody in Chicago, Milwaukee, Minneapolis, that whole area."

In the early twentieth century, Charles K. McNeil either invented or pioneered the point spread. Odds, on either side, had been most common. The mathematical whiz, with a master's degree from the University of Chicago, polished the point system. As a securities analyst at a bank, in down time he concocted odds on who at the firm would next get the sack. He put three-to-one on the bank president. When that man discovered McNeil's extracurricular activity, he sacked McNeil—who was more upset that he had so poorly miscalculated his own odds, which he had set at eight-to-one.

In the late 1940s, Minneapolis gambler and bookie Billy Hecht adopted that "line," also dubbed the "Minneapolis Clearinghouse," making that city the de facto national capital of sports betting. Leo Hirschfield's *Green Sheet* was the first national football-betting publication.

Lem Banker was familiar with all of that. It is not surprising to hear him wax, with some sentiment, about the benefits of doing business in Las Vegas when its machinations were largely controlled by the mafia.

Boxing and pro football were his specialties to bet and favored sports to watch. Benjamin Banker also took Lem to Rocky Marciano bouts, informed Lem of all the turn-of-the-century greats, like Sam (Boston Bone Crusher) Langford, and immersed his only child in the fascinations of the sweet science. Lem began boxing early, never losing a street fight.

He was fifteen when he had had enough of Whitey Ushack, maybe nineteen, pestering him and his friends. He invited Whitey outside a dance hall. "A town bully, like Richard Widmark," Banker says of the old-time actor who played smart-mouth toughs. "I was in great shape. I broke his jaw, knocked him the fuck out. He never came back." Banker ended his final two years of post-WWII army service with the Military Police, when he also boxed for the base team and mostly fared well. Against one behemoth, Banker got knocked down seven times. "In Yokohama, Japan," says Banker, wincing and shutting his eyes as if he had just relived each of those kayos. Pugilism, he realized then and there, would not be his avocation.

Banker would befriend boxers all his life, and he became close with Joe Louis and Sonny Liston. He did well betting on boxing. He had heard that Thomas Hearns had sustained a mouth injury in sparring before an April 1985 fight, with three middleweight belts on the line, against Marvin Hagler. Hagler almost got knocked out in the first round, in the outdoor arena at Caesars Palace, but would wallop Hearns in the third. Fight over. Banker won about a hundred and fifty grand.

He was sad to see Muhammad Ali fight Larry Holmes, also at Caesars, in October 1980. "I knew Ali had been taking water pills, and he was only jogging at night. He'd seen his best days." Banker put two hundred thousand dollars on Holmes. He also finagled a press pass. Phyllis George, former co-host of CBS's *NFL Today* studio show, and husband John Y. Brown, the Kentucky governor, slid by Banker en route to their seats on press row. Brown leaned into Banker's right ear. "Lem, who you like?" Banker said, "I like Holmes."

At that very moment, "a beautiful black girl," Banker says, leaned back and frowned at Banker. It was Veronica Porché Ali, the third of the heavyweight's four wives. "I said, 'Ohhh, I *love* Ali. I *love* Ali!' I was so embarrassed, but what happened? They stopped the fight in the tenth; a shutout." Holmes had not lost a round. "Ali *couldn't* fight anymore," Banker says. "He *had* seen his best days."

With Mike Tyson, Banker would discuss some old-time fighters—Joe Genet, Sam McVey, Jack Johnson, and Bone Crusher Langford—in detail. Tyson had seen skittish footage of some of them, and he thirsted for personal accounts from Banker, and what Banker had heard of them over the years. "According to my father, Langford was the greatest of them all," Banker says. "I knew Genet. He retired and owned a gym in Union City, New Jersey. I worked out in his gym, went through his scrapbook; he fought in France in World War II. He told me all the stories."

The elder Banker tried to transfer his sports-betting acumen to Lem. It worked. To this day, Lem recalls the main lessons, like not betting what he'd like to win, but what he could afford to lose. Also, the harder a person works, the luckier he gets. And when someone gets behind, he should not try to get even all at once . . . just a little at a time. Money management, he says, is imperative. As is passing on games rather than betting just to have action.

I inquire which is more important, guts or luck? "Guts . . . oh yeah. I don't believe in luck." He agrees with the Japanese proverb that goes, Luck is like having a rice dumpling fly into your mouth.

The wisdom of going against, or fading, public opinion sticks with Banker, serving as the "essence" of his betting style, he wrote in his entertaining and informative *Lem Banker's Book of Sports Betting* (1986).

Going broke, he wrote, is never the end of the world; penury makes a person readjust, hungrier. That is just what he faced at the end of the 1964 football season, when Notre Dame played at the University of Southern California. The Irish were undefeated and opened as an eight-point favorite. Banker had it figured as an even game, so he took the Trojans and the points, for ten grand, about all the money he had. He bought six tickets and hired a limousine to whisk him and friends to the Los Angeles Memorial Coliseum.

"If I was going out, I was going out in style," he wrote. Notre Dame led at halftime, 17–0. Lem was down. He left his pals to get some air and did something that was rare; he bought a hot dog. (He has always tried to eat healthily.) In the concourse, he was chewing and contemplating life when he heard some people talk about how the Trojans had not been playing poorly, which lifted him. He returned to his seat with optimism, and USC scored twenty in the second half while keeping the Irish off the board.

Once, he almost did time. The Federal Wire Act was used against Banker, in 1978, when he had arranged a bet, on the phone, on a Pittsburgh Steelers game in a Las Vegas book for an acquaintance that, unbeknownst to Banker, was in Rhode Island. That guy had been the target of a federal probe, and investigators had picked up Banker's voice on the recording. He was fined ten grand and given two years' probation.

The impact Banker has had on sports gambling has been significant. When it appeared senators John McCain (Arizona), Jon Kyl (Arizona), and Sam Brownback (Kansas) would go all out to bar sports books from offering collegiate games on their boards, Banker says he contacted Nevada senator Harry Reid, who directed Brian Sandoval, then chairman of the Nevada Gaming Commission, to fly from Carson City to Las Vegas the next day.

Banker met Sandoval at a Ruth's Chris steakhouse, where Banker implored that University of Nevada and UNLV games be returned to those betting boards. That it had been illegal in Nevada to bet on those in-state programs, since the 1950s, would be used as evidence by the political troika as to why it should be illegal to bet on all college sports.

In January 2001, after a unanimous vote by NGC's five members, it became legal to wager on UNLV and Nevada football and basketball games. "That was huge," Banker says. "Thanks to me!" He laughs.

Banker also thanks himself for thinking, and acting, quickly way back—in the sixties, he says—when an All-American team of collegians played an annual football game, at Soldier Field in Chicago, against the reigning NFL champions. He had bet the wrong side, but a deluge had called this game early. Banker rang a twenty-four-hour hotline at the *New York Post,* got the sports editor, and exclaimed, as officially as he could muster, that a game must be played fifty-five minutes to be official. The *Post* ran with it, as did many other papers in the country. With a sly grin, Banker says, "Saved myself a loser."

He takes credit, too, for concocting a similar forty-three-minute rule in the NBA. Many Las Vegas books have those time thresholds in their rules, and one controversial incident, involving a game being called official, even occurred within their valley.

In September 2002, Wisconsin's football team had a 27–7 lead over UNLV, at Sam Boyd Stadium in Las Vegas, when the lights went out with seven minutes, forty-one seconds to play. A car had reportedly smacked into a nearby transformer, zapping two of three power lines to the stadium, the backup system was weak, and officials from both teams agreed to calling the game.

The Badgers had been favored by four and a half to seven points, but swarms of Wisconsin fans who had made the trip were unable to cash their betting slips, as winners, because the game had not lasted fifty-five minutes; it finished a hundred and sixty-one seconds from officialdom. In several sports books, many Wisconsin supporters were furious to only get their money back. Banker says he heard that Billy Walters, the pro handicapper doing time in Florida for an insider-trading scheme, might have been behind those shenanigans, but proof of any foul play has never been documented.

Banker had an effect on baseball, too. On August 31, 1956, Harvey Haddix had been the scheduled starting pitcher for the Philadelphia Phillies—on whom Banker, in New York, had made a bet—but Haddix hurt his arm during warm-ups. Second baseman Granny Hamner took to the hill, instead, and threw into the fifth inning. He was the losing pitcher of record in the Phillies' 6–3 defeat in Pittsburgh. Banker was among a group that successfully argued his bet was null and void, since Haddix had not started. It worked.

He says that was the seed that sprouted into today's baseball-betting guidelines, in which punters can choose sides, or null-and-void a bet if one, or both, of the starters is a late scratch.

The stories, and nicknames, flow. Banker knew of an Icepick Willie, a Sleepout Louie . . . once he drove into the Catskill Mountains, in New York, when a big limousine cruised by. It slowed down, "and there was Babe Ruth, a month before he died," Banker says. "There he was! We blew the horn, and he gave us a big wave." He called Joe DiMaggio a friend. "Joe, he never tipped anyone." Banker laughs, then becomes serious. "Joe married Marilyn Monroe, of course. He came home early one day to find [Frank] Sinatra in bed with Marilyn, and Joe never talked to Frank again."

Banker calls sports betting a fascinating occupation, "and it's just as interesting as a hobby." He required twenty years to eventually earn a reliable income from wagering on sports. He stuck with it, he wrote in his book, "because I liked the life and always was lucky enough to win when I had to. In the latter experience, I'm definitely the exception, not the rule."

Key elements of his tactics have trickled down to Jonathan Ribaste, who admits that it took a long time for some of them to sink in. Like many, Ribaste was an ardent fan of the Chicago Bulls and Michael Jordan, and that passion conquered all reason. Today, Ribaste tries to parrot his grandfather's level-headedness—betting with the head, not the heart—and thorough examination of power ratings, and mitigating factors, all of which result in sound plays.

His favorite team, Ribaste says, is the one that covers and makes him money. That took a page (twenty-one, to be exact) from his grandfather's playbook, in which Banker penned, "A pro gambler can't afford to be [a fan]."

Lem Banker, however, did enjoy his friendship with Al Davis.

He accepted every invitation the late owner of the Oakland Raiders sent his way, from celebrations at the Bellagio and Caesars, to flights and overnight stays in Oakland, sometimes with grandson Jonathan in tow, to watch games in the owner's box. The Raiders' new Las Vegas stadium will begin housing them for the 2020 season, but Banker does not ever recall Davis talking about aspiring to one day move his team to Las Vegas.

Banker says Davis told him that at the Citadel, where he got his first post as an assistant football coach, he sometimes talked with Gen. Mark W. Clark, the military school's president. He cut such an imposing, impressive figure that Al named his son after the man who led the capture of Rome from axis soldiers in 1944.

The gambler isn't so impressed with the son. "I loved Al Davis; his son is a fucking jerk-off," Banker says. "He's getting ripped off, giving this guy [coach Jon Gruden] ten million dollars a year for ten years. He coulda gotten him for five [million] . . . he overpaid." Mark Davis hired Gruden, whom Al Davis had paid to coach the Raiders from 1998 through 2001, to lead the team again before the 2018 season.

Banker highlights teams that have strong rushing games. Watch closely, too, he suggests. Officials and referees are only human, so mistakes are inevitable, especially in basketball. He does not infer untoward activity, just basic errors in judgment. The home team, he says, will get the best of that maybe two-thirds of the time. Such insight will enable the handicapper to make better decisions about the true ability of a team. And seeing something on the TV screen that is totally missed by the announcers is an additional source of value. If Banker likes a team getting five and a half points, he'll wait it out to get six or not get involved in the game.

In pro football, he'll add three points to a team's home power rating if it is strong in its own building, ranging to nothing. On average, he gives the home squad two points. In college football, that figure ranges from two to four points, the latter most often in a non-conference game. He makes no adjustments for artificial-turf scenarios or weather. "Nobody likes playing in cold weather," he wrote in his book, "no matter where he's from. I think it's an equal disadvantage."

He noted that most people overestimate injuries, so some of his biggest bets have been on teams that have been knocked down in the public mind, "and in the point spread," which will be further addressed in specific situations with the handicapper-bettors Kelly Stewart and Paul Stone.

Banker says he never kept meticulous records, tracked certain plays or angles, or entered debits and credits into a spreadsheet. He did not stick to a bankroll, separate from money he used for the mortgage and bills and food, or a unit, generally one or two percent of a bankroll that represents an average bet. He just went with it, depending on which turf club had what numbers. He sought to "scalp," or engage in "arbitrage"—using numbers at two books against each other, to ensure a profit—whenever possible, and on the slimmest of margins.

For example, he would bet thirty-three hundred dollars on the Pirates, a $1.10 favorite at one book, to beat the Phillies and win three grand. At another book, he'd put three thousand on Philadelphia, a $1.15 underdog, to win three thousand four hundred and fifty bucks. He will either push or win a hundred and fifty dollars, which "pays for dinner."

Veteran handicapper Dave Cokin has bottomless admiration for Banker. "Might be the best storyteller I've ever heard," Cokin says. "So many great stories. He goes way back to the old days, and he knew some pretty shady guys."

Beyond the entertainment value, Cokin respects how Banker operated. Once, Banker allowed Cokin into his lair. Long before the Internet and widely available statistics, Banker compiled information from his many sources around the country, who fed him newspaper accounts and inside dope on a daily basis. It boggled Cokin to see such in-depth work and how Banker used all of it.

"He rated every baseball player," Cokin says. "He knew what he was doing, handicapping baseball. He basically power rated every guy at every position, that's how he did his baseball matchups, every day. Back then, there was no access to lineups. You had to assume each team's probable starters, and he'd come up with his number on the game. Then he'd bet it. He was way ahead of his time."

Because of his familial drama, Banker was forced to become involved in something he had always abhorred. He sold his picks. He became a tout. "Ninety-nine percent of them are garbage," he wrote in 1985. "I've known dozens of guys who've run tout sheets, and I've been impressed with very few of them."

## THE SKINNY

Veteran handicapper Lem Banker has always done the dirty work, always computed his own power ratings, for players and teams. Way back before computers and widely available statistics, he compiled his own individual baseball player ratings, from box scores and his many sources around the country. Lineups were not released early, so he'd have to guess, as best he could, what they'd be, weigh the matchups against the Las Vegas numbers, and bet accordingly. That greatly impressed fellow professional bettor Dave Cokin.

Banker has come to rely on power ratings from *The Gold Sheet,* and he also favors the college basketball and football ratings compiled by Jeff Sagarin. Pay attention to the players and games, Banker says, and it will become possible to tweak and twist those numbers to personal preferences, in injury or home-road situations, and discrepancies with the Las Vegas lines just might lead to profits.

Mort Olshan, who founded *The Gold Sheet,* produced one of the few tout pages he respected. Banker liked the sheet's statistical information, and he found that Olshan's basketball and football power ratings often mirrored those that he produced. (Banker also favors Jeff Sagarin's ratings.) Since Olshan's death in 2003, the publication has been in the very capable stewardship of editor Bruce Marshall, who had been writing for Olshan since 1981.

It's difficult enough to win at sports gambling, to hit better than fifty-three percent at straight-up picks, which is barely breaking even. To compound that by paying someone for picks, in what will be a recurring theme on these pages, and making breaking even that much more difficult of a proposition, is asinine, says Banker and many others.

He had always sided with the little guy, the squares out there scratching and clawing just to make a few bucks, which is why he never hesitated to dole out his best selections, for free, whether that was to friends, on TV shows, or in newspaper columns. He wanted to give "Joe Blow"—his words—a chance, a fighting chance, to make money.

So undertaking his own tout service, website and all, proved somewhat embarrassing. A year-long subscription cost three thousand dollars, but it was nothing but headaches for Banker. In 2010 and 2011, as recorded by The Sports Monitor of Oklahoma, an independent monitoring service, Banker went 217–220 (49.66 percent) in his collegiate and professional football selections. He shrugs, conveying that he derived no fun from the venture. There were too many moving parts, too much to constantly update and review. The website LemBanker.com had its own Twitter handle, and its final entry was in October 2011. *Win with me tomorrow,* it reads.

"You're competing with a bunch of liars," he says of competition. "If you try to be honest with these guys . . . I want to be honest with the [customers]. I'd play an odd amount, five games or seven games, and try to go three outta five, or five outta seven. The line is tougher now than it was years ago. That was a pain in the ass."

Did you make money?

"Not really."

Jonathan walks me to the door. He tells of how he had bet the Milwaukee Brewers, in the 2018 baseball playoffs, because of the value, the plus price, he had received. His grandfather followed suit and was rooting for the Brewers, even more since he discovered my Milwaukee roots. (The Brewers would lose the National League Championship Series to the Dodgers.) That's what led to discussions about the Braves, in the 1957 and '58 World

Series, against the Yankees, and Bones, from whom Lem would ultimately receive, thanks to Lefty, that thirty grand. Jonathan appears genuinely proud of the family patriarch.

"I learned everything from my grandpa," he says. "He's taught me a lot, everything I know. It takes a while to understand it all, but this is a family business." He grins wider. "We're just looking to keep the secrets."

# THREE

# Blue Suede Shoes

THE MIAMI MARLINS AMBLED into Busch Stadium III in St. Louis on the morning of Thursday, June 7, 2018. The mercury hit ninety-two degrees, clouds formed a constant canopy, humidity hovered a bit above forty percent. The Marlins had defeated the Cardinals on Tuesday and Wednesday evenings, so the visitors, who had been stumbling around before this trip, were finding their sea legs along the Mississippi River. They were seeking an improbable road sweep against one of the game's most durable, and winning, franchises. From most angles, the midweek day baseball game in the nation's heartland did not demand much attention.

Even though it was anything but just another ball game to Van Smith, more than two months later he will recall nothing about it. He is nonchalant, business-like, with the icy detachment of an assassin. In betting, his aim mirrors his life philosophy—never high, never low, keep it steady, no surprises. It's a glance at how he operates from which much can be gleaned.

The series presented him—barely—with a betting opportunity within the rigid guideposts to which he adheres, since Miami was among the bottom-feeders of Major League Baseball, among the six worst teams, while the Cardinals' winning percentage established them as the tenth-best team. Van had unearthed a dandy of an angle; when a bottom-six team plays at a top-ten squad, bet the home team in the second game *only if* it had dropped the opener to its meeker foe.

His general belief, proven in his notebooks over the years, is that the price might be better (maybe minus-180, for example, as opposed to minus-220, the difference between laying $180 or $220, which can accrue considerably when compounded over four or five months) on the home favorites in the second game, since it is coming off a loss; moreover, the general public latches onto streaks, potentially further shaving the price of the home team in that ensuing game. And that home team, off a stinging defeat, will have had its attention piqued.

Due to success after twelve months with a grand as a unit, or average bet, Van had bumped his unit to two thousand dollars— one percent of a two-hundred-thousand-dollar bankroll—during his second twelve-month stay in Las Vegas. That is, he set out to win a unit, two grand, when he participates in an average sports wager.

Betting home favorites in baseball is dicey because, unlike football or basketball, a point spread is not involved. There's no ten-percent vig, or the basic laying of a hundred and ten dollars to win a hundred. Throw a stout starting pitcher into the equation, and a winning baseball team at home could be favored by as much as minus-300, laying three dollars to win a mere buck— even minus-400, and up, when the hurler on the bump is élite. I've seen north of minus-500, when Clayton Kershaw was in a stellar groove. In those games, the foes will offer sweet returns as underdogs.

St. Louis lost the first game of that series to the Marlins. Gears clicked, the green light flashed. Van went into action. He wagered four thousand, at a money line of about minus-200 (or one-to-two odds), to get six grand back—representing the unit, or two thousand, he set out to net. But the Cardinals lost, 11–3, that Wednesday night. According to his time-tested rules, he'd have to fire back in the third game, Thursday, sufficiently enough to win six thousand dollars; to recoup that four grand, plus gain that two thousand that he had hoped to make as a profit.

The odds on St. Louis starter Miles Mikolas against Miami pitcher Trevor Richards (winless on the year, so far) were about minus-220, meaning to win a hundred bucks required a wager of two hundred twenty. Van put approximately thirteen thousand dollars on the line to gain that six grand; risking thirteen grand, essentially, to win the single unit that served as the point of this entire ordeal. Van will play it out even if it involves a four-game series, which could prove nerve-racking to the average punter. The Marlins and Cards, however, were only playing three.

The line on that third game at the Westgate SuperBook, whose mobile app Van favors, made a significant jump (to make St. Louis even more of a favorite) one hundred and two minutes before the scheduled first pitch, and another with forty minutes left. Either of those bumps could have reflected the single wager that Van made with a few taps of his mobile phone. José Martínez hit a two-run homer in the bottom of the first inning for St. Louis, Luke Voit smacked a pinch-hit solo shot in the seventh, Mikolas handcuffed the Marlins over seven innings, and relievers Jordan Hicks and Bud Norris did their jobs in a 4–1 victory for the Cardinals before a crowd of 41,297. Because Van netted the two thousand dollars from the series, he marked it as an overall win, a single triumphant notch in the baseball victory column.

Van recalls not a single detail from that particular game, couldn't even remember if it had taken place in cloudy daylight or under the stars. "No idea," he says. "The game I *do* remember . . ."

That one involved Boston ace pitcher Chris Sale at home against the Chicago White Sox. The Red Sox won. That improved Van's record with that particular asset, in baseball, to 5–0. It ran to 10–0. In mid-August, another green light flashed after the New York Mets won a series-opening game at Philadelphia. That meant the Phillies were ripe for a wager in the second game, and Philly—and Van, of course—won. "Boom," he says as he points at the particulars of that play in his notebook. "There. It hits. A beautiful thing."

It would become even more attractive. Van would typically halt his baseball action at Labor Day; September call-ups, or roster expansions during the final month of a season, can tend to toss wrenches into the routine of any given team, altering chemistry that had been established between starters, affecting game outcomes. However, he made an exception. The Yankees were in play, on August 28 and September 1; they won both games.

## THE SKINNY

How Van Smith attacks his sports gambling presented a revelation. I had believed, had drilled in me over decades, that the 52.38 percent barrier, factoring in the typical ten-percent vig on the average sports bet, was critical to experiencing success, to reaping profits. Bet the side or total on an NFL game? That'll be $110 to win $100, please. It's that ten-percent "juice" that makes it such a challenge.

However, Van's approach rendered that thinking obsolete, and that was refreshing. What else did I not know? Not a short list. His tack is about units, get 'em and get out, with little allowance for greed to muddy his strategies or endanger potential winnings. Yet, even he had flex points, signals that allowed for some bending to his rules. In sports gambling, flexibility is key.

The strict guidelines of one of his main baseball approaches usually limit Van's average action in the sport to maybe a game a week, so he made some further exceptions to his Labor Day Rule when several golden opportunities presented themselves. He pulled the trigger on Cleveland on Tuesday, September 4. Indians starting pitcher Mike Clevinger had won three of his previous five starts, losing none, with an earned-run average of 1.76 over that stretch. Kansas City starter Danny Duffy had been on a mediocre run. The impetus for the action, however, was that the Royals had defeated Cleveland in the series opener the previous day.

In that second game, Cleveland was a favorite of about minus-230, so Van had to risk forty-six hundred dollars to gain that unit, or two grand. The Indians won, 9–3. As Roxy Roxborough reinforces often, echoing bookmakers like Jay Kornegay, sports wagering is a moving target, for the buyer and the seller. Everything, always, is changing, so flexibility is imperative. That is why Van pulled the trigger an additional two times, more post-

Labor Day violations. He won them both. Van finished his 2018 baseball-wagering campaign, on this specific angle, with sixteen victories and not a single defeat (remember, it's a singular victory to come away from that specific type of wager, on a certain series, by netting two thousand dollars, and he never lost one in 2018). Thirty-two grand secured in his coffers.

A machine.

The Veer Towers are considered the Leaning Towers of Vegas, engineering feats of marvel that lean at opposing five-degree angles. They are equal parts glass, greenish-yellow panels, and steel. They were the sole vision of daring Mexican architect Francisco Gonzalez-Pulido, his first major project to advance from figment to blueprint to fabrication. He calls them utopia, surrealism, and great ambition, apt summations, too, of this city and some of its inhabitants and visitors.

A strict check-in policy awaits at the ground-floor foyer, straddling the east and west towers, before passage is granted to the elevators. At that front desk, the bi-monthly *High Rise Life* magazine contains features on the Porsche 911 Speedster Concept, a private aviation service, a new Bijan branch at the Wynn designed to mirror its flagship boutique on Rodeo Drive in Beverly Hills, and must-see beaches in Bora Bora, Fiji, and Greece.

Elegance on a grand scale, but Van belies his surroundings. We've only met once, and he seemed affable and engaging at that pool party. On the phone, he sounds as if he were willing to delve into his sports-wagering tactics, and he does not disappoint.

He is welcoming, more interested in his guests or dining mates, or new faces at a pool party, than he is in hearing his own voice. He knows the secret of the sharpest CEOs and heads of state, the premier hosts and maître d's—who frequently make it about the other person, deflect attention, shift the spotlight; make *them* the focus, make it about *them*, make *them* feel important. According to the British conduct manual *Don't*, first published in 1880, if someone wishes to be popular, "Talk to people about what interests them, not about what interests you."

Over four hours, Van is neither boastful nor predisposed to hyperbole. It's all in the notebooks. He is comfortable discussing his sports betting, which he did matter-of-factly, if briefly, at that pool party, because he has known discomfiture in talking shop. He managed a strip club in the Chicago area for six years, the first three of which he kept mum about because his mother was alive; he did not want to have her, or the family name, sullied in any manner. He kept the gig to himself for those final three years, too, due to the unsavory nature of the business.

"It wasn't underground," he says. "They're there. People who go to them just don't talk about it. But when you talk to people from Texas, or Florida, or Atlanta, nobody in Texas calls them strip clubs; they're *titty bars*. I hardly told anyone that's what I did. Friends didn't go to strip clubs, so I never was going to run into them anyway. I never would have wanted to embarrass my mom or make her feel bad. Me? I don't care. I didn't go bragging about it, because it wasn't an acceptable form of entertainment in the Chicago area.

"Most people outside of Las Vegas, it's just easier to say I'm retired than saying I bet on sports. But *here*, it's cool. People understand that. Maybe in time, in other places, it'll become more acceptable. Personally, I'm not embarrassed about it or anything. Also, I always like to project a nice image. I want people to think well of me, that kind of thing."

His abode is simple, spotless, white walls surround the Spartan square footage. The kitchen off the entry is bathed in white custom cabinets and stainless steel, as if never been used. Like a model home. Not a plate in the sink, not a glass on a counter. It's open to the dining area on the other side, part of the living space. Two square pieces of art, of vertical earth tones, hang on the wall over the wine racks—whose favored Cabernet Sauvignons are Caymus 2015, Silver Oak 2013, Justin 2014, Chimney Rock 2014. On two shelving units stand fifty-one photographs of family and friends, all in similar white frames. A corner bookcase displays volumes about actor John Wayne, director Howard Hawks, studio mogul Louis B. Mayer, and Clara Bow, who once extended ranch invitations to Fred Balzar, the Nevada governor who signed gambling into law in 1931. Bow's son autographed the tome. Van prizes a coffee mug from a recent Turner Classic Movie film festival, of which he's attended a few.

Out his windows, the Bellagio fountains are to the right, the Spring Mountain Range (including the southern wing of the Aria hotel) straight ahead, the T-Mobile Arena to the left. He passes a bogus Eiffel Tower and a counterfeit New York skyline, too, during any given five-mile morning walk, in which he wears no ear plugs that feed him music or inane blabber. He wants to be alert, as much about his surroundings as about his thinking, sifting through the possibilities and probabilities of his betting guidelines, noting a twist on a tendency and researching the tidbit when he returns to his nest.

Van settles in after a morning in Church. He has settled into Las Vegas, where he has earned Master Freemason status. We are about four thousand feet—and nearly on a direct parallel line—north of the Mandalay Bay perch that, almost a year earlier, a monster utilized to harm hundreds, transforming a concert venue into a killing field. Van might have strayed into crosshairs, had he known Big & Rich was slated to perform at that festival.

The NHL-expansion Vegas Golden Knights also played a preseason game that day, but its earlier start meant that much of that crowd had very likely already departed, avoiding potential tragedy. Van has two Knights season tickets, but he gave those ducats to a bartender pal who took his father—neither were near the nightmarish events late October 1, 2017, a Sunday. Van also has owned Cubs season tickets, at Wrigley Field, since before the light stanchions went up in August 1988.

He was a rookie when he tended bar at Sweetwater, a popular North Rush Street establishment that would become Gibsons Bar and Steakhouse in 1989. Even as Sweetwater, it was choice for people watching, a fine martini, a succulent filet. One night, Gaylord Perry strolled in. A fun place on any given night, on this evening it was downright boisterous. It could have been Thursday, April 30, 1981; Van was twenty-two, Perry forty-two, a North

Carolina native in his twentieth major-league season. Van and Perry hit it off, as did others. When Sweetwater closed, they made the rounds into the wee hours. Van knew what Perry did for a living, knew he had been a five-time All-Star, knew he was a pitcher for Atlanta, knew he was starting for the Braves the following afternoon against the Cubs.

The carousing did not end until around four-thirty in the morning, and Van and some colleagues started spreading the news. "We were all calling our friends, [to] 'Bet on the Cubs! We were out with Gaylord Perry all night and we got him all fucked up!'" They figured Perry would be in sorry shape on the bump in a few hours.

Perry, in what would represent his final start in those hallowed confines, allowed two one-out singles in the bottom of the first inning, and both moved up a base when he unleashed a wild pitch. The fog of a wild evening? An error by the shortstop allowed a run in, but on a single to left field Billy Buckner was thrown out at the plate. Chicago led, 1–0. Van's prognostication, however, disintegrated when the Cubs, winners of only two of their first fifteen games, were stymied by Perry the rest of the way. He went the distance, walking none, striking out four, and limiting the Cubs to that single run on nine hits in Atlanta's 2–1 victory before a crowd of 2,656.

"The guy pitches like the Hall of Famer that he is," says Van of the two-time Cy Young-award winner who was inducted into the Baseball Hall of Fame in 1991. "The only time in my life when I *ever* . . ." His voice trails off. It represented the rare occasion when he thought he had some juicy inside information, stuff mortal locks are made of, only to have it backfire. He laughs at the memory, how he had been just starting out in the business world, as an adult, so his loss was petty. "Back then—Jesus, over thirty years ago—I was probably betting twenty-five dollars."

Do not get him started on the ludicrous, exorbitant gaming taxes of his hometown region. "Las Vegas, for the most part, embraces [sports wagering], 'We want to be your partner. We aren't looking to be your enemy,'" he says. "In Illinois, it's, 'We want to be your enemy. We don't want to be your partner. We want to squeeze you. We want to get every nickel out of you that we possibly can.' It's this adversarial relationship, and it's terrible."

He believes he saw right through what MGM did in 2018, when it aligned itself, in some vague data-relationship multi-year arrangements worth millions of dollars with the National Basketball Association, NHL, and Major League Baseball. "These sports leagues thinking they should get a stipend, or a percentage, of sports wagers . . . go screw yourself," Van says. "I understand what MGM did, paying out that pittance. All that is so they [MGM] can use the [league's] official logos on statistical sheets. If [the leagues] want to get crumbs that way, okay. But this is just a way for these guys, the casinos, to appease these leagues."

Many frustrating years were required to transform Van into a cut-throat figure who could attempt to prop his retirement lifestyle in Las Vegas. As a stark example of how he once operated and whom he used to be, he points to Seattle's baseball series that began in Houston on Thursday, August 9, 2018. The Mariners had started well but were slipping, having won back-to-back games only twice over the previous five weeks. The Astros were the game's defending World Series champions and had won six of their previous seven games, all on the road.

A younger Van would have called his bookie, saying little other than his account number, the play, the money. That's how a buddy of mine in Dallas operates with his local bookie. An arm of that system, however, has evolved into a kind of offshore operation in which the customer is given a number and a password for access to an online site, with an arranged "bankroll" and limits, where plays are recorded. Money is not exchanged between the two parties. "Nobody can kick the bookie's door down," says Van.

The company responsible for that Internet operation would receive, typically, twenty or twenty-five bucks per patron, per week, by the bookie. With fifty customers, that's a decent take for the coordinator of the website. Bookies' rosters, however, often are much larger. The lifeblood of their business is credit.

Another pal, in Southern California, wagers via the online site GoBlueCC, which appears to have a server situated outside Wichita, Kansas, but whose offshore site could not be determined. Every Friday, he meets with an agent, presumably the local bookmaker, to dispense or collect cash. In early December 2018, that friend's younger brother successfully lobbied that local bookmaker to configure a PayPal system to ease such payments.

In Chicago, Van also met with his bookie once a week to even his account. "You would meet up and pay them, or they pay you. I always arranged it to be a weekly thing. It kept me in check more. This is the ultimate, here in Vegas, or with the offshores, because you set up your account and if you don't have it, you can't bet it. Nothing is better than that. Bookies will never go out of business, because of the instant credit. And probably ninety percent of the people want that."

The SuperBook gets most of Van's business due to favorable lines. "That place is a godsend, because of its ten-cent line on hockey and baseball. Nobody else has that, and it saves you money." A ten-cent spread—rare in and around Las Vegas, but not exclusive to the Westgate—between favorites and underdogs connotes that a customer will get $1.30 on a $1.00 bet on the underdog, while the favorite will cost $1.40 to gain $1.00; the "dime" difference is between the $1.30 and $1.40. Should a bettor be faced with a $1.20 underdog price and a $1.40 favorite number, bells should begin ringing—that twenty-cent difference will, in the long haul, cost the player.

When a book on the East Coast began doing business with a thirty-cent baseball line, *Las Vegas Sun* scribe Case Keefer, who earned some fame in 2017 by topping five dozen national journalists in an NFL against-the-spread pick'em contest, rolls his eyes. "But I know that's kind of the growing process."

Doug Fitz, a retired Cleveland and Las Vegas police officer who has earned respect as a handicapper, is more incensed by what he views as an attempt to gouge an unsuspecting public, "a bunch of novices, people who don't know any better. 'We'll soak as much as we can out of them, till the jig is up,'" he says. "A lot of these people probably didn't know the difference, probably didn't even know what the hell a money line entailed. Now, out here [in Las Vegas], they wouldn't have been able to pull that off for five minutes. Nobody with any amount of sense would play into that kind of stratagem."

Veteran gambler Lem Banker says a twenty-cent line should make customers sprint out of a shop. He writes, *There's just no way you can beat it day in and day out, a sucker bet if there ever was one. And it's your fault if you take it.*

Longtime bookmaker Art Manteris, in his *SuperBookie,* wrote that the house's hold, or net revenue it can expect to make, on a twenty-cent line is 4.5 percent; at ten cents, it dips to 2.4. In 1991, the Barbary Coast introduced a nickel line. That tends to keep customers and endear the shop to new patrons, but, *whether they made money is something only they know,* wrote Manteris of the Barbary. So it isn't surprising today, with the same Gaughan-Vaccaro-Andrews-Magliulo group manning the ship, to find an occasional nickel line at the twenty-four-hour South Point.

## THE SKINNY

Most books display baseball and hockey odds, which come in money-line form, as, say, minus-130 for the favorite and plus-120 for the underdog. That's a ten-cent difference between the two, which is a ten-cent line. Like the favorite? It will cost $130 to win $100. For the dog, a $100 bet will gain $120. As the price of the favorite increases, as it always does when it features a dominant starting pitcher, the difference will reflect a ten-percent edge for the house. At times, South Point book director Chris Andrews and senior lines-maker Jimmy Vaccaro will okay a nickel line, or minus-120 for a favorite in a game and plus-115 for the dog. Over the long run, that would represent huge value for the player.

A twenty-cent line, to which Lem Banker alluded, should be avoided at most any cost by the long-range punter. Now, if it's purely a recreational activity and a home team is fancied because it has an underdog price to it, and the first pitch will be hurled in a matter of minutes, the fact that it's a twenty-cent line should not be a deal breaker. Banker simply wants the public to know what it's dealing with, that the books are a business, a ruthless business. So perk up when they post thirty-cent lines, which the professionals consider felonious. When one director of a new book in the East expressed ignorance about a sixty-five-cent line, that self-indictment should have served as a warning sign to many: to shop elsewhere.

Van also has accounts with the MGM, CG Technology, and William Hill, all of which he retains mostly for amusement. Offshore, he has access to BetUS, a privately held online gaming company based in Costa Rica that has been around more than twenty years and was recommended to him by trusted friends. He has no offshore horror stories.

Others have reported winning a big one, then the offshore entity says it has no record of such wager, or of having difficulty retrieving large amounts from those companies. Tom Barton, the professional bettor in New York, says it is prudent to extract funds in an amount less than five thousand dollars. "I've never heard of someone saying, 'I couldn't get my three thousand out.' Never. It's always, 'I have thirty grand, and they're saying it's going to be a hundred and twenty days.' I've heard that. If you are going to do it, pull out [less than] five grand. That's the only big thing. And I don't think you'll have a problem."

Most often, Van says it isn't worth the extra time involved, to gauge for the best lines, to make the bets, to go through the process of retrieving money. So he focuses on the Westgate. He'll do business offshore when he travels. When he does make a withdrawal, the company responds by sending him a gift card, equal to the sum it owes him, via a banking institution based in Gibraltar.

"A MasterCard gift card," Van says. One side of the card always features the limestone landmark at the mouth of the Mediterranean. "I take out about two grand at a time, and they charge me twenty dollars. It takes about three days. They'll load it, and I can use it just like a credit card."

Barton believes the offshores, like BetUS, will suffer most as sports wagering proliferates in the U.S. "It might devastate them. Are their halcyon days over or coming to an end? Who knows?" Those offshore operators might encounter problems with U.S. authorities, since their business is considered illegal on these shores, upon returning to the States. "[Will they] have issues with citizenship, if and when they want to come back? Absolutely. Authorities know who they are, how deep it goes."

Back to Seattle–Houston. The Mariners won the first game, 8–6, and the second, 5–2. This was a four-game series, and in the old days Van would have latched onto the Astros, displaying a complete lack of discipline by firing major ammo—two or three times his usual wagering amount—on Houston, with a bookie, in the third game. No *way,* he would have deduced, that the Astros would lose a third consecutive game, at home, to the Mariners. Seattle won, 3–2. The Astros, at *home,* getting swept by *Seattle* in a four-game series? He would have lobbed even more money on Houston in that fourth game.

"There's no *way* they can lose again," Van says. "Well, guess what?"

Houston lost that fourth game, 4–3, in ten innings. The Astros had tallied three in the bottom of the eighth, to take a 3–2 lead, only to fold, allowing Seattle a run in the top of the ninth, on a Ryon Healy two-out solo home run. The go-ahead, and ultimately deciding, run scored in the top of the tenth, when Mitch Haniger doubled in Dee Gordon, who scored all the way from first base, with one out.

That particular series would not, today, have met Van's stringent baseball requisites, of a top-ten squad playing host to a foe in the bottom six. He admits that, not so long ago, such a matchup would have landed him in trouble as a form of martingale, perhaps in a subset of that theory termed d'Alambert's equation. In a martingale example, I bet twenty bucks on a hand of blackjack, lose, then bet forty in an attempt to make a profit (a win covers losing that first twenty and earns me twenty), and if that loses I double up again, to eighty. The losses pile up fast, which is the inherent danger of the play.

Van tries to recall the exact title of that off-shoot angle, instead saying *D'Arban-something-or-other*. Team A, at home, can't possibly lose to Team B in back-to-back games, correct? And, if so, it can't happen a third time. Correct? A bettor doubles down after the first, again after the second, more swift kicks below the belt, if not financial disaster. Chasing.

This gaffe—the Gambler's Fallacy, or betting that a streak is bound, or about, to end—has some roots at the Casino de Monte-Carlo on August 18, 1913, an infamous evening in which the ball dropped into a black number on the roulette wheel twenty-six consecutive times. The chances of that happening are one in 136.8 million. When the ball settled in black for the fifteenth occasion in a row, there was a "near-panicky rush" to bet on red. Gamblers doubled and tripled their stakes. The casino made millions of francs. The BBC ran a WHY WE GAMBLE LIKE MONKEYS headline.

Shayne Brown, whose path has crossed with Van's, knows why. The chief Nevada representative for the ever-popular Tito's vodka, based in Texas, he has a home in the exclusive Spanish Oaks section of Las Vegas. In 1997, he had begun apprenticing in the liquor industry in Southern California, taking home about four hundred and twenty-five bucks a week. He had a bookie and enjoyed taking chances betting on sports. When the Colorado Rockies made a late-season visit to Atlanta, he straightened his back and phoned his bookie.

He knew the Rockies, in their fifth season as a major-league franchise, usually played horribly against the Braves. In its début campaign, Colorado lost all thirteen games it played against Atlanta, which sported one of the finest starting rotations of pitchers in baseball. And the Rockies were playing *in* Atlanta? Easy pickings, Brown thought, even though as such home favorites the Braves would command a big price. "[Greg] Maddux, [John]

Smoltz, [Tom] Glavine," Brown says. "How could Atlanta lose, *at home*, with *those* pitchers?"

Forgive Brown for not recalling the precise series of Atlanta hurlers that Colorado would face; it's a gash that has yet to fully scab, a nightmare that still induces sweat, a lesson he will never forget. Betting what you don't have does belong in a special classification of exhilaration—you don't know what pressure is, golfer Lee Trevino famously said, until you play for five bucks with only two in your pocket.

Brown wagered two hundred dollars on Atlanta, and ace Maddux, in the Friday night game. He was about to be gifted a hundred-dollar bill, he believed unequivocally. The Rockies won, 3–1. Brown doubled up on Atlanta, and starter Denny Neagle, in the Saturday tilt. Colorado won, 10–6. On Sunday, Brown again doubled up on the Braves and Smoltz. But the Braves couldn't even score, as Colorado plated four runs. Brown was down more than a grand, which he didn't have, to his bookie. He borrowed the money from a friend, whom he repaid in installments over the next several months.

Baseball's version of a martingale zap, with a slight nod to a diabolical roulette wheel in Monaco. Whenever he develops an inkling to throw good money after bad, or chasing, to recapture the principle in one fell swoop, Brown recalls those Rockies games in Atlanta, and the subsequent cold, cold sweat.

At Brown's party for Super Bowl LI, when the Atlanta Falcons had taken a 21–3 advantage over New England into halftime in Houston, I inquired with him, knowing he had access to several casino apps in town, about the money-line odds on the Patriots to outright win the game. With super quarterback Tom Brady running New England, it seemed a fitting scenario to take a chance. Especially at sixteen-to-one odds, which Brown found at a shop. We put a few acorns on it and were rewarded when the Pats and Brady put it in overdrive to win in overtime, 34–28.

That's entertainment. Van once sought other potentially profitable outlets, like playing poker and counting cards. He inspected two Texas Hold'em books penned by the expert David Sklansky, to understand that game's dynamics. "To understand what you'd have to go through. Afterward, I decided it didn't interest me enough to dedicate myself to doing that."

He visited with noted card counter Frank Scoblete to scrutinize his methods, nearly convincing himself to give blackjack a go. He had never reviewed the Kevin Spacey movie *21*, about a team of students from the Massachusetts Institute of Technology knocking over Las Vegas casinos for six million dollars, but he didn't have to. "I started thinking, 'All that bullshit, hiding *this* and *that,* we've got a *signal* . . .' You're still dependent upon other people, as well as the casino could shut your ass down in two seconds if they want to, even hassle you. Independent casinos have their own jails, and god only knows what could happen."

He determined that, in the best-case scenario, he could make eighty dollars an hour, playing at least four hours a day, five days a week—with a unit spread of one hundred to eight hundred dollars, specific to the card situation—to make a living. About eighty thousand a year. With a bankroll any bigger, say, a unit spread of five hundred to four grand, the payoff of four hundred grand would be enticing, the scrutiny untenable. "They're going to be up your ass," Van says. "A [cashier] at the Westgate told me, 'You have the mind for this stuff.' She always argues with me. I'm like, 'Honey, you're the one still working here. I'm the guy who comes in every two weeks and takes out five or ten grand.' Who's right? Who's wrong?"

(Van is wise to restrict casino visits to cash retrievals, because their perils run beyond the obvious. Do not engage just anyone. When some red-eyed half-wit inquires what I do, and I make the mistake of telling him, he says, "That gets you hard?" Huh? When it's in the one-teens outside, when shorts and flip-flops are *de rigueur*, and stray spray from the next stall—below the partition that ends mid-calf—in the gents catches your bare feet . . . yeah, special. Ladies, you do not want to begin to divine the ratio of those in that room who do not wash their hands to those who do believe in hygiene. Oh, and the chatter. "I was a great baseball player, but at thirteen or fourteen I couldn't hit a curveball . . . pop won twenty games, in back-to-back seasons, but ruined his arm pitching in both games of a doubleheader . . . about twelve years ago, I had a full body-scan . . ." The drunk imploring all in the room how great he is at betting is a too-frequent breed.)

The absence of a state income tax in Nevada helped lure Van to Las Vegas. He does not instruct his accountant to list gambling as a profession on his federal tax return. He is retired, so this is a hobby. He does declare winnings as income, per the advice of a former Las Vegas CPA who specialized in such minutiae. "What she told me was, 'Make *sure* you pay tax. Acknowledge it. That way, if somebody—well, the IRS—wanted to do a roundabout and start checking, they'd say you underpaid, that you still owe *this* amount. What happens, in that case, is you pay back taxes, [and] the fine [and/or penalties], but you don't go to the can. If you don't pay [any up-front tax], you ignore it, you avoided paying *any* tax . . .' "

Such foolish, reckless, and highly imprudent behavior could result in undesirable consequences, involving more than steep financial ramifications.

"Trust me. I'm no accountant, but that resonated with me."

Van knows his limitations. "I know I'm not going to turn into Billy Walters."

In July 2017, Walters, known for massive wagers that altered point spreads, was sentenced to five years in a minimum-security federal prison for his supposed role in a forty-three-million-dollar insider-trading scheme that involved the professional golfer Phil Mickelson. Micah Roberts, a writer and one-time book director under Art Manteris, called the Walters-Manteris duel the "biggest feud in Vegas." Manteris, who does very few interviews, told ESPN, "I respect what [Walters] has done, but that doesn't necessarily mean I want his business."

Van keeps a lower profile, so he will never be found at a roulette wheel in Monaco or, as will happen later regarding another subject, as the subject of an Art Manteris quote. "I don't go to Europe," Van says. He travels to California a few times a year and might attend another TCM Festival, staying at the stately Hollywood Roosevelt Hotel, site of the first Academy Awards gala in 1929. He visits friends in Arizona, Nashville, and Memphis, a short drive from more pals in Tunica, Mississippi. Buddies are always up for going to Cubs games in Chicago. The Golden Knights keep him busy. The Palm and Del Frisco are favorite Las Vegas culinary haunts.

Van strolls to the lower-right drawer of his TV cabinet. The notebooks, with all the secrets, lay at the top. Four hours would be required to peruse them, to gain context on how he wound up here, twenty-three stories above the mecca of U.S. sports gambling.

To Case Keefer, the sportswriter, those notebooks are conspicuous. Of the several professional gamblers with whom Keefer has come in contact, computers serve as rudders. Van does employ one, but only for general player or team research, and his laptop is nowhere to be seen inside his apartment. "They do exhaustive research, making formulas, [the computer] spits out a number, and they go for it," Keefer says of the common pro-bettor profile. "Doing it all by hand, having those notebooks, that just seems less and less the approach. That differentiates his story. I do not think there are many guys doing it the more old-fashioned way."

As he has raised his stakes, Van has become seasoned and sophisticated. As I sit with him in the fall of 2018, for his third twelve-month stretch in Vegas he will most often bet four thousand dollars, with certain situations warranting wagers of a grand, three grand, or five grand. But that's in the future. For the internal governor that has guided him for the past fifteen years, especially the past few, he thanks Joe, a good friend with whom he speaks regularly. Van had been frustrated and irritable. He was making horrible picks, having trouble separating smart plays from the sucker games on a long college football menu, losing lots of money. Joe sensed the misery.

"You know what I do?" Joe said. "I started looking at rankings and power ratings." He explained that he simplified his sports wagering by concentrating solely on those ratings and rankings, with the understanding that much information was contained within those specific numbers—statistics, patterns, power factors, injuries, weaknesses, and other nuances that would be very time-consuming for him to disseminate, if that were even possible, and track. Many people will tailor power ratings of others, adjusting accordingly to information that they value to a greater, or lesser, degree, and tinkering with them throughout a season.

Alas, power ratings are major factors in how the oddsmakers and bookies establish their lines.

Joe devised strategies from there. Van thought all of that sound. "I knew there were fellas who used computers. They can throw every game in there and come out with something," Van says. "But I'm not that guy. I told Joe it sounded like a solid way to proceed. It was a great thing for me."

## THE SKINNY

Power ratings are common in a bettor's arsenal. They can either be derived from scratch, using elements that have been proven to be useful, over years or decades, in dissecting the key elements of a team's performance and using that against another team. The home team will have a factor that reflects whether playing in its own stadium is an advantage, or it's just another field. If the Miami Dolphins have been designated as a 36, for example, and they're playing at the Texans, which have been pegged at 31 but plays exceptionally well in Houston over recent years, warranting an extra half a point on a home-field advantage that typically is three points, then Miami can be designated as a 1½-point favorite: 36 minus 34½.

Should the early-week spread come out with Miami as a 5-point favorite, the handicapper who performed the above math and established those power ratings will see that 5 is greater than 1½, so the clear theoretical betting value here would be to take Houston and the five points at home. If the power ratings are keen, Miami should win by a point or two; by taking five points, the bettor has gamed the system with his knowledge and experience.

Some will take power ratings from *The Gold Sheet,* an established, decades-old newsletter, for example, and tweak them just a bit with personal touches. Or, punters will take power ratings from *TGS,* or one of the many other publications and websites that supplies them, and apply them straight up in relation to the upcoming weekend's games. There are different ways of developing them, but power ratings are the backbone of many gamblers' prognosticating methods. Moreover, they can be valid, and deftly applied, for other sports.

He began implementing Associated Press rankings for college football and college hoops, and he used ESPN power ratings for the professional sports. He tested situations, explored tendencies, charted them with the ballpoint pen in those notebooks. Today he has a system that makes him laugh at himself for thinking he could get one over on a master like Gaylord Perry, an investment plan into which blood has tapped.

In the summer of 2017, Van's brother inquired if Van could make some money for him. He gave Van ten grand, hoping to capitalize on the notebooks, the discipline, the winning. Twelve months later, that seed funding had become fourteen grand. Van asked him, You want the money, or should I roll it over? His brother said, Roll it over. What do you think you can do? "Well," Van said, "we'll bump your unit from one hundred dollars to a hundred and fifty, so you should make six grand. In two [total] years, you [will have] doubled your money."

Van had his first client, albeit pro bono. Double the principal in two years? What particular stock, or other conventional investment vehicle, could accomplish that feat? For the record, Van's retirement funds, and other investments, increased a total of seventeen percent in the 2017 calendar year. He did not touch any of them.

For all the success he has experienced in baseball, he considers it to be a minor arena for him. His main attention, remember, is the weekly power ratings on ESPN's website. The top ten teams and the bottom six squads are his focus. They alter a bit every week, and he changes course—in his notebooks, every Monday—accordingly.

The play once involved teams in the bottom ten, but he found that trimming four from that list produced better results, streamlining his exposure to needless plays. Several years ago, he tracked many angles. His shorthand relies on acronyms that, to a layman, must resemble some sort of WWII code: *THF,* for Top (a top-ten-ranked team) Home Favorite; *BAD,* or Bottom (bottom six) Away Dog. His baseball notebook is lined with *BHD, TAD, BAF,* etc., along a left column. The overtaking of enemy airports? Initials of double-agents? "I tracked everything," he says, "every friggin' thing. Each week would require four, five pages for all the games. It just got to be too much."

A thorough analysis of more than ten years' of his baseball notebooks revealed that a bottom team plays at a top team about thirty times a season. The nonchalant wagering on the home team in that first game, however, did not prove to be prudent because, according to his statistics, that home team won about twenty of those games. The problem, again, is that home baseball favorites command such a high price, of minus-200 or higher. That's why those ten defeats are costly, not making those twenty victories worth the trouble of betting on them.

"And I found that, one or two times a year, the bottom team will sweep the good home team. So, since the first game is such a break-even proposition, I started waiting until the second game. If the good team lost that first game, now I'll make that bet [on the home team]. And the whole point is getting to those fourteen units."

In five of the ten seasons before 2018, that particular baseball play did not lose. The price of doing business in that sport, however, is the high price on home favorites. "When it loses, it costs you money," he says, "and it's going to eat up about half of your winnings. However, in those five years that it did not go undefeated, it did still make some money once or twice. Say, six units; that's twelve grand. Thank you very much. Twice, it lost money.

Once, I broke even. Didn't make any money. But, okay, I didn't lose any money. So I'll take that."

Van also lops football, collegiate and professional, among his minor action. It bears repeating that these revelations represent a portion of the angles, and games, on which he acts.

In the amateur ranks, he studies the Top 25 rankings, every Monday, every week. He will take home dogs—*FHD,* in his notebooks, meaning For Home Dogs—and go Against Away Dogs, or *AAD.* In 2017, he was 12–3 wagering on home dogs and 17–11 going against away dogs, a combined 29–14. Including the vig, he cleared roughly thirteen units, when a unit represented a thousand dollars. "So, beautiful," he says. "I made thirteen grand, just on that."

In the NFL, he has an angle in which he will go against the Super Bowl loser in the first six games of the following season. In the 2017 season, that was Atlanta, and the Falcons only won twice against the spread in those six contests. It netted him nearly two units. (In 2018, New England, which lost a thrilling Super Bowl LII to Philadelphia, split its first six games against the spread.)

Using ESPN's power ratings, another of his NFL plays is betting on top-ten teams as home favorites. In '17, that went 35–26, netting him more than six units. He takes top-ten teams when they are home dogs; it went 2–1. He goes against top-ten away favorites when they're playing teams not in the top ten, but only until he is ahead two units. That was achieved quickly. That's approximately seven units, or seven grand.

In just those actionable football situations, Van netted twenty thousand dollars. He will not bet on college football bowl games, because too much time elapses between the end of the regular season and those tilts. And he will not play anything in the NFL during the last weekend of the regular season, when who will play is such an iffy proposition, or the playoffs.

Onto his Big Three, beginning with the NHL, "where I try a lot of things." He displays the notebook for the 2016–17 season. In ESPN's weekly power ratings, he circles the top ten organizations. In certain circumstances, he knows the teams so well he will alter those ninth and tenth teams, when their inclusion seems "absolutely crazy." He will replace them with teams he deems more worthy. He tracks, as usual—in terms of home, road, favorites, and underdogs—the top and bottoms squads. He wagers on the top-ten teams at home when they're playing host to a fellow top-ten squad. Like baseball, hockey does not involve point spreads; they are straight money plays in which home favorites typically are pricey.

He bets out of the gate, according to those ratings, and the notebook shows he went 11–1 in the first week. "I'm already up nine point eight units," he says. The second week, it was 7–3, for a 1.8-unit net. That's 11.6 on the young season, with that predetermined goal of fourteen. The third week was a loser, at 8–6; because of the price, he lost 1.15 units. He's 26–10, up 10.45 units. In the fourth week, he went 11–4, for a 4.4-unit gain. That put him close to fifteen units, a net of almost fifteen thousand dollars, so he was finished with that particular play.

"I'm done," Van says. "Bye."

He continues detailing the outcomes, writing results on those pages in black ink. He will follow the second half of NHL seasons independently of the first. "Because what I found is, in the second half that thing that *worked* usually goes to shit."

He opens the 2017–18 season by hitting his fourteen units by December 6. He follows his notations, which show that his net profit would have peaked at 32.6 units. However, it went south after that, and the second half would have ultimately netted him less than a unit. That reinforced his research into the sport over the previous ten-plus years, which revealed that the very best he could hope to profit—"the plateau," he says—was sixteen units. He scaled back his cut-off point to fourteen, to be safe, as a guard rail against greed. "What's more important to me is to win that money and put it away, rather than putting it at risk."

Hockey might be his favorite sport, and the Golden Knights season-ticket holder was happy to be taken along for a magical 2017–18 ride—all the way to the Stanley Cup Final, against Washington—with the rest of a wild fan base thrilled to be a part of one of the four major North American sports leagues. The summer before that smashing début, the Westgate SuperBook had the Knights listed at five hundred-to-one to lift the cup. Thirteen tickets were written at that price, and no matter how much that payoff got whittled by book director Jay Kornegay and his staff, money kept pouring in on the first big-time Las Vegas sports franchise. Had Vegas won it all, some book directors estimated that it would have been a five-million-dollar hit to their city-wide tills. But Van never took that futures lure, never entertained the possibility of such a big hockey payday.

"Doesn't bother me," he says. "I don't make bets like that."

Those are for tourists, he adds, not for someone who tracks diligently a precise set of circumstances worthy of risking his money. It's an investment. That's the common theme among those who consider themselves hardcore professional sports bettors, like legendary Las Vegas figure Lem Banker—they want nothing to do with parlays, teasers, or futures. Fools errands. Van might put a twenty on the Knights if he's headed to the game, or a similar wager on a baseball game if, say he's headed to the Palm, at Caesars, and he knows the game will be shown in its bar area.

"I'm just not a person who bets on futures, like, Who will win the Heisman Trophy? or Who will win the World Series?" he says. "I don't make those bets. Like guys who do the fantasy stuff. I don't have any interest in that whatsoever. The most foolish . . . the *worst*."

He closes the hockey notebook. He mentions how he has befriended many athletes, umpires, referees, officials, executives, celebrities, and other public figures over the years, in the prominent positions he has held. "And none of them know that I do this. I don't discuss it." With the sports figures, "I would never want them to get into trouble" by knowingly fraternizing with someone so involved with sports betting.

In the NBA, Van relishes the bad squads, "the crappy teams," he says. A bottom-six team (ESPN power rankings) on the road catching less than ten points has proven its value, to him, over the years, and he bets it until he has earned five units because he does not want to belabor the play. At the start of the 2017–18 season, that gem went 5–1 in the first week, 3–2 in the second. "I'm eight and three, up about five units," he says, "and I'm done. An awesome two weeks!"

Yes, that would seem to be a counterintuitive action; a bad NBA team getting fewer than ten points, away from home, no less. But that's the point, Van says. "It's that sometimes you get a late backdoor cover or the good team rests players, or doesn't take the other team seriously." It happens frequently enough to have become part of Van's repertoire.

He highlighted another gem out of a column by Todd Dewey, an exceptional writer who covers sports wagering for the *Las Vegas Review-Journal*. In one of his columns, he wrote of Steve Fezzik, a well-known bettor and handicapper who hesitantly revealed a play in which the wise move is taking the Under in a game featuring two teams that both sport a winning percentage of at least sixty. Like many gamblers, Fezzik might have been loath to reveal such a successful angle; not that he did not enjoy sharing the sugar, with amateurs, but the less the guys on the other side know, the better.

Van studied that play going back more than five seasons. "I found out that it works. Some might think those teams will go out and play like gangbusters, for some reason. But that also artificially inflates the line a little bit." He also confirms that top teams in the league usually have some sense of how to play defense; when two of them collide, an Under delight.

He employs it on or about the third week of the season, allowing teams to settle into patterns and identities. Fourteen units, again, is his approximate bail-out point. By Week 18, it's 23–10. At 19, it's 24–11. Week 21 results in a 29–14 mark for the season. He quits. At two grand a unit, those two specific plays netted him 18.3 units—at 37–17, the twenty units are whittled by 1.7 units, the vig on those losing wagers. However, his bank book benefited by $36,600. For someone playing the long game, that is what matters.

The previous season, that sixty-percent Under play had paid off by the sixth week, when it had gone 19–6. At a grand a unit, he was up $12,400. He stresses every angle is pliable, that $12,400 might not be $14,000, but he called that one quits because he has developed a near-fatal allergy to avarice. This is his business, and he molds its boundaries and dynamics as he pleases, with absolute devotion to profit.

Years ago, during that morning walk, he pondered if that sixty-percent-teams-to-the-Under angle would also be valid in the college game. He went to work, called up the sites, scribbled in a notebook. *Voila!* It did work, he says. To allow programs to settle into styles, he employs the move at the first of the year, when teams typically begin their conference schedules. And it is not restricted solely to games between teams in the same league.

When the calendar flipped to 2018, he bit. It went 17–16 the first week, 18–14 the second. He was barely above water. However, the third week brought him glory, at 23–7. The play had gone 58–37, for a net profit of 17.3 units. The fourteen had been reached. He was up $34,600 on that singular action.

He played it out, on paper, and his notes show that it went 172–143 on the season. That's twenty-nine units minus the 14.3 on the vig from the losers, for a net just below fifteen. Again, his fourteen-unit threshold proved wise. "Beautiful," he says. He has a Bad Away Dog angle that he bets until he's up five units, which he hit in the ninth week.

The NCAA basketball tournament—whose first weekend is a four- or five-day extravaganza in Las Vegas, since forty-eight marquee games fill the big screens and sports books—does not interest Van. He does think the two-sixty-percent-Under angle might pay dividends in the first- and second-round games, but he will continue testing it for another year or two to gain more of a sample size. He does, at times, feel as if he's a scientist, shifting the different sports under his microscope with the seasons.

"That's how I do it," Van says. "What I like about living here is, in Chicago, when I started betting more money, I wasn't feeling safe anymore. Sometimes, I didn't get paid on time. Also, being limited; 'You can't bet *this* much.' For me, I've been making a good living. I haven't worked, in the conventional sense, for four years. I look at it as a great return on my investment, as well as not taking up a tremendous amount of time. If I wanted more, I could find more angles. But as long as the angles I'm using stay successful, and I increase [annually] the amount that I bet; I'd rather do it that way than look for more things to bet. Because, to me, these are proven winners."

He has pondered selling his picks, entering that vast gray area filled with loudmouth touts and pushy peddlers—*never* give these people a ring or a phone number, unless you're lonely and desire infinite return calls—who smear the few who treat it as an upright, transparent business, who are accountable. Once, at an Easter gathering at a friend's house in Las Vegas, Van met veteran handicapper Jim Feist. They had a cordial discussion.

Van went deeper with Wayne Allyn Root, the former sports handicapper who found additional success as an author, television producer, media personality, and political commentator. Van was curious about the vagaries of selling picks, the prospects and perils of operating his own handicapping service. To do a big operation, as Root once ran and which Feist currently partakes, would cost millions to start, to hire capable and trustworthy people, to arrange infrastructure, advertising, marketing.

Now you're an employer, Root told Van. Now you're running a business. Could you make money? "Yeah," Root said. "You probably can, but it's going to be a lot of work for you. Can I ask you, is there any ego involved?"

"To be honest, Wayne, no. I don't want to be famous. I want to be rich. What I mean is, fame gets you certain things, but money can get you almost anything. No. There isn't any ego involved."

Root recommended that he continue making bets for himself, and for a relative or friend who might like to get in on the action, and for dividends. "But don't waste your time and money trying to get involved in that. All you'll do is give yourself headaches."

Van assented.

He rings me near a deadline, at the end of November 2018. His report is stark. Corresponding to an increased bankroll, his average unit had been bumped to four thousand dollars. He went 28–20 in his major college football action, which netted him twenty-four thousand dollars. Not bad. His NBA efforts, however, had been middling, so he suspended betting pro hoops to research how a new hand-checking rule, or lack thereof, might be responsible for a boost in scoring.

He had just read an item in one of Todd Dewey's columns whose evidence pointed to taking the Under in an NBA game in which a road team is favored by at least seven points. Since 2004, those games had a seventy-two-percent Under success rate. Van was diving deep into its research.

The NHL, though, had been cross-checking him into the boards without remorse, leaving him bowed and bloody. Through the start of November, he had dropped eighty grand, which included defeats in fifteen of sixteen games.

"That's the frustration and danger of betting," Van says. "I don't know why [hockey] started like that, but that's the business. I pulled all of my NHL books together and reviewed everything. I had been getting annihilated. I questioned everything I had been doing. But that's the benefit of having a bankroll. It's also a lot like counting cards: you can get your ass kicked, but you still have to push it out there when it's time to push that [big] bet out there."

Over the previous two weeks, his hockey action was in the process of righting itself. He had won thirteen consecutive NHL plays, on a track toward recouping nearly every penny of that eighty thousand dollars. (In fact, part of that serious regrouping tack included whittling his net goal, in that singular NHL play, from fourteen units to twelve, which he would be ecstatic to hit in early February 2019.)

"I feel a million times better," he says, "than I did two weeks ago."

# FOUR
# The Mostest Book

PAM KORNEGAY SIGHED as her husband, yet again, glanced at his phone and began tapping at it. They were out to dinner. It was a quarter to eight, at least, long past business hours. Even though she had long known the deal, that his business can be as round-the-clock as a surgeon's, this was still supposed to be personal time, a rare night out. Just for an hour or so? Can we eat in peace?

This was nothing fancy. No view of frolicking fountains or a slowly rotating view of the entire Las Vegas Valley hundreds of feet above it. In fact, they could see TV screens—sports, of course—from their table.

Jay Kornegay had a pressing issue. He apologized. Minutes later, they locked eyes. That was ESPN, said the executive vice president of the Westgate SuperBook. "They just needed something." In fact, the network hoped to gather some odds, a point spread or something, on an upcoming game. To enhance its discussion of it, they needed those up-to-the-second Las Vegas numbers.

The eight o'clock SportsCenter started on many screens inside the restaurant. Pam Kornegay saw the Las Vegas odds flash beneath an ESPN talking head.

"Did you just do that?" she said.

"I just did that, right here from my phone."

"Wow. Okay. I won't say another word."

\* \* \*

ESPN executives tapped many resources, did their due diligence, canvassed sources in Las Vegas, executed exhaustive research, and called Jay Kornegay and some of his superiors. "Out of the blue," Kornegay says. "They stated that they were looking for a new partner, they wanted the best, the market leader, 'And you guys are it. Can we use your odds for our networks?' "

Kornegay laughs, recalling the conversation. He said then, "Sure. Absolutely."

There was a bit more to the negotiations that occurred around 2013. Then again, it was simple. No money has changed hands. It is quid-pro-quo perfection, designed for each company to pump the other's brand. The network's viewers know they will see WESTGATE SUPERBOOK at the bottom of every gambling-related discussion, and that constant reinforcement makes the property something like the McDonald's arches in sports-betting recognition and reliability. The cost of doing business, on occasion, means the appetites of Jay and Pam Kornegay will be curbed a bit.

"It keeps us busy," Jay says of his SuperBook team. "As the climate has changed over the years, more and more people want to know this side of the business. That's why ESPN expanded its coverage; their [feedback] and their [social-media] 'hits' showed that people want to know about the gaming side of things. They want to know what the spread is, what the total is. They used to put [our numbers] up every third week or so, but it's pretty much become a daily routine."

Presiding over the city's preeminent sports book comes with constant challenges, and Kornegay's duties only expanded when SCOTUS extinguished the Bradley Act in May 2018. Westgate superiors devised bold strategic plans for a national expansion of the brand, a logical move considering the SuperBook's relationship with ESPN.

Kornegay was tapped to lead the charge. The first step was to add USA to its domain name (SuperBook USA) and social-media platforms (@SuperBookUSA on Twitter, for instance). The next steps, well, they're being written by the day. There is no guide-book.

"I have to re-boot a little bit," he says. "There is a lot of great opportunity. We're certainly excited about all the things we've done over the past thirty years, which will benefit us moving forward with this expansion across the country."

Unlike some critics fifty years ago, Kirk Kerkorian saw great opportunity by building the first Las Vegas mega-resort to the east and north of the Strip—it's actually in Winchester, Nevada. He valued independence, its proximity to the convention center, and believed it could be its own draw if it were spectacular. It opened, as the International, in 1969. Elvis Presley set attendance records there and lived in an extravagant five-thousand-square-foot pent-house—the thirtieth-floor Imperial Suite. Through double doors, it featured a marble entryway, leading to an even larger entryway, which led to an even larger foyer.

In the top drawer of the nightstand to the right of his king-size bed he kept his essentials—Quaaludes, biphetamines, Placidyls, spansules, Demerols, Dexedrines, Dilaudid, injectable drugs, syringes. The private elevator bore a bullet hole, owing to The King's impatience; drywall all around the pad had further served as Presley's targets, as did a television set or two. Three Sky Villas, for high-rollers, replaced the suite in 1994, seventeen years after Presley's death.

It reigned as the biggest hotel in the world for most of the sixties and seventies, and it has matched Calvin Broadus in name changes. It became the Las Vegas Hilton, the LVH, and, in 2014, the Westgate Las Vegas Resort & Casino. Barron Hilton presided over the grand opening of the SuperBook in December 1986. It would be remiss not to mention the hotel's formidable silver-screen cameo, as The Whyte House, in the 1971 James Bond flick *Diamonds Are Forever.*

The actor Sean Connery, at one point, drives an orange beast of a muscle car east, past the intersection of Las Vegas Boulevard and Flamingo Avenue—which Michael Gaughan would monopolize, in regards to sports betting, for several years. In a Westgate corridor today hangs a framed photograph of Connery in a gas station, petrol 35.9 cents a gallon, beside that orange rig, the property in the background. That movie was Connery's last as 007.

Kornegay's path to the trident-shaped building began in 1987, when he and seven Colorado State pals voted on where to spend spring break. Jay yearned for warmth, sun, sand, and Mexico, any Mexican coast. Everyone else voted for Las Vegas. They were all twenty-one, and they checked into Bally's for a week of fun.

They had played poker every Thursday. They followed point spreads in *USA Today,* making dollar bets. But *this?* He never left the sports book. "I had no idea," says the diminutive, bespectacled, mustachioed Kornegay, with a horseshoe ring of cropped hair and a quick smile. Those features are depicted, quite accurately, in his own bobblehead doll, a first for a Las Vegas sports-book director. A cardboard cut-out facsimile of Kornegay somehow did not last long on the SuperBook floor.

After graduating, he and girlfriend Pam Dean, who would become his wife, bolted for Lake Tahoe. He had studied business management, to prep for the restaurant business, but Food and Beverage ideas duly disintegrated at Bally's. His eyes fairly glisten as he recalls how that week changed the course of his life. Thirteen months in Tahoe and he was ready for the majors in Las Vegas. He got a job hand-writing sports tickets in the Bally's book. He frequented the Marina, where he'd sometimes point out that they had the wrong team favored on their boards. And six months later, Kirk Brooks and Vic Correll invited him to join them in starting the Imperial Palace sports book. He'd be a supervisor. He didn't hesitate.

At the IP, they built the city's first drive-through ticket window, a system that relied on tubes and pneumatics. Kornegay and his team earned a great deal of press by offering a variety of Super Bowl proposition wagers. Locals dubbed it Imperial Props. In 2004, Kornegay moved to the SuperBook. Ed Salmons and Jeff Sherman were two key IP figures who currently work for Kornegay. They continue to produce a mini-book of Super Bowl props every late January. For Super Bowl LII, that was a thirty-page packet.

During his first year at Elvis's old stomping grounds, according to Kornegay, he and Kenny White went to Indianapolis to participate in a two-day seminar and meet with an array of league executives, NCAA officials, authorities from the Federal Bureau of Investigation and Royal Canadian Mounted Police, and Canadian Lottery representatives. White is a second-generation Las Vegan and bettor with a storied résumé, as an oddsmaker, crack tactician regarding power ratings, former Las Vegas Sports Consultants owner, and back-to-back victor in a prestigious Stardust pick'em contest.

The guests included NHL executive vice president for security Dennis Cunningham, officers of the NFL, NBA, and Major League Baseball, and Rachel Newman Baker, then the NCAA's managing director of enforcement for development and investigations, now an athletic director who oversees compliance at the University of Kentucky.

Until those meetings, Kenny White had never known that the FBI considers a bookmaking operation illegal when it consists of at least four people. "If one person worked on his own, gave people phone numbers and booked bets, they'd never arrest him for bookmaking," he says. "If he doesn't pay his taxes, the IRS could come in. But if you pay your taxes, you can be a bookmaker, anywhere. Four or more involved is a bookmaking operation; that's what they're going after and what they're looking for."

White gave a presentation on his forte, how odds are made, and Kornegay spoke about the bookmaking industry. They fielded questions about every facet of their operations.

"They [didn't] really understand," White says. "It looks like nuclear science to them. They're getting better at it. Boy, they're learning more and more, but they knew nothing about sports betting back then. They thought it was such an underworld, shady thing that they really didn't want to know how it worked and what it was. But they learned more, then, and they've learned more now. They know more about it than ever now."

Kornegay still fields phone calls from people he met on that trip.

"That is when we were trying to tell them that integrity is our product, as well," he says. "We don't want to take bets on something that's predetermined. Who gets hurt? I understand a 'league' [would take] a hit on its reputation, but the bookmaker also takes a hit because people think things are fixed. But if you look, over time, there really haven't been many [nefarious incidents]. Now that we are more transparent than ever, I feel like it will be very, very difficult for [people] to 'set up' a game, whatever you want to call it. We all take precautions to make sure that games are fair and true."

David Siegel, Westgate Resorts founder, president and CEO, capped off a recent nine-figure overhaul of the company's Las Vegas property with an eight-figure refurbishment of the SuperBook— somehow, its pitiful stuck-in-the-seventies facilities were overlooked in those upgrade plans. That gents room aside, the SuperBook is the toast of the town's sports-betting establishments, according to an overwhelming consensus of professional bettors. Jay Kornegay presides over it, and he has seven friends to thank for steering his career path toward Las Vegas.

The SuperBook is so popular, it is a high point of guided tours offered to guests upon checking in to the Westgate Las Vegas. Late Thursday and Friday mornings, when many people arrive, are so busy that guides can be heard finishing sentences that others had just started. This is what *thirteen million* dollars can buy . . . the world's *largest* sports book . . . at *thirty thousand* square feet, this is the world's largest sports book . . . the latest refurbishments only cost *seventeen million* dollars . . . for *fifteen million* dollars . . . and *there* is the world's largest indoor television screen.

That two-hundred-and-twenty-foot 4K video wall is, in fact, the largest indoor TV screen in the world not in an arena or stadium; from left to right, it curves like a J. It can be divided into seven separate screens, each displaying its own NFL game. But each of those seven screens can be divided in multiple ways, which can

SPORTS BETTING FOR WINNERS

induce whiplash when there are two dozen games airing on college football Saturdays. The far right one typically posts spreads and odds, and one or two on the far left will show races from various tracks for horse players.

That's where visitors will find a life-size bronze statue of Man O' War, created in Italy at a cost of a hundred and fifty thousand dollars. The chestnut stallion's lone defeat, in twenty-one races, came in the 1919 Sanford Memorial Stakes, at Saratoga, to hundred-to-one longshot Upset. A plaque on the statue reads, THE MOSTEST HORSE.

This, then, is THE MOSTEST BOOK. In wooden slots by an entryway, sheets with games and point spreads and odds are sorted, their sheer variety astounding. In world *futebol* alone, the usual suspects—England (Premiership), Spain (La Liga), Italy (Serie A), and Germany (Bundesliga)—appear. But Kornegay's charges also supply lesser-known leagues in Belgium (Jupiler Pro League), Turkey (Super Lig), Sweden (Allsvenskan), and Norway (Eliteserien). "We pride ourselves on having the largest betting menu, giving people offerings they might not find anywhere else," Kornegay says. "Some things have worked out over the years; some things did not take off."

About a hundred and fifty individual leather chairs occupy the front row, with two rows of booths, executive and VIP, behind those. Behind the booths is a bar a hundred and twenty feet long, video-poker machines at each stool. Behind that are stand-up stations with narrow shelves to place drinks and elbows. Behind that are many tables and stools, and behind that are various dining options. If all of that is packed, typical for a fall Sunday, there is a separate theater within a short walk that seats fifteen hundred and can show a dozen games on its movie-theater arrangement.

The SuperBook is a massive, dark airplane hangar. Best of all, the place is smoke-free. In a corner to the far right is a small glass-encased room for smokers and those who vape, with small TVs on a wall. Or they can mosey outside. One irate person wrote a well-crafted letter to Kornegay, protesting that prohibition. You're going to lose business and you're going to lose my business, he penned. Kornegay wrote back that he understood, but that it wasn't a subjective, personal decision made my him or another executive.

"It's a decision made by the masses," Kornegay says. "I told him, 'I know we won't please everybody, but I think we will please a lot more than we fail.' And it's really turned out that way. People love it, especially the younger generation. You'd be surprised how many of them don't smoke."

## THE SKINNY

Before anyone walks into the SuperBook and reaches the ticket counter, the Eyes in the Sky likely already know everything the staff needs to know about that customer. The sharpest of the sharp players will have registered with employees behind the walls, so there is some preparedness involved with being ready to counter-balance a big wager on a certain side, or total. There's fast, and then there's bookmaker fast.

Medium-range players will be known, too. And anyone making a large bet, of ten grand and up, will be required to fill out IRS paperwork. So they will be known, too. Anyone else will not register as a key player with the house. A so-called Bettor X made headlines around the 2017 World Series and the Super Bowl played in February 2018. He was making seven-figure wagers, and winning most of them. During the 2018 football season, a Duffel Bag Bettor was making consistent rounds in certain Vegas books. He literally plucked stacks of cash from said duffel bag, and though he started poorly, over the last two weekends of October it's estimated he earned about $2 million.

"I know who he is, uh-huh," Jay Kornegay says of DBB. "Average-looking gentleman. I think we'd have an idea what he does, [but] I don't like to talk about our customers, for obvious reasons."

He did talk generalities, like what tips him and his colleagues to suspicious activity. "Like a guy works at McDonald's but he's betting $40,000 a game, right? That doesn't add up. I'm a little more concerned if [a bettor] were a minimum-wage person or I can see warning signs, as in, I hear he's trying to pay his rent, something like that, his source of funds doesn't add up. We might have to talk to him. We do that on a regular basis. We look at source of funds. Some of them are just professional gamblers. Others can explain it, whether it's an inheritance or [other] funds. Others can't, and from that point we can't accept their wagers anymore."

A prime business rule is refusing service to anyone, anytime, for any reason, and Kornegay concisely sums up his book's position about its ability to refuse a wager from anyone, anytime, for any reason. He says, "Yes."

The sports-betting boom was reflected in an all-time number of entrants for the SuperContest (three thousand one hundred twenty-three, with a thousand-dollar buy-in) and SuperContest-Gold (one hundred twenty-eight, with a buy-in of five grand). The former pays $1.42 million to the victor, who also gets fitted for a championship ring, while the latter winner will receive the winner-take-all $640,000. In each, patrons must pick five NFL games a week against the spread. They received a gray T-shirt— GOOD TEAMS WIN on the front, GREAT TEAMS COVER on the back, mimicking the title of Pat Hagerty's 2016 book—with each entry.

"How many will not submit their week-one selections?" Kornegay wrote on his Twitter account. He set the total at two and a half, for entertainment purposes. He is always entertained by those few who enter such high-dollar competitions but fail to submit their five weekly selections. Once, such a customer was sitting in the book, with friends, completely oblivious to the fast-approaching deadline. It came and went. At some point, it dawned on him to approach the counter. Kornegay raised his palms to the ceiling. Rules are rules, which his veteran player knew.

As legal sports betting settles into more and more jurisdictions, Kornegay believes the day might arrive when the Super-Contest goes national, with Powerball-type hysteria and tens of millions—A hundred million? A quarter or a half a billion?—at stake for the winner.

The whole SuperBook setup gob-smacks Hank, a financial analyst who, until his wife's disapproval ten years ago, had dealt with a bookie near his Southern California home. He had last been on this property when it was under the Hilton umbrella. He is half speechless. We stand beside each other in the back of the book. A fan of the New England Patriots, he is pleased that their game in Chicago takes center stage on that video wall, meaning it has one of those seven gigantic screens all to itself, and its audio sprays from every SuperBook speaker. Kornegay decides which games receive that star treatment.

The Patriots go off as three-point favorites. However, Chicago goes ahead, 17–7, early in the second quarter. After the Bears' point-after kick conversion, the TV screen goes to commercial. The in-progress figures flash on the big electronic board not far from us, up to the right. I ask Hank if he has ever seen those in-game numbers that can be sources of income with proper diligence and speed. That is new to him. On that line, New England is a five-and-a half-point dog, plus-200 on the money line to win outright.

The Patriots plus points is always enticing, since quarterback Tom Brady had made them an élite team for many years and he's a comeback king. The Bears, giving those five and a half points (at eleven-to-ten odds, or, lay a hundred and ten dollars to win a hundred), are minus-250 to win the game outright. They own a ten-point cushion and are at home, so to win a hundred a punter must risk two hundred fifty if he believes Chicago will win outright. But New England plus points, I tell Hank, looks like a golden play because of Tom Brady.

Hank perks up. He dashes to the counter, since that window closes when the game resumes. When it resumes, a Patriot runs the Bears' ensuing kickoff back for a touchdown. Hank is happy. Brady throws a touchdown pass with about four minutes left until halftime, to give the Pats the lead. Hank beams. He leaves for five minutes, returning with two pieces of pepperoni pizza and a Coke—for a mere seventeen bucks, but the pizza is excellent—for me. My pleasure, he says as he fetches his lunch. He does not divulge how much he wagered, but he says he had bet on his team plus those points and on the money line during that brief commercial break. At intermission, he keeps thanking me. He is certain New England would win another football game. I have another engagement and jet. The Patriots win, 38–31.

Kornegay leads a private tour of one—me—past those deli chairs, high-back stools, the long bar, the VIP booths, those comfy front-row chairs. He taps a code into a metal door pad and we're behind the curtain. We stroll left, right, and left, into his headquarters. How much deeper could I burrow into the central nervous system of the world's most impressive sports book, into the netherworld of those computers and algorithms, the very triggers that determine the flow of millions of dollars?

An Air Force brat born in Missouri who has lived all over the U.S., and in Germany, Kornegay considers Colorado to be home. His wife, and adult son and daughter, all support Colorado teams. In his office, he keeps narrow-framed photographs of the arenas, or stadia, of the Broncos, Rockies, and Avalanche. His favorite piece of art, however, is a framed *ESPN the Magazine*, NBA commissioner Adam Silver on the cover and dated February 16, 2015, hanging on the wall behind me.

## THE SKINNY

The Kornegay family has a unique Thanksgiving tradition, which could become popular as sports betting takes hold in new jurisdictions across the country. It might even serve as a tryptophan antidote. A few days before the family, and their friends, gather at the Kornegay compound, Jay purchases a small stack of ten-dollar parlays tied to that day's NFL games. When everyone has showed, he bends them in half and dumps them in a hat. In turn, each guest plucks a ticket, and it goes around until the hat is empty.

"Now my father-in-law has a ten-dollar parlay in his hand.

My mother-in-law has one. And you know what? NOW they really want to watch the games," Kornegay says. "If you want your family to watch the games with you, do that. They enjoy it and have a lot of fun with it. When you have a vested interest in the game, it's totally different."

"Really proud of that," Kornegay says. "He was the first one to acknowledge that sports gambling wasn't such a horrible thing, that 'We need to look at it and possibly put our arms around it,' to a certain extent. When they did that, a spread about sports gambling, that was the beginning of the climate change. I told them, 'As far as the entertainment value, nothing surpasses sports gambling. You bet ten bucks, you're good for three hours.' "

The first myth he dispels is the notion that all books attempt to balance every game with equal amounts of wagers on both sides. For an extremely basic example, I inquire if it's optimal for his book to take in a hundred ten dollars (to win a hundred, remember the vig) on both sides of a football game whose line ends in a half point; it's guaranteed that one side will win. So, the book takes in two hundred twenty dollars in bets and will pay out two hundred ten. That ten bucks in profit represents a 4.54 winning percentage—the hold—for the house in the totality of that transaction, the basic average it can expect to net. Is that 4.54 percent the magic number, generally, that books strive to make in any given game or on any given day, even over the course of every fiscal year?

For posing such a softball question, I am somewhat mollified to discover that Elliot Frome, a casino-gaming analyst who is the son of the late video poker hall of famer Lenny Frome, believes the above to be true. "In the sports books, [the goal is] getting half the money on each side of a wager," Elliot wrote in the November 21, 2018, issue of *Gaming Today*.

According to the engaging Kornegay, that line of thought is too general, too basic. "Nowadays, I think that's a little urban legend that's out there, that we just want to balance every game," he says. "In a perfect world, yeahhh. But in a perfect world, it just doesn't happen. You go through every single game today and probably none of them, down to a gnat's ass, are balanced on both sides. That scenario right there, it just doesn't happen. I don't want to sound corny, but it is somewhat of an art form. You're dissecting the money, you're dissecting the market, you're dissecting the betting patterns that we're seeing between the sharps and the general public.

"What we're trying to do is put ourselves in the best possible position to win, not necessarily balancing both sides. We're trying to increase *this* price when we see a lot more money on *this* team, and decrease the price on *this* so people will want to bet *that* side. You're trying to get to a comfort level of where you want to be on a particular game."

(Some books, during some dry stretches, would not mind netting 4.54 percent every single year. In the middle of the summer of 2018, Jimmy Vaccaro says the South Point held about three and a half percent in the fiscal year that had just ended. Over the previous five years, that shop's annual figure had been around five percent. Kind of ironic, then, that at a UNLV seminar, attorney and professor Greg Gemignani estimated that, since 1984, the average hold of a Nevada sports book has been 4.5 percent.)

Kornegay knows different companies have different tacks, different philosophies. Prime on his list of priorities, he reiterates, is to put the SuperBook in the best possible position to win.

"What does that mean? It means we know where the sharpest guys are, right? We know where the general public is, right? We're trying to be in the same position as the most respected players that we know of. They're the ones that find the loopholes. They're the ones who find the weak points in spreads, and we respect them quite a bit."

He's monitoring a dozen games on the large cabinet opposite his U-shaped desk. The Missouri-Georgia tilt is his biggest morning decision, and the Bulldogs are fourteen-point favorites. (That will be their final margin of victory.) His Rams of Colorado State, a four-and-a-half-point favorite, take a 6–0 lead over Illinois State. He grins. But the Redbirds will romp to a 35–19 victory. Nevada at Toledo just started. Kornegay—or, rather, his employer—needs Nevada plus ten. But on a bad day for the house, due to one single game—not this one—the Toledo Rockets will blast Nevada, 63–44.

The one conspicuous game at the SuperBook is Stanford at Oregon. It will determine the book's bottom line for the day. Kornegay is perplexed that just about every square and sharp dollar has been directed toward the Cardinal, which is a 2½- to 3-point favorite. That's right where Kornegay knows the sharps have pegged the game. He is reluctant to push it to 3½ or 4, because that would expose the book to middlers on a key number or two; giving 2½ points and then taking 3½ or 4 is a staple move for professional bettors, giving them a two-way win if Stanford wins by three (the most common final margin), and a win and a tie if that spread lands on four.

In the third quarter, Oregon has a touchdown overturned that would have staked it to a 30–7 lead. Stanford roars back and gets handed a gift when Oregon running back CJ Verdell fumbles at the Stanford 40-yard line with fifty-one seconds remaining; the Ducks were in position to bleed the rest of the clock. Instead, the Cardinal race down for a field goal that ties it, 31–31, and Stanford wins in overtime, 38–31.

Kornegay typically departs the office on Saturdays anywhere between six and nine at night, depending on many factors. This night, he watches the end of that game at home. He confirms that his book lost a six-figure amount, on that game alone, that was healthy, which probably means approximately two hundred thousand to three hundred thousand dollars, at least.

## THE SKINNY

It's difficult enough to pick a single game, so why complicate the task by adding another game or two, at least, to that equation and playing a parlay? It's a basic statement heard often in every Vegas book, but Jay Kornegay says players come in all shapes, sizes, denominations, and intents. He is asked about the customer who has been doling out tens of thousands of bucks on two- and three-team parlays during the 2018 football season.

"Ten thousand [dollars] to this guy is ten dollars to that guy, so it's all relative. It happens on a daily basis, okay? Five-figure parlays, right? Two-teamers, three-teamers, four-teamers, whatever it is. Pretty much happens on a daily basis. Everyone is on a different level. There are some just having fun. You see it. But we're looking at our background checks. We would know if *this* guy can justify those type of wagers."

"I've seen plenty of these happen over the years," he says. "Doesn't faze me. More or less, I'm just shaking my head, you know, 'Why didn't [Verdell] get down,' or, 'Did the coaches reiterate about holding onto the ball when he fumbled?' Biggest decision of the day, and it went against us."

He long ago stopped sweating about the outcome of any particular game, or even a day or a week. Like professionals on both sides of the counter, it's all about the long game. But as I ask him about sweating, he's scanning those dozen screens. "Just looking at how we're doing; oh, we're winning, losing, winning, losing, losing, winning . . . that one's a push." He laughs.

Kornegay does admit, though, that there are certain times when he will slip a DVD into the contraption. "[Like] when we're having a bad day," he says, "I'll just start watching a movie. I'm done. At other times I'll watch a game not because it's a big decision, it's just entertainment. I still like to see who comes out ahead and who wins. But the sweating days, I don't know. I'm long past that. I don't throw things because a kid just threw a pick and it'll cost us a small fortune, because I know in the long run it will just equal out."

To keep his shop on the right side of the balance sheets, Kornegay knows computers, the algorithms, the thresholds must all be accurate and in synch, a constant symphony that the shop owners cannot afford to have misfire.

Mistakes in the new markets, as sports betting claims new U.S. territory, might be expected, but they've already been costly. At the Meadowlands Racetrack in New Jersey, Newark resident Anthony Prince pulled the trigger on a bet of a hundred and ten dollars on Denver as it was driving to take the lead at the end of a game against Oakland. Prince was handed a ticket that paid him the ridiculous odds of seven hundred and fifty-to-one if it hit, or eighty-two thousand dollars. The Broncos do beat the Raiders.

FanDuel disputed the ticket, saying the odds should have been more like one-to-six. During an eighteen-second glitch, Prince was one of twelve customers to have received those stratospheric odds. Not only were its systems not clicking, but FanDuel spun its PR wheels in handling the affair. After some delay, the company made a face-saving maneuver when it agreed to pay Prince the full eighty-two grand. It also distributed a grand to eight-two random customers.

Nigel Seeley, the British journalist and punter who has worked in the U.K. sports-gambling industry, said there is no way—absolutely no bloody way—the English bookmakers would ever pay out a mistake like that. "They would hide behind the *palpable error* rule, which means, 'We can make mistakes if it's glaringly obvious it's a mistake.' That [ridiculous payout] would never happen in England. Never, ever, ever. That's what it was, the PR standpoint. [FanDuel] didn't want the bad press. Whereas, in the U.K., they don't give a sh . . . monkeys about the press. They couldn't care less. 'We're not paying you. We've made [the decision]. Balls up! You're not getting paid! Do one!'"

Exhibiting a bit more diplomacy, Jay Kornegay had just met with his team, of about eight souls he trusts for expert analysis and insights into what shapes the SuperBook's point spreads and odds, about that very messy situation in which FanDuel found itself. A voice in the industry had speculated about foul play, an inside job, in the incident, but Kornegay says he believed that was a knee-jerk reaction, as well as a dangerous and probably unfounded position, and he planned to talk to the person who voiced it.

His employees make thousands of line changes a day. "And

there will be errors," Kornegay says. "It's just human nature. It's not so automated to where, *Beep, beep, beep, You moved it the wrong way!* It doesn't happen that often, but it will happen." If, say, a respected bettor lays a bundle on Georgia giving fourteen points, and in a flash that game moves to the Bulldogs minus thirteen and a half points, someone just made an error. A big, smart wager like that, of course, would have moved that line the other way. "But we have a couple of eyes on it and we can correct it right away."

That specific FanDuel glitch, however, went deeper. Such a major, glaring error revealed an internal issue with software thresholds, not to get too nerdy about the failure.

"I guarantee you they [have by now] looked over their thresholds, and when a bet comes up and it has a high-risk limit, it's going to be needing approval from a supervisor," Kornegay says. "We do have something in our rules that, if we have a mechanical or human error, that's obvious. But once it's a ticket written . . . it's a slippery slope. I get it. But as far as a ticket written, that is punched out, it's pretty much action.

"A ticket for eighty-two grand? It wouldn't have been printed out [at the SuperBook] unless it was approved by a supervisor. In that case, there would be other ramifications for that." He subtly tilts his head, raises an eyebrow to convey that, under that circumstance, someone just might soon be unemployed. "I just think it's a new platform they're using out there, and they didn't have an approval process. Their thresholds were not addressed."

I press Kornegay. He does not show agitation. Yet.

Computers are relied upon to make snap decisions, taking into account—supposedly—every element of what two teams have done and balancing that against what's most likely to happen next, or the rest of the game. More and more, they are being relied upon to set the odds, drawing the ire of some like Jimmy Vaccaro at the South Point. A computer, Vaccaro has already expressed with much disdain, can't match what he knows, what's he's seen and experienced, what he feels in his gut about what's about to happen next. The U.K. quants and computer geeks are becoming so pervasive that Roxy Roxborough calls this "the British Invasion II."

Like most books in Las Vegas, the Westgate taps StadiumTech, based in Las Vegas, for risk-management software that creates systems designed to protect the house. Thresholds can be personalized to meet each book's individual demands and requirements, which can be accentuated by a staff's specific computer expertise. The live numbers—in-person, or in-game—are generated by SportRadar, headquartered in Switzerland with an office on Fifth Avenue in New York.

## THE SKINNY

Betting on a game while it is taking place can be as dangerous as it is exciting, the obvious advantage being that a punter can see how the teams have been performing and, from that, drum up an informed opinion about how the action might unfold. A healthy wager on Team A could be horrific if it staggers out of the blocks, say, and is trailing by two touchdowns before long. With these options, a "layoff" on the other side could recoup what appears to be a surefire loss, or at least not make that debit hurt so much.

The in-person, or in-game, option is offered when a timeout is called or between the first and second, and the third and fourth quarters. Halftime numbers have the benefit of time, to digest the first-half action and the second-half spread without having to rush. With the in-person option, two minutes is average. Strike fast, though, because others will and the best number can fade away in seconds. Live betting, which William Hill features, is constant. As the game proceeds, the computers are factoring in what has happened, and what is most likely to happen the rest of the way given the amount of time remaining.

Many pros do not partake in this type of betting because, at worst, they're dealing with thirty-cent lines and low maximums. Remember, this genre of bettor is in it for the long haul, the marathon, and consistently dealing with a thirty-cent line is anathema to how they must operate to pay the mortgage and bills. There's an art to everything, and it's best to monitor such action, maybe with a friend who has had some experience, before participating in this type of excitement.

For these purposes, and for simplicity, we will refer to the Euro algorithms as the British models. Apologies to Bulgaria and Switzerland. "As far as game situations or live betting, they have a long way to go," says Kornegay. In European football, cricket, tennis, and Formula 1 racing, he says, those computers are spot on, very efficient.

But there are holes in the system, he says, in relation to some U.S. sports, and he illustrates his issues by pointing to baseball and football. Most Las Vegas books that allow in-person and live betting limit the damage that can be done by restricting wagers, thousand-dollar to three-grand maximums at many properties, depending on the sport, and by having humans constantly monitor them.

"[The British machines] don't understand that [Dodgers starting pitcher Clayton] Kershaw is at ninety-five pitches right now, and it's 1–1," Kornegay says. "They do not understand that Kershaw will be out of the game shortly, and it'll be up to the bullpen, at that point. It's already a pregame-set algorithm, that goes for the whole thing." Therefore, such a book is susceptible, in that short window, to a wave of bets being placed against the Dodgers.

Someone savvy, behind the desk in the darkroom of the Super-Book operations, would have to be paying attention to what's unfolding and make the necessary adjustments to such live number postings. It's the ancient man-versus-machine riddle.

Kornegay was just getting warmed up.

"They [computers] do not understand that if a [college football] team is up 56–0, like Ohio State likes to be, they don't realize that those scenarios, teams with those leads, tend to take the foot off the pedal, put backups in, they just start running nine times out of ten. Some of the calculations just keep running, 'God, they're going to win this game 98–0!' No, no, no. [Those teams] tend to back off.

"So a lot of these models need to be Americanized. That's what I like to call it. That's what others call it. Because they don't get that, even in basketball," when a team is up by a bundle, the algos stay on a steady course, with little concept that the winning team is about to back off as the foes fight to save face, to earn a modicum of respect, and tally more points.

According to Kornegay, the Euro models were paying for it, most dearly, by savvy punters turning profits in baseball and basketball.

"It's going on right now," he says. "They need to know how American sports works. You have to list pitchers, we tell them. Well, they say, why do we list pitchers but we don't list starting quarterbacks? Well, that's somewhat valid. Then again, eighty percent of that [baseball] line is made because of that pitcher."

About those relievers.

"It doesn't factor that the bullpen went sixteen innings, or whatever the case, last night, and got worn out. So Kershaw is going out but his bullpen is just exhausted from last night. I don't think it takes those situations into consideration. They really need to fine-tune it. But they'll get there. They'll definitely get there."

On risk management and exposure and thresholds and quants and sweating, Jay Kornegay is nearly on tilt. He's watching games, but there are still a few hours until Stanford–Oregon, which will deliver some late drama, to Kornegay's consternation. The family dog will not be in any jeopardy. Right now, though, one of the most important figures in Las Vegas has had enough of me. It's taken two months to sit right here, in his bunker-office, and I might be pressing my luck, even though he is far too gracious to reveal exactly what's on his mind.

"You know, this is a long conversation, trying to explain what we do . . . it's not the easiest thing and probably not complete to a point that everybody will understand."

Kornegay's ears have become finely tuned instruments. They inform him as he strolls the grounds. "I can just hear this roar, and I don't even need to look at the screen. I'm pretty sure I know what happened." He laughs. "Or, it's quiet." He knows exactly which side the shop needs in every game and exactly what the sound of the crowd means. "It goes both ways," Kornegay says. "The average bettor will be really close fifty percent of the time. You win some, you lose some."

Sometimes, Kornegay is square in the bull's-eye of an irate customer. Inside the Imperial Palace, the final seconds of Denver's 34–19 victory over Atlanta in Super Bowl XXXIII, in January 1999, produced such antics. The house had listed Yes or No prop options on whether Broncos reserve quarterback Bubby Brister would have a rushing attempt. "He was the backup to [John] Elway, and we thought they'd take Elway out [at some point, with the Broncos comfortably ahead] and put Bubby in there, and he'll take a knee or two. We had put KNEEL DOWN as a rushing attempt."

That is exactly what happened, to the dismay of a punter who had wagered that Brister would not have a rushing attempt in the game. The patron, with a full house and many of Kornegay's colleagues watching, gave it to Kornegay full-throat.

"He knew I was from Denver and he believed I was friends with [Denver coach Mike] Shanahan," Kornegay says. "He accused me of calling Shanahan and telling him to put Bubby Brister in, because we needed Bubby Brister to have a rushing attempt. Everybody was like, Are you serious? Yeah, I had a direct hotline. It was great. During the Super Bowl, I just picked up the line, 'Hey, Mike. I know you're in the middle of the game. It's Jay in Vegas. Umm, could you put Bubby in? Appreciate it, thanks.'"

Wouldn't be doing my job unless I asked Kornegay if, in fact, he even knew Shanahan.

"No," Kornegay says with a grin. "Never met him in my life. Anyway, it was pretty hilarious. A lot of people use that F-word, meaning the 'fix' word, over the years. I'm thinking, If the games were fixed, how does that happen? The guys that fixed the games, what, they met with the kicker at the local IHOP? They told the kicker to not only miss, but make it look good and hit the post? There are a lot of stories that are R-rated that shouldn't be in there. Wish I had jotted it all down over the years. Pretty much every two weeks we have a new story.

"Yeah, it's been crazy."

# FIVE

# Guys from Australia, Guys from Antarctica

A SHORT GUY, CARRYING a worn backpack, asks a female clerk at the South Point about betting limits, compelling her to interrupt Jimmy Vaccaro, who has been engaged in a serious discussion.

"What, baby?" Vaccaro says, slipping his left hand on the right shoulder blade of the attractive woman in a black-and-white referee top. "The limit? Right now? Fifty thousand."

Vaccaro returns to the conversation with a visitor, about quants and those damned British computers, when the referee top slinks back next to him to whisper something.

"How much could he bet, on the World Series, right now?" Vaccaro says. "If he wants to bet it today, while I'm here, he can have fifty grand. How long will I be here? All night. How long will I *really* be here? At least until six, honey."

The line of chatter completely broken, Vaccaro pauses for a second to glance at the quiet man about thirty feet away, nothing garish about his garb, nothing that would tip off anyone about the contents of that backpack.

"Let's say," Vaccaro says to me, "this youngster would come up and bet fifty thousand on the World Series. In two minutes, I'd go back [behind the counter], look at it, and adjust it. I would see what other places are offering, because I'd probably like to take about twenty percent back, to earn a little bit on the bet that was made. I'd go in there with a decent rooting interest. My thing has always been very simple; you've got to keep writing tickets. If you keep writing tickets, it'll work out in the end."

The punter bit, placing twenty grand on the Dodgers, at plus-131, to win Game 1 of the World Series in Boston. A Dodgers' victory would net him twenty-six thousand two hundred dollars. Los Angeles would lose that game, 8–4. Early the following afternoon, the Backpack Kid returned, betting fifty thousand bucks on the Dodgers, at plus-145, to win the series. They'd lose Game 2, too, before the series shifted to Southern California. Boston would win the series in five games.

You never know, Vaccaro always says, about players, games, or sports. The author Michael Vernetti summed up the conundrum well, as noted earlier, by calling it "the predictable unpredictability of athletic contests" in his biography of Howard Cannon. The Nevada senator influenced the lowering of the federal tax on race and sports wagers from ten to two percent, in 1974, and then to a quarter of a percent.

## THE SKINNY

Nevada's state betting tax is 6¾ percent, the federal tax is one-quarter percent; so books are on the hooks for seven percent total tax. They grossed nearly $5B in the most recent fiscal year. Compare that to Pennsylvania's thirty-six percent—and a $10M buy-in fee—and Rhode Island's proposed fifty-one percent surcharge, and it's a wonder how private entities will even deal with those overheads. It's been estimated that the Keystone State might soon gross $12B, but in that ESPN story the ridiculous tax rate was buried in the next-to-last paragraph. Nevada books are fortunate to net five percent, and are much more inclined to make three to four percent annual revenue, from which all of their salaries and expenses derive. Take a third of that in extra tax, and a slim margin becomes even slimmer. The Westgate SuperBook's Jay Kornegay says the Pennsylvania demographics "are there," so maybe the volume will offset that narrow percentage gain.

Roxy Roxborough says those are "irresponsible" tax rates,

in that they make the eleven-to-ten wagers, the typical vig-induced ratio on NFL sides and totals, problematic. "Books will have to dance around [the eleven-to-ten] by either taking a hit themselves or taking small limits on straight bets. The most logical way would have been a sliding-scale tax rate; less on straight bets, more on parlays. It would have achieved their goal and made players, the state, and bookmakers happy. Too easy of a solution."

Vaccaro returns to serious business, of naming his favorite *Columbo* episode. Five of them, he says, are pretty darn good. But the one with the actor Burt Young (Stallone's future brother-in-law in *Rocky*) as Moe Weinberg, in which Peter Falk (as Lt. Columbo) goes undercover as a street burglar, "that was pretty good," Vaccaro says of the episode called "Undercover," which first aired in 1994.

That is Vaccaro's favorite show. When it's a snoozer, he will awaken to *The Rockford Files,* maybe even *The Honeymooners.* He is fond of another era, in many ways, and he is the Las Vegas manifestation of the past clashing with the present. His passion for sports betting has impelled him since he moved here from the Pittsburgh area in 1975. In certain ways, Vaccaro has come around to modern technologies.

When he joined a certain social-media outlet, Jimmy Vaccaro didn't care much for it. Eventually, he did come around and wrote, *when they first ask me to twix i said no but with response you guys have given has changed me 100% . . . you guys got a voice . . . i truly thank all of you.*

His "twix" (er, Twitter) voice is endlessly entertaining, as he has highlighted driving into the shop late, at one-thirty in the afternoon, only to be told by the valet, You're late. Only thing that meant, Vaccaro wrote, is he'd have less time to spend in the spa. He'd write that he's gotten a steam and a massage at least once a week since coming to Las Vegas forty-three years ago. "Kids, get a rubdown once a week, especially during football. Take it out of your wife's purse, go to Quicken Loans, go to a shylock, cash a bad check, but get a rubdown."

When *Thursday Night Football* kicked off the 2018 NFL season, he suggested telling *the wife to order out for the next 5 months on Thursdays.* He called the 3270 Club he often patronized in Campbell, Ohio, in the sixties, "the nuts," but it had only one way in, the same way out. "Fire breaks out upstairs, your [*sic*] gonzo. No backdoor."

Those previous two paragraphs are cleaned up, somewhat, in grammar and punctuation. Feast on the raw version: *be careful kids*, Vaccaro wrote on the first day of NFL exhibition games. *i was sitting in steam room when 2 things came across this old coconut the amount of people betting 5 team money line parlays for 4 figures and kids under 10 yrs old in casino's . . . big decision for us was back door cover with ucla sometimes they help sometimes they don't . . . bad beats happen on both sides easy to complain from either side of the counter so just pay or collect and move on.*

Vaccaro is such an iconic Las Vegas character, he guest-starred—in real life, wearing a light-colored sports coat and a buttoned-up pink dress shirt, before a huge odds board at the Mirage—on *The Simpsons* in 1995. An in-the-flesh human, a Western Pennsylvania falsetto-lisp—which tends to flourish on VSiN when he misconstrues a good-natured Brent Musburger tease as a jab—on a cartoon show. For the episode "Springfield's Most Wanted," he set the line on who shot Mr. Burns. He suggested putting a few quid on Crusty the Clown.

He was responsible for most of the Mirage's book design. "Yeah," he says, "that was Jimmy's! My fingerprints. I'm proud of that." On VSiN, where his title is senior lines-maker, he saddled next to Brent Musburger one late afternoon and immediately flipped a switch when Musburger, giggling a bit, segued to Vaccaro for another fantastic "anecdote or two." What, Vaccaro squeaked, "is an *anecdote!?*"

One morning, the stream-of-consciousness gem watched a patron approach the window and ask for a three-team parlay for five dollars—the guy plopped twenty quarters on the counter. "I guess if you want to play you are going to play, even if that is all that is left in your kick," he wrote. "But we all have been there." He reiterated a common line he had heard from the 1970s when he wrote, "Kids, this ain't Green Stamps you're dealing with." Later that day he told Patrick Everson, of Covers.com, about Philadelphia moving to minus-eight against Dallas, "Everyone is on the Eagles. Wiseguys, the public, guys from Australia, guys from Antarctica . . . everybody."

On Thanksgiving morning, after line updates of three NFL games and two in college football, he wrote, "What a day! Drumstick in your left hand and a 3 teamer" in your right hand. "We got a lot to be thankful [for], guys and girls."

What Jimmy Vaccaro thinks is what he says. Been that way all his life, says seventy-nine-year-old brother Sonny Vaccaro. "No filter," Sonny says from his home in Cathedral City, California. "That's him. Whatever he's thinking, he says. He has never gone by a script in his life. A character. Jimmy's a character, with a lot more integrity than Jimmy the Greek. Just being honest, because I knew Jimmy the Greek."

Jimmy Vaccaro did not hold back four months earlier, as one of a featured group of speakers on the final afternoon of a two-day seminar, Understanding Sports Betting, sponsored by the UNLV International Center for Gaming Regulation.

With the wave of sports-betting interest and intrigue since the Supreme Court wiped out PASPA, the center's various seminars on the industry—ranging from two to four days, costing $925 to $1,495—were becoming more popular by the quarter. In this one, tribal representatives from Minnesota, New Mexico, and Oregon comprised part of an audience of about thirty, as did representatives from private companies, members of police organizations, and two other scribes.

Three people from a major sports league attended, but the response to a request for an on-the-record comment—What had they learned? What were they hoping to learn?—was met with resounding disapproval, so anonymous they will remain. The placard for business development director Taylor Silva's employer read LAS VEGAS RAIDERS—two years before the official move. Asked if he might entertain a future interview, Silva nodded and politely offered a business card.

Five guest speakers covered, among many topics, the history of betting and the various types of wagering that are engaged across the globe. At the apex of Roman power, the city boasted of seven chariot race tracks. Australia banned in-play wagering in 2001. In China, latest figures show that ten billion, in U.S. dollars, is wagered annually; in Japan, where boat racing is a popular betting pastime, eighteen billion; in the U.K., where gambling winnings are not taxed and it is legal to accept credit cards for bets (which is illegal in the U.S.), forty-three billion is wagered yearly. The world-wide annual figure is three trillion dollars.

(When the topic of exotic wagering, as in parlays and teasers, is broached, a speaker says this is when "things get really exciting." To a seatmate, someone in the audience mock-whispers, "*really* exciting . . . think of all the fun!")

It was during that first seminar day that I learned how every bet I had placed on an NFL game, since December 19, 2011, had constituted an illegal act. That was the issuance day of the two pieces of stock—*the no par value common stock of Green Bay Packers, Inc.,* it reads—my late father, an Ice Bowl attendee, had presented to me that Christmas. Speaker Greg Gemignani, the attorney–professor, had been raised in Wisconsin, is a Packers fan, and he, too, owns stock in the team. "Owners," he says, in his finest Captain Louis Renault (Claude Rains, *Casablanca*) impersonation, "can't bet on games."

It's a strict rule in every sports league, but there's a wink involved, since the *no par value* qualification makes the stock essentially worthless. The league's lone publicly owned franchise has a unique grandfather clause that enables it to raise funds, via stock sales, that can be applied only toward stadium enhancement. There have been five such sales since the first one, in 1923, that kept the franchise solvent.

Fans of other teams can scoff that it isn't bona fide stock, that can be sold for profit or transferred, but they will never be able to own such a memento. Jealousy. And if not for that grandfather clause, details of the NFL's TV-revenue dispersals to each of its thirty-two members (about a third of a billion dollars, lately) would remain mum; as a publicly held nonprofit, the Packers are America's lone major sports franchise that annually releases its financial ledgers.

The only other sports organizations of significance whose operations are conducted in a somewhat similar manner are FC Barcelona and Real Madrid, two of the world's most valuable soccer clubs owned and operated by their supporters. Barça, however, is a cultural touchstone beyond its sporting heritage, with a rich history of Catalan independence that rails against Spain's crown and provided inspiration to a people during Franco's oppressive regime.

As far as being cuffed by police or NFL security, neither Gemignani nor I actually fear any ramifications of wagering on a pro football game. For a business day and a half, speakers like Gemignani describe industry challenges, and low points, like an Arizona State basketball point-shaving scandal in 1994 that had been uncovered by hawk-eyed sports-book directors, including Jimmy Vaccaro, and regulators in Nevada.

The hand injury sustained by LeBron James in the 2018 NBA Finals is addressed as a curious case, since the Cleveland Cavaliers did not disclose it during the last three games, against Golden State. The Cavs lost those three contests, failing to cover underdog spreads in all of them. The topic is a mere mention in the classroom on UNLV's campus. But when the seminar shifts to the South Point, for a round-table discussion—conducted in a massive square of adjoining conference tables—with three of the property's executives, Jimmy Vaccaro bellows about Cleveland failing to disclose an injury to one of the game's best players.

Which is the entity lacking integrity? Some leagues had frothed about the fount of riches that widespread sports betting would surely produce, masking their intended money grabs as "integrity" fees. (I would pause, only slightly, upon discovering that one very successful bookie, east of the Mississippi, is friendly with several members of an NHL team. That is offset, in spades, by the sloppy performances of officials in just about every NFL game. Integrity?)

When integrity is mentioned, Vaccaro raises his voice about LeBronGate. Anyone within six degrees of a loose-lipped assistant Cavs trainer, say, might have had access to a valuable piece of information, redeemable for cash at a Las Vegas casino, neighborhood bookie, or offshore site.

"It's unbelievable that it wasn't reported," Vaccaro says. "Made us look like fools. I can't believe there wasn't a full-blown investigation into how they basically screwed us."

Vaccaro gets nearly as incensed about the rise of the machines, the computers, that are becoming such a prevalent part of his business. His primary issue is that no machine knows what he knows, what he feels in his gut, or can react to certain situations that he's been watching play out on fields and in arenas all of his life. "A computer doesn't know if it's raining," says Vaccaro, "or if someone got hurt."

Or, as expressed by the SuperBook's Jay Kornegay, if Cleveland's relief pitchers got pounded last night, so the odds on its game today in Detroit had better reflect that frail aspect of the Indians' bullpen. Hint: in the United Kingdom, that aspect is not exactly represented in Cleveland's opening line, giving an edge— to those alert to it—to Detroit's number.

The other side of that conundrum is in-progress—in-game, or live—betting, where the computer can—theoretically and supposedly—produce in a millionth of a second an alteration, a reaction to the events in a game or the direction of money being wagered, quicker than any human being.

Vinny Magliulo caps the two-day seminar by imploring how wrong it would be for anyone in the audience to assume that running a sports book can be easily achieved by just shifting a keno manager into such a new wing of a casino's operations. Don't do that, he says twice. "Okay," he says as he rises from his chair, "who's ready to bet?"

\* \* \*

Three months after that seminar, Jimmy Vaccaro stands in the South Point sports book and reports that the property's initial runs with in-game wagering have been glitch-free, largely successful. The South Point has been slow to move in this area of betting, but it's a dangerous arena. Man and machine had better be spot-on and fool-proof, because this is where the sharps pounce for profit.

For the first time, the South Point began such offerings during the 2018 football season, with ten games on Saturdays for college football and ten NFL games on Sundays. He says two tellers were hired—he nods toward the backroom, behind closed doors—to control, monitor, and manipulate those point spreads and prices that can change, with waves of cash in one direction or the other, instantaneously.

"It's been fine," Vaccaro says. "Everything is good."

Over a few months, he seems to have somewhat mitigated his stance against those machines, but he says he will never relinquish total control to the inanimate objects. Vaccaro aims to retain a role, his gut feeling, in determining a game's numbers.

"Twenty-five percent of that 'old feel,' where it's going and what you're doing with it. You can't rely totally [on computer algorithms]. I think there are some people that do that. I could never live by that, by making a decision because some computer told me to. There's nothing wrong with seeing what their decisions might be, but I'd never, ever do that. I am not stubborn. I've crossed the bridge from the old time to here. I still have a lot of old times in me, but I listen to everybody."

Derek Stevens has been gauging the man-machine dilemma. The edgiest Las Vegas hotel-casino owner (brother Greg is a mostly silent partner), Stevens has transformed the downtown area. He kind of fell for the city the summer before his senior year at the University of Michigan, when he and a buddy met other friends in Los Angeles. They made a spontaneous trip northeast, and twenty-four hours in Las Vegas became forty-eight when Stevens, then twenty, scored at Sigma Derby, which allows multiple players to bet on little plastic horses scooting around a glass-encased track. Today, there is one Sigma Derby left in Las Vegas—at The D.

After making his fortune in auto parts, in his native Michigan, Stevens returned to Las Vegas, first purchasing a fifty-percent interest in the Golden Gate in 2006, buying Fitzgeralds and turning it into The D, obtaining the other half of the Golden Gate, and devising his grand 18 Fremont plans. He became the first hotel owner to accept Bitcoin for room bookings. He does what he says he's going to do, so nobody should discount his vow to make the future 18 Fremont sports book the finest in the city.

"The one thing that maybe connects me to the old school is I'm still a privately held, privately owned casino [owner]; I'm not publicly traded or a large corporation," he says. "When you run your own company and you've got ideas, you can be aggressive. Usually, our committees are much smaller and we make a lot of decisions quickly. So I guess that's an old-school element to it, more independent and entrepreneurial. I'm definitely bullish on downtown. But I'm bullish on Las Vegas, overall, as well."

His undertaking at 18 Fremont, set to open in 2020, has compelled the ambitious Stevens to set his own lines, to have his own independent odds-making operation to service the new property and his existing casinos at The D and Golden Gate. Stevens, who had been using William Hill to handle that business, hired Matthew Metcalf, from Jay Kornegay's roster at the SuperBook, to run his book. Metcalf, Stevens says, blends the right level of experience with the right level of youthful enthusiasm.

Stevens agrees with Vaccaro about gut feelings.

"I would not want to get into the bookmaking business if all we had were computers, great software, some great data analytics, and algorithms I would trust," says Stevens, fifty. "I think that's a recipe for disaster. I also think, without those, you don't have much of a chance, either. This is where sports betting is evolving. You've really got to have both. When you have a bad day at the book, you want to be able to look at two or three Jimmy Vaccaros and say, 'What just happened?' You need guys who have lived this for decades. So I actually agree with both points. Both elements are critical today."

He relates *Moneyball*, the book about Oakland Athletics general manager Billy Bean and a somewhat revolutionary approach to the application of certain statistics, to the state of bookmaking today.

"It was all about analytics, and some of the old-school baseball guys didn't buy into it," Stevens says of Michael Lewis's exceptional tome that became a film, starring Brad Pitt as Bean. "The right answer comes down to the fact that there's a happy medium. You have to have the newer-wave analytics, but you need to have an old-school baseball guy who can see if you're warming up your closer and, all of a sudden, one day he has the yips. You're not going to get that off an algorithm. You need to have a blend.

"We've seen how baseball has evolved over the past twenty years, where you've got old-school gritty veteran baseball guys that can work in conjunction and tandem with the data–analytics guys. That's the model that we're now showing is superior. And I believe sports betting is going down the exact same path."

Not so long ago, Stevens knows, the decisions were so much simpler. Sides and a total would be posted, halftime numbers would be devised and etched on the chalkboard, and in a reasonable amount of time after the game the book would know whether it was a winner or loser on any particular game or day.

"Now, it's different. Now, you're going to take more in-game wagers than you will pregame and halftime bets. At every element, it's much more of a true market. Just the sheer volume is not something that can be handled by any one particular human. I mean, you might be looking at taking sixty bets a second. There is no human that can do that. So you have to have some experience and wisdom to go along with the technology to accomplish what needs to get done."

Nigel Seeley, the Briton hired to work that BetCast in Las Vegas, understands Vaccaro's contention about a computer's inability to factor weather, injury, and other subjective factors into the line of a game. He also has experience working at Stan James, the independent U.K. bookmaker, and he spent some time compiling odds for the sports division of IG Index, a trading company. His father was a longtime director at Ladbrokes.

"Jimmy is right," Seeley says. "The computer is making calculations as the clock is ticking down. Certain things do influence games, like what Jimmy refers to. But the computer has its price, and it will work [properly] ninety-eight times out of a hundred. There are reasons why these companies make so much money. They know their computers win them money; it's small margins of massive, massive, massive turnover."

A most contentious aspect of the business is that some veteran handicappers and experienced bettors believe the computers and offshore entities have ruled Las Vegas for the past ten years. That the books and oddsmakers of Nevada take their cues from the offshores, post those numbers as their own, then massage them as patrons bet the games.

In Long Island, New York, professional handicapper Tom Barton says he was astounded, if not incensed, when the manager of a new book on the East Coast admitted to him that it retrieves all of its opening lines from offshore accounts. Way offshore. "Bulgaria!" Barton says. "And he told me it's easier for them to get off their debt that way. So not only are they taking an offshore fuckin' book's [odds and spreads] in Atlantic City, but they're also saying that they'll off-put that and put it on somebody else. They *lay off* there, which is insane."

Roxy Roxborough, Las Vegas royalty, believes it would indeed be rare for one of the major Las Vegas books to rely—solely—on an offshore, in such a blatant manner, for such figures. Roxborough writes in an email from Thailand, "But they still look at them!"

Vaccaro nods to all of that, agrees that it happens, and that it happens too frequently. No, he says, the South Point does not operate that way, not with director Chris Andrews, oddsmaker Vinnie Magliulo, and Vaccaro—about a hundred-and-twenty-years' worth of casino experience—guiding the operations.

"It's hard not to look at [the offshores]," Vaccaro says. "Everything is everywhere, anymore. It's not like it was forty years ago. That was a little bit different; there wasn't no [computer] screen, there wasn't no Internet, there wasn't anything. You did what every other little kid did when he got home from school; you'd bring out your little pencil and chart things out. Now, you just fucking hit a button, and everything is in front of you.

"You see everything else, but you don't live and die by Pinnacle, you don't live and die by The Greek." The Pinnacle offshore site is based in Curaçao, while The Greek is headquartered in Jamaica. The Unlawful Internet Gambling Enforcement Act of 2006 made it illegal for U.S. citizens to conduct direct business with such offshore companies. Of his main objective, Vaccaro says, "You put the place you're fronting for in the best possible position."

Vaccaro is typically transparent, often divulging quality information when asked a basic question. He's a rich trove of Las Vegas and sports-gambling history. When he offers only a three- or four-word answer, he has something on his mind. He's either got a pending meeting, odds on a certain game are requiring his attention, or, well, he's ten minutes late for his afternoon steam. Late October 2018 provides extra distraction as a Showtime film crew has been spending many hours, on consecutive weekends, interviewing Vaccaro and his colleagues, and punters in the audience, for an in-depth documentary about the industry.

He is a product of his environment, a smelting-pot nook encompassing Western Pennsylvania, Eastern Ohio, and that vertical sliver of a West Virginia panhandle—where the Mountaineer Casino, in New Cumberland, began its sports-betting operations a day before Thanksgiving 2018—in which gambling is as much a part of the bedrock as steel mills and coal mines.

Sonny and Jimmy watched their father, Natale, go to and come from one of those mills for many years. Natale Vaccaro, who had migrated from Calabria, Italy, to the U.S. when he was eighteen years old, never once complained. In forty-three years, he missed only one day of work. At Duquesne Steel Works, he directed the twenty-seven-hundred-degree molten steel, or "lava," into casts.

"In the sixties, he bought his own home," says Sonny Vaccaro. "That was a big breakthrough."

Those mills and mines, and the many immigrants they employed in the late nineteenth and early twentieth centuries, were, according to experts, responsible for the explosion of vice in the region. Meyer Lansky, and LaRocca and Genovese crime-family subordinates, would dig their claws into Steubenville—birthplace of Jimmy the Greek (born Demetrios Georgios Synodinos), where a young Dean Martin learned about gambling and odds, working as a croupier for ten years—and Youngstown, in Ohio; Wheeling, in West Virginia; and Pittsburgh.

Its well-earned moniker is the Cradle of Bookies.

Vaccaro was among a vast exodus of gambling enthusiasts who have relocated to Las Vegas, which includes Scotty Schettler, Richard Saber, Jack Franzi—the famous "Pittsburgh Jack"—and his nephew Art Manteris (Stations' race and sports vice president), cousin to Chris Andrews (at the South Point). Nicholas (Nico) Sfanos is another club member who, in the fall of 2018, left Las Vegas after a ten-year run to direct the new DraftKings at Scarlet Pearl Sports Book in D'Iberville, Mississippi.

Sfanos, who calls Manteris "Archie" and Andrews "Chrissy," told *Gaming Today* that he takes immense pride in being included with such luminaries. "There's a special thing about being from Pittsburgh when you're in this industry. Pittsburgh and sports gambling, they go hand in hand."

In his *Always Bet on the Butcher,* author Warren Nelson wrote, about Franzi, "One of the smartest and most knowledgeable guys in the business." In his nineties, Pittsburgh Jack—the first of the bunch to look west, in 1972—still frequents the South Point to play the slots. "He taught me composure," says Vaccaro, "the idea that, if there's nothing there, don't push it." In other words, if a game is getting scant attention, don't tweak the numbers just to attract action.

Bert Osborne, Robert (Muggsy) Muniz, Johnny Spot, Jerry Ludt, Tom Blazek, and Tommy Saber were some of the other notables on a deep list of transplants who climbed out of that cradle.

"There are so many people in this town from Western Pennsylvania," says professional bettor-handicapper Ron Boyles, a native of New Castle, Pennsylvania, whom Jimmy Vaccaro has called "Skinny" for decades. "It's incredible how many moved out here right at that same time. You can go to any sports book in Vegas and you'll find someone from Pittsburgh."

The region has produced quarterbacks at an even more outlandish rate, namely Joe Willie Namath, Dan Marino, Joe Montana, Jim Kelly, Johnny Unitas, George Blanda, et al. Kids latch onto that kind of hometown publicity, listening to games that starred those figures, maybe wagering the lunchtime milk money on the hometown hero.

Vaccaro started betting in his youth at the billiards tables, for twenty-five or fifty cents a game, in Louie's Pool Room at 412 Cavitt in Trafford, his hometown, a dozen miles east of Pittsburgh. At ten, he bet ten dollars—on credit, through Sonny, who would make a name for himself in the sneaker business—on the Colts to beat the Giants in the 1958 NFL championship game; he still beams about Alan Ameche running it in from short yardage in overtime to win it for Baltimore. He made his first hundred-dollar wager when he was thirteen or fourteen.

He and friends would zip across the border to Chester, West Virginia, to engage in barboot, a Greek game involving two miniature dice. For the shooter, only four combinations (3–3, 5–5, 5–6, and 6–6) are winners, and only four (1–1, 1–2, 2–2, 4–4) win for the field. A second figure, the fader, sets the odds.

In 1972, Vaccaro was driving around with his dog in a station wagon as he listened to the Steelers' playoff game against the Raiders on the radio. Its television broadcast was blacked out in the area. The Immaculate Reception ensued, causing Vaccaro to lose the four hundred bucks he had placed on Oakland. At an early age he knew to bet point spreads, not teams, even the popular one in his backyard. He had dropped twenty-four hundred dollars on the Baltimore Orioles when the underdog New York Mets won the 1969 World Series; that one took Vaccaro a few months to square with Irwin, his bookie.

"It was every day," Vaccaro says of gambling's influence on his hometown. "It was just always there. As a kid, I knew about people betting numbers. I knew about people playing pool for money, playing short cards, gin rummy. There was a natural attraction. When business was really good and the steel mills were working, there was just money everywhere. You just got grounded to it. It perked my attention."

He came to Las Vegas in 1975, hooking on with Michael Gaughan at the Royal Inn, just as the state repealed a law that forbade sports books in casinos. The Royal became the third such property with a book, after the Union Plaza and Stardust, where Lefty Rosenthal set a high standard for future sports books. Till then, they were stand-alone shops, smaller than 7–Elevens. Lefty designed expanses with large-screen televisions, chairs, desks, long bars, and other inviting amenities.

"I knew exactly what to do," Rosenthal said in Nicholas Pileggi's *Casino* (1995), the book that director Martin Scorsese would develop into a film starring Robert De Niro. Rosenthal had spent a lifetime in those inhospitable, sawdust-infested, stand-alone joints, which were invaluable to him when he finally got the chance to design, and run, his own shop at the Stardust. "I can't tell you the hours I spent going over the design, just the hours going over the right kind of seat to buy, the space, height, the boards, the TV screens. I wanted them to be like theaters."

Large, impressive, and welcoming books today—from the SuperBook to casinos along the Strip and on the periphery (M Resort, Red Rock, Green Valley Ranch) of the valley, to what Derek Stevens is developing at 18 Fremont—owe a debt to Lefty Rosenthal, grandfather of the modern-day sports book experience.

Roxy Roxborough tells people *Casino*, the movie, is about as real as Hollywood could ever make something, "without the way Hollywood likes to mess up everything. Once [authorities] decided to go after one of the guys who was mobbed up, they went after Lefty. The idea was to change the way casinos were run . . . that started a crescendo of events where casinos turned corporate over, I'd say, the next five to seven years. Of course, nobody called him Lefty. We only called him Mister Rosenthal."

Lefty warned his barrister, Oscar Goodman, to always shoot straight with him. "As long as you tell me, it's okay. Just don't ever try to hide anything from me," Goodman recounts, in his book, Lefty telling him. Goodman added that Rosenthal wasn't an intellectual but was a smart man.

Michael Gaughan has no issue calling Rosenthal by his nickname, deigned presumably for the simple reason that he was left-handed. "He wasn't a good guy," says Gaughan. Rosenthal's long résumé of questionable associates and activity got him banned from Las Vegas casinos in 1987. He died in Florida in 2008. Gaughan says the movie was eighty-percent accurate.

Scorsese and his location crew had discovered that the five-acre Las Vegas ranch on which Gaughan's wife, Paula, had been raised would capture perfectly the gruesome end scene in which this fictional Anthony (the Ant) Spilotro and his brother would be discovered to have been beaten and buried alive—which really happened to the siblings, in Iowa. Short, mouthy actor Joe Pesci played the role of the Ant with aplomb.

Donate twenty-five grand to the UNLV rodeo team and leave the land the way you found it, Gaughan told the Scorsese crew, and it's a deal. "They come by and lay down five acres of re-bar. They bring down a trailerful of corn from Sacramento. Nice, green corn. Took two or three days to shoot. Well, Mike Toney, [late UNLV basketball coach Jerry] Tarkanian's ticket guy, is the guy who kills Spilotro, or Pesci. When Pesci was in that hole, Toney fell on him and broke a couple of Pesci's ribs. They had to stop filming for two and a half or three weeks. They come back to resume shooting, and the corn had yellowed. The next day, they drove down another trailerful of corn from Sacramento. What a pain in the ass."

*   *   *

In personality and experience, it would be very difficult to top Jimmy Vaccaro in Las Vegas acclaim and lore. Gaughan took Vaccaro with him when he opened the Barbary Coast in 1979.

On the northeast corner of Las Vegas Boulevard and Flamingo Road, the Barbary's intersectional neighbors were Caesars, the Dunes, the MGM Grand, and the Flamingo Hilton, with the Castaways, Sands, and Aladdin within healthy walking distance. The competition all sat idly by, with no sports books, for about six years. When Caesars finally installed a sports booth, it was so tiny customers could reach around and alter lines when employees were distracted. On many mornings, Barbary officials would stroll into those hotels to cash in rolls of their own chips—Gaughan accepted enemy chips in his book.

Today, a Las Vegas real-estate expert estimates land in that vicinity to be worth north of ten million dollars an acre. In the expansive office he shares with business partner Frank Toti, in the back of the South Point overlooking the pool area, Michael Gaughan nods at that figure. He does not prefer cameras and microphones, and he deflects sports-book inquiries to Vaccaro. "Nobody knows more," Gaughan says of Vaccaro.

Gaughan is gracious to allow a stranger into his lair.

"What a corner!" Gaughan says. "The Dunes, Caesars . . . they never fooled with a sports book. Churchill Downs was down the street, between MGM and Aladdin. There were maybe eight stand-alones around then. But at that corner, nobody [else] had a book. [Federal taxes were] two percent at the time, which nobody wanted to pay. It took hotels a long time to figure this out, the geniuses . . . this is important, which I taught at [UNLV]. Sports books are supposed to do three things for you. They're supposed to bring people into your place. They did that. Two, you accommodate the people you have. And, three, it makes a little bit of money. They all finally realized that."

Gambling is in the Gaughan DNA. He keeps a big black-and-white framed wedding-day portrait of his paternal grandparents on the wall across from his desk. He points to that grandfather,

Michael J. Gaughan, when asked where this thread began. Michael J. owned, and made book on, horses, and he was involved in another notoriously dubbed Chez Paree club, this one in Carter Lake, Iowa. He suffered fatal injuries, says the South Point owner, when he was pushed from a moving train. Burial records show that Michael J. Gaughan died, in Omaha, on March 6, 1944. "It was a lot tougher back in those days," says the grandson. Was the tragedy gambling related? "Yeah." He does not care to further discuss the matter.

Gaughan and Vaccaro witnessed an all-time zany Las Vegas chapter in 1981, when Hollywood writer and director James Toback, wearing headphones connected to a Walkman hooked to his belt and carrying a knapsack full of cash, walked into the Barbary. For that reason, Vaccaro, supervising the sports book, dubbed Toback "Music Man." Art Manteris devotes eight pages of his *SuperBook* biography to detail the subsequent events.

Toback's credits would include *Bugsy,* the popular 1991 release that starred Warren Beatty as the mobster Bugsy Siegel. A quasi-autobiographical 1974 flick called *The Gambler* starred James Caan. Toback, in Las Vegas, was a six-week tornado, wagering seven figures a day on baseball just at the Barbary. Pittsburgh Jack was there and marveled that Toback would increase his bets as his offered odds worsened. On the same game, at minus-130, he wagered the limit (three grand), as he did at minus-135 (five grand). Then, with a no-limit stipulation, he'd fire thirty thousand at minus-140. His largest wagers were on the worst numbers. He'd bet two million a day, with wild mood swings. "Docile to crazy," Vaccaro said in *SuperBookie.* "And everything in cash."

That was the year of baseball's mid-season baseball strike, and Music Man hit the Barbary for five hundred thousand dollars on a Cubs game, the last before the strike. He soon cashed tickets worth about a million and a half dollars, so many hundred-dollar bills that he wound up stuffing them into his boots, socks, and underwear for the plane ride home to Southern California.

He'd lose it all, ending the chapter by making five-team baseball parlays for twenty-one bucks. A wild man, Vaccaro said. "As coldhearted as anybody I've ever met in my life. . . . an absolute stone-cold player with nerves of steel."

Vaccaro has seen abject fear in those on the other side of the counter. Those nerves can affect anyone, from the amateur approaching the ticket window for the first time to a veteran of the industry, fumbling with the computer keyboard on the business side of the counter. From the brain down through the larynx, the voice grows hoarse, slightly nasal. Sensibility at the external auditory meatus (ear) and back of the pinna (ear canal entrance) can be nullified, triggering imbalance, upsetting the stomach and digestive tract. Liquids might be regurgitated through the nose during the act of swallowing.

Impairment to the vagus nerve (actually two clumps of complex nerve tissues, stretching from the brain into the abdomen), according to *Harrison's Principles of Internal Medicine,* as related above, is not so dissimilar to the testing of one's Vegas Nerve. Chad Millman presented the corollary in *The Odds* (2001), about a wild college basketball-betting season in Las Vegas. Blurred vision. Dry mouth. A migraine. Retching and heaving. Legs give way. You hit the floor. Welcome to Fabulous Las Vegas. Engaging in sports wagering can have consequences. A select few can sustain themselves.

Toback did, well, for a little while. His rise and fall were spectacular. He appeared to be the reincarnation of James Caan, playing English professor Axel Freed, in *The Gambler.* "I've got magic powers," Freed says in the movie. "I'm searching. If you're smart, you'll play these, too." Freed has gambling issues, to the extent that sultry girlfriend Lauren Hutton becomes an afterthought.

He makes three hoops bets—Harvard over Brown, Georgia Tech over Auburn, UCLA over Oregon—then takes Hutton to Las Vegas. From a bar, he watches as all three take early leads. They hit the tables, and Caan actually doubles down on eighteen; he yells, "Gimme a three." He gets dealt a three. Zany, to be sure, but so was Toback's tear through the city. Jimmy Vaccaro once had to run Toback down across the street, at a blackjack table at Caesars, to fetch the nearly forty grand he had owed the Barbary.

Caan and Hutton go home, only to discover those three basketball games, at fifteen grand a pop, all lost. His bookie wants the forty-five grand. She goes to bed. He gets into the tub, listens to a Lakers-Jazz game on which he had bet. The clunky radio sits precariously on the edge of the tub. James Worthy, with Chick Hearn on the call, misses late free throws, Utah hits a shot at the buzzer to win the game, Caan loses another bet. He kicks the radio, and it crashes . . . to the tile floor.

"I like the uncertainty, the thrill," Axel says, "and I love the winning."

That, in a nutshell, was Music Man, real-life drama played out before Jimmy Vaccaro's very eyes. The older brother marvels over the younger brother's life.

"He's come farther than anyone would have expected, in life," says Sonny Vaccaro. "He's the biggest celebrity, without being a celebrity. One of the most interesting characters. He's been everywhere, done everything. He was not born into it, and he worked his way up. It was just natural for him to get into that business."

Jimmy Vaccaro has some steadfast rules that are inimitable, and at the very top is the fact that Joes bet teams, Pros bet numbers. A cliché, certainly, but he has seen it every day of his professional life, for decades. It's very simple, he says.

"If the Cowboys are three-point favorites and you got a smart guy in line, he's looking to lay the three but by the time he gets to the window the number goes to three and a half, he gets out of the line because he missed the line that was three. The guy who's yapping and drinking his Corona, he says, 'Cowboys.' He's laying the three and a half. So, yeah, smarts bet the numbers and the recreational guys bet teams."

## THE SKINNY

Jimmy Vaccaro, who earned legendary status during a long run making odds in Las Vegas, has one golden rule that has been confirmed multiple times a week for more than forty years—Joes bet teams, Pros bet numbers. That is, the recreational player, tourist, or public bettor will visit from Dallas, Pittsburgh, or Green Bay and just blindly put money down on the Cowboys, Steelers, or Packers, respectively, to win this weekend's game or to get to the Super Bowl, or to win the whole thing. No shopping for the best number, no hesitation in the action. It's about sentiment, the heart.

Professionals, by contrast, use only the noggin in determining the destination of their money. The so-called "sharps" don't mind giving three points, because if their side wins by three then they get their money back. Three and a half? If that's the spread by the time they reach the ticket window and ask for it, they will politely decline, turn around, and live to fight another day. Over the long haul, over the course of twelve months of wagering, or decades, those half-points add up and mark the difference between a losing or winning effort when that year's ledger is totaled.

That goes right along with covering the key numbers. The NFL, by far, gets the most wagering attention, and in football there are some very basic rules to looking out for yourself and making the wise selection, if it exists. Vaccaro does not outright dismiss teasers as goofy tourist attractions, either. In teaser parlays, the patron plays with additional points, typically six or seven, in his favor, at a reduced payoff. With the Lions plus eight and a half, a teaser pumps that to plus fourteen and a half, covering the key numbers of ten, thirteen, and fourteen.

Of course, teasers require action on more than one game. And, of course, the payoff is diminished; I follow Roxy Roxborough's advice, on occasion, and play NFL two-team home teasers that do not even return even money—but I'm cashing tickets, which is nice. (More on Roxy's teaser tactics later.)

And, of course, Vaccaro represents the house, and parlays and teasers are very profitable for the casino. However, he does not discount the value added in a teaser.

"Especially if you're first in line," he says. "You'll get the best number, either way. If you're looking to bet the underdog, in most cases, especially on Sunday morning, if you're looking to add you're probably, seven out of ten times, going to get a better number. Instead of taking seven, and adding six to get thirteen, on Sunday morning when that favorite is seven and a half, now you're getting thirteen and a half."

Over the long run, if scores are being kept, half points are vital in Vegas.

"So, yes, that's smart. More people are betting teasers than ever before. They never, ever, ever have the worst number. If betting Pittsburgh minus seven, they're only going to have to give a point. Smart."

Other rules are not so steadfast, not to be found in any manual. At the Barbary Coast, Art Manteris once goofed, taking in only sixteen thousand five hundred dollars from a punter when he should have collected seventeen thousand six hundred. "I simply screwed up," he wrote in his book. Tallying the till that night, he was mortified to learn of the shortage and knew exactly where his error had occurred. Jimmy Vaccaro, Manteris's supervisor, fixed it and did not reveal how he had done it. Later, Manteris discovered that Vaccaro had made up that difference out of his own pocket.

Vaccaro verifies the story and says he did so on many occasions. "Back then, with no computers, and the rush you would get . . . when things were going on, kids were working their asses off." So they were entitled, he figures, to some leeway if not forgiveness.

He glances at the South Point counters, six windows open, each at least six deep, on a weekday afternoon.

"Look at this," he says. "It's two o'clock in the afternoon, and this joint is a firecracker to begin with."

A striking female assistant strolls by.

"Hey, cowgirl," Vaccaro says, "what you got going on there?"

Michael Gaughan's theory about females being the optimum sports-book employees gets a ringing endorsement from the first person he hired at the Royal way back in 1975.

"Yes, you got it," Vaccaro says. "I talk about it all the time.

They're ten times better workers than guys, cuz guys got a fuckin' ticket [on a game] or they want to go out [and watch a game] . . . or, [they say] 'Look at this guy, betting ten thousand, and I only got ten dollars.' "

Vaccaro tries to treat all customers, from the ten-dollar parlay bettor to the guy laying fifty grand on a side, the same. Even the Duffel Bag Bettor, an anonymous punter who made headlines during the 2018 football season by wagering huge amounts—in cash he plucked from a duffel bag—on various bets, including parlays. His actions fluctuated wildly, unofficially, from losing a million or two over the course of two weeks to winning a couple of million over another two-week run. Duffel, however, lost some stature—at least, to some pros behind the counter—when he bought himself a half-point on a pick'em college football game that could not have finished in a tie.

Punters can reduce a spread, say, from three and a half points to a flat three, at a cost, typically moving a minus-110 wager to minus-120. If that team wins by three, the fortunate bettor would have bought himself a tie, and get his money back, rather than lose it. On his "twix" feed, Vaccaro referred to this particular customer as Duffel Bag Nutball.

"He comes in and gets treated the same," Vaccaro tells me. "I holler at him, too, if he does something stupid." I press Vaccaro, asking what that shadowy figure is like? "Duffel Bag is a pain in the ass. But he bets a lot of money, so I respect him." What does he look like? "He looks like you would give him money if he were standing on a street corner."

For a few weeks, until he was left standing on a street corner, he says, Jimmy Vaccaro believed he was going to be a casino owner. At the end of *The Odds,* author Chad Millman errs, according to Vaccaro, when he describes a Last Supper type of gathering, called to bid Vaccaro adieu as he was supposedly leaving Las Vegas to go back home to Pennsylvania. This was around 2000. Millman quotes Vaccaro saying, "I can't stand this fucking place anymore."

Except, Vaccaro says, it didn't go down that way. He never left, and never intended to leave. That was a period in which he gave notice to Mirage owner Bobby Baldwin, he says, and planned to join Vic Salerno and a relative, and Roxy Roxborough, in buying a Howard Johnson's property by I-15, at Tropicana and Dean Martin.

The majority owner, with seventy-five percent, would have been Salerno, and Roxy would be number two in the hierarchy, says Vaccaro, who would have received seven and a half percent. He had a lag time of a month to recharge before a lot of work would have to be done. Salerno turned it down, Vaccaro says, when political forces raised an already-agreed-upon rent.

Salerno gave Jimmy a job at his Leroy's property. Vaccaro would matriculate to William Hill, and land back with Michael Gaughan, at the South Point, in 2015. The collapse still stings Vaccaro.

"I thought I was going to be a fucking owner! Still, to this day, when I see [Salerno] I kick him in the ass. He says, 'Awww, you don't know the deal; they changed it on me.' Are you kidding? Me [as an owner] in a sweatshirt and jeans? I woulda been great!"

# SIX

# An Accomplished Gentleman

HAD CERTAIN DEALT CARDS been played a certain way by an ancestor nearly a century ago, Michael (Roxy) Roxborough could today very well be a managing general partner or the chief executive officer—both?—of the Toronto Maple Leafs, in charge of hiring the proper people to draft and obtain the proper people to keep the once-storied organization in its rightful perch atop the NHL.

Instead, with his Thai wife, Alise, he splits time between her home in hectic Bangkok and his property in the tropical paradise of Phuket. Roxy has called Thailand home for about twenty years. Instead, he earned legendary status in Las Vegas, where for a spell he carried the title as "nation's oddsmaker," providing point spreads and information to the bulk of the Nevada market via his independent Las Vegas Sports Consultants, Inc. Instead, at this writing, the Leafs continue to languish.

While visiting his many friends in Las Vegas, on May 28, 2018, Roxborough attended a Stanley Cup Final game between the Washington Capitals and the Vegas Golden Knights. He sat in a choice T–Mobile Arena seat and marveled that this was his first NHL championship-round game since 1964, when he sat in Maple Leaf Gardens to watch beloved Toronto play Detroit in a Game 7. The Leafs won, 4–0, to claim their third consecutive cup. Roxy was thirteen. Toronto returned to hockey's penultimate playoff round in 1967, defeating Montreal for the organization's thirteenth Stanley Cup. Toronto has not returned to hockey's showcase event.

"I thought it was sort of ironic," says Roxborough, "that here I am in Las Vegas, and Las Vegas is in the Stanley Cup Final, and the Leafs have gone through God knows how many hundreds of millions of dollars, probably billions, trying to win, or get there, since sixty-seven, and haven't been able to do it."

When Maple Leaf Gardens was being constructed, as the calendar flipped to 1930, Roxborough's grandfather, Edgar, owner of Roxborough Electrical in Toronto, was hired to install wiring inside the edifice. The Depression was thinning bank accounts, so when it came time for the team owner Conn Smythe to pay Edgar, funds were lacking. Smythe offered Edgar—as well as bricklayers, masons, carpenters, and most everyone else who played a role in building the Gardens—stock in the franchise.

Edgar Roxborough declined, demanding to be paid in cash, because his employees would not exactly accept little torn pieces of stock certificates as compensation. "He got the money," Roxy says, "much to his regret later, as events unfolded." In thirty years, the value alone of that stock—had it been sold—would have increased by a multiple of thirty.

The Roxboroughs would become part of the Maple Leafs' ownership group. In 1961, Doug Roxborough, a great uncle to Roxy, represented a consortium that would eventually own the second-largest amount of team stock shares. That, of course, did not constitute controlling interest. What if Edgar had been in position to accept that stock offer thirty years earlier? Would that have led the family on a path toward one day running the Toronto Maple Leafs how they saw fit?

To this day, Roxy ponders what might have been. "A major mistake," he says. However, he harbors no regrets about the course his life has taken. In Thailand, he consults a few British operations on cricket and Euro *futebol* odds, has some dealings with Australian firms, and enjoys an exotic lifestyle. The disintegration of PASPA has created a brave new sports-betting world, he says, which will be intriguing to observe. "Right now, this is probably the new Golden Age."

\* \* \*

Hockey and mathematics course through the Roxborough lineage. Henry Hall Roxborough, a great uncle to Roxy, was a hockey historian. In 1964, he penned a book about the Stanley Cup that, for a time, served as the definitive source about the imposing trophy. A track-and-field official at the 1936 Berlin Olympics, Henry Hall wrote for the Maple Leafs' program, was a regular guest on Toronto's intermission radio shows, and he ghosted other books.

Henry relished challenging equations, digging into probabilities as they pertained to hockey. He once determined that the team that scored the first goal in an NHL game had a seventy-percent chance of winning; when a team tallied the first two goals, its odds of winning increased to ninety percent. He also analyzed the wisdom of pulling a goalie, in the final minute or two, when facing a one-goal deficit, or even trailing by two.

Roxy Roxborough's father had a Harvard MBA, and he restructured and bought businesses, a takeover maven. Relatives own NHL season tickets in Toronto, Vancouver, and Miami. Stephen, Roxy's brother, wrote a comprehensive hockey anthology. Roxy spent some time as the statistician for the Vancouver Canucks of the old World Hockey League.

Roxy studied probability theory and behavioral psychology at American University, in Washington, D.C., and UNLV, critical assets that would pay dividends in the casino business. At American, as a dormitory bookie he was beaten for about four grand when the 1969 Mets upset the Orioles in the World Series, a gut-punch that would require a year to pay off when he borrowed the cash from another party. All of it was education, prepping him for his career. He'd teach a course in race and sports-book management at a Las Vegas junior college.

He bought into American Wagering, Inc., the Vic Salerno property that would become Leroy's, and they would corner the market with a ticket-issuing apparatus. "We had a monopoly," Roxy says. "And after the Stardust sports book opened [in 1975], business started growing so fast it would make your head spin."

After Bob Martin, of the Union Plaza, got popped in 1983 for violating the Wire Act and was sent to a minimum-security facility in California, Roxy would fill an odds-making gap. It would take a few years, in which a soft line would be exploited by syndicates and computer groups, but Roxborough's Las Vegas Sports Consultants would become the industry's established lines-maker.

He had started the company, in 1981, in his kitchen, logging spreads and results by hand into notebooks, a practice that continues today in some circles, and on the twenty-third story of a high-rise on the Strip. In the last half of that decade, Roxy would earn that nation's oddsmaker status by not just supplying thirty-five Nevada properties with the latest point spreads, odds, and lines, but also providing them with the latest information, injury and weather reports.

What's more, it was a full-service outfit as Roxy and his team—he had six full-time employees and six part-timers—consulted on gaming strategies, management, marketing, and personnel. In his book, Art Manteris said Roxy has done more than anyone else for the development of the Nevada sports-gaming industry. "He commands respect within an industry that simply wouldn't be where it is today without him," Manteris wrote. "To me, that's major impact."

The sixty-seven-year-old Roxborough has logged time at all angles of sports betting, as amateur to professional bookmaker, bettor, oddsmaker—and, with Vic Salerno, hotel–casino owner. His credentials to comment on the industry are supreme. His Twitter feed must be followed for pithy insights. Looking to lose weight? *Eat less, exercise more.* Want to have more success betting on sports? *Bet prices, not teams. One day soon*, he tweeted on November 16, 2018, *you will be able to go to a mini-mart, get a five-team parlay, a joint, and a six-pack. So this is what America wants?*

When Roxy visits, he might be the most dapper man in Las Vegas. He rarely saw his grandfather or father wear anything but a suit and tie, and that's how Roxy dresses. "Family tradition," he says. Lean, hair trim, bespectacled, often in bespoke splendor, the finest cottons, linens, and worsteds, silk tie and pocket square, perhaps a bowtie, light Panama hat with a dark band. "The perfect sartorial expression of an accomplished gentleman," wrote the talented Savile Row tailor Richard Anderson of true elegance, the cut highlighting the person, and vice versa. That's Roxy. Much of his attire has been designed or produced by Alise Roxborough, an accomplished fashion designer.

"She picks them out, makes my clothes," he says in early September 2018, a day before he and his wife were leaving Las Vegas for Thailand. "That way at least I get the right color of socks. These days, though, that might even be a bit of a fashion statement—different-color socks."

Roxy Roxborough knows all about trend-setting, as he has made a living spotting them, catching and riding them, and bucking them, with proper tea leaves and timing. Parlays are a case in point, as many professional handicappers despise even hearing the word. But Roxy takes them a step further by having zeroed in on teasers. In the proper circumstance, they can be advantageous for the bettor as reliable investment opportunities.

Some background will give the play proper perspective.

In his youth, Michael Gaughan became fascinated by the football parlay cards at the Saratoga, his father's joint. Hit a ten-team winner, multiply your wager by a hundred-to-one. Old cigar-chompin' guys consistently put two or five bucks down on those plays. Sucker, thought the young Gaughan, who knew the true odds from his pop. When he grew into the business, Michael bumped that payoff to three hundred-to-one. Live here just a short time and the mantra becomes rote—it's tough enough to pick just one game correctly. Ten? Well, step right up.

## THE SKINNY

Parlay cards have long been big-time moneymakers for the house, dropping tens of thousands of dollars per week into the kitty for Michael Gaughan when he was just starting out in the business. They still offer thick pads to any casino's bottom line, but a review of the true odds shows just how sweet they used to be to management. As Art Manteris pointed out, the true odds of picking ten games against a line out of ten is 1-in-1,024. Long ago, the payoff was only a hundred-to-one. Even when a customer hit one, the book made out by not having to fork over the extra 924-to-1 true payoff. A license to print money? Just about.

Gaughan would increase those odds to 300-to-1; tripling the payout, but still not coming close to true percentages. Today, Gaughan Gaming, and other properties, offer 800-to-1 odds on connecting on a ten-team half-point (ensuring there are no ties) parlay, but even those figures fall short. Along comes the squashing of PASPA and other states getting into the act, and now the true odds—paying out 1,024-to-1 odds—are being rewarded at the Biloxi Golden Nugget in Mississippi.

As some states struggle with the sports-betting equation, and others stumble, at least the expansion of the business in the U.S. has resulted in an evening of the playing field, in at least one aspect and in at least one shop, for the Average Joe.

The adrenaline rush and excitement in maybe hitting one, though, is a powerful aphrodisiac. "Extremely popular with non-serious bettors," wrote Art Manteris of parlay cards. "[They] attract the unsophisticated bettor and offer high yields for the sports books." Manteris knows the true odds on hitting ten out of ten is one chance in 1,024, with a theoretical house hold of 70.7 percent. Even when someone connected on one the book made out, not losing an additional 924–1 odds, relating to those felonious turf-club odds. Gaughan might have looked like a prince of the people, tripling those odds. Yet when someone hit one at his shop, he was still short-changing patrons by 724–1 odds. Today, Gaughan Gaming pays 800–1 odds on hitting all ten parlay picks, still unrepresentative of true odds. The Station properties also offer those odds on going ten-for-ten.

The expansion of the industry has duly rectified some of that imbalance. Maybe others will follow the lead of the Biloxi Golden Nugget sports book manager Brad Bryant, who announced, in the fall of 2018, that his property would offer true odds on parlay cards with up to fifteen selections—that's one chance in 32,768; wager five bucks and hit it, get $163,840 in return. Score one for the player, even though the house is still, and always will be, way ahead in the parlay-card long game.

It is crucial, Roxborough says, to have knowledge and a feel for the odds, the numbers. Those lessons are typically learned, at a price. John Scarne, known as an internationally renowned gambling expert in his day, implored the importance of knowing the proper odds. In 1952, he miscalculated such figures in a dice game and lost forty-nine thousand dollars—the equivalent of nearly half a million bucks today. "In gambling, you got to pay to learn," he wrote in *Scarne's New Complete Guide to Gambling* (1986). "But forty-nine thousand was a lot of dough to pay just to learn that."

However, Roxy does not dismiss a specific parlay maneuver. He discovered a gem, a two-team NFL home teaser parlay—let's name it the "Roxy Special"—in which the bettor can jimmy with six points in his favor. Like the Bears at Soldier Field minus four points? This teaser option alters that to Bears plus two. That eliminates the four-point victory as a push, and covers the Bears winning by common slim margins while making it a winner in the event of a Chicago defeat by a point. Don't fudge with three-teamers, Roxy says, because that eliminates the player's edge. It's the two-team home-side NFL teaser that, to Roxy's meticulous computations, gives the gambler a nifty—and rare—edge of 8.1 percent.

## THE SKINNY

The Roxy Special defies conventional reasoning when it comes to parlay wagers. Specifically, action involving teasers. Professional bettors in the game for the long haul shun even the mention of such plays, because they know the odds favor the house to an overwhelming degree. Roxy Roxborough, however, has computed a gem of a bet during the course of his rich, well-rounded career in the business.

By laying money on a two-team NFL home teaser, by Roxy's abacus, the player has an approximate advantage of 8.1 percent. I've had success with this angle, which, of course, comes with a price. Hit a $100 two-team NFL home teaser parlay, and the net will be about $85—paying less than even money. However, my main goal is to cash tickets, and those additional six points in my favor for NFL home teams are golden. On Thanksgiving 2018, I stretched my luck, teasing all three NFL home squads. Detroit lost to Chicago, 23–16, but I had teased the Lions from plus-three points to plus-nine; Dallas defeated Washington, 31–23, and I had teased the Cowboys from minus-seven to minus-one; and New Orleans beat Atlanta, 31–17, after I had teased the Saints from minus-thirteen to minus-seven. That's how $100 becomes $250.

I despise sweating, and the Roxy Special is an effective antiperspirant. In addition, some of that careful investment approach must stem from my late father, whose speculative motto was "belt and suspenders," or being careful. (He also savored buying low. A stock has dipped precipitously? He never panicked. The perfect time to buy more, he'd say. Even though I have seven bookcases in the pad, I also despise expensive bookmarks. Roxy has helped both of those goals. Grazie, Roxy.

Applying the Roxy Special from the fifth through the fifteenth weeks of the 2018 NFL season, home teams with the additional six points in their favor covered one hundred thirteen of a hundred and sixty-two games, with two ties, for a success rate of 70.37 percent. Remember, two teams must be picked to cash the ticket—selecting one can be accomplished with relative ease, but there remains an art to nailing that second leg.

Unless someone had the prescience to select the fifth week of that season to employ the Roxy Special, when home teams with the added value of those six points covered fourteen of fifteen games; four of those winners would have been, using the normal point spread, losers, but those additional six points made them teaser victors. And in those fourteenth and fifteenth weeks, home teams with that additional six points covered twenty-four of thirty-two games.

I have been stuck behind a poor soul, or two, who finally gets to the counter and becomes paralyzed. Either their desired pick has increased half a point or its price has inched up or their second- and third-guessing has frayed the wiring between the pons and medulla. They're the opposite of that devil-dowager with which poor Michael Gaughan had to joust in his final ticket-writing epi- sode. Those in line become agitated. The ticket writer frowns. Once, one told a chap, "If you so dislike what you wanted to do, go the other way!"

Roxy has borne witness to this scene too many times. His les- sons from the frontlines of the business can help many bettors, and price is at the top of his list. Bet prices, he recommends, not teams, and be definitive.

"It goes a long way, doesn't it?" he says. "It does, because peo- ple get obsessed. One thing is, any team can be a bet if you're getting enough points or getting enough price. But a lot of ama- teur handicappers get married to teams. They get married to two things: they watch games on TV, and it makes a bigger impression on the games that they don't watch. Everybody has a visual bias, anyway.

"The other one is, they have ideas that they want to bet teams. They look at the point spread and say, 'I can't bet that team. It's too high.' But they never think about betting the other side. It's a beautiful thing of sports betting. If you think the odds are bad, you can go with the other team. But a lot of amateur bettors get tied into teams. They don't think too much about prices. To me, the whole game is price."

Money management is imperative to having an enjoyable expe- rience that, maybe with some fortune, could be worthwhile to the bank account, too. Roxy advises basic strategy to avoid danger.

"You can't be betting one hundred dollars on one game and five hundred on another, simply for the fact that nobody's opinion is five times better on one game than the other. It's really hard to make a living at sports betting, but to think one bet is five times better, or even to think that one bet is three times better . . . until they understand gambling a little bit better, I think most people should be flat-betting; if they're going to bet a hundred dollars, keep betting a hundred until they find out whether they have an edge or not."

Insights must be culled about the game behind the game, why numbers move, and how to respond to myriad situations on the field and on the big board.

"Of course, everyone wants to win," Roxy says. "They should have a good time doing it. But if you think you can be a professional, and you don't have a degree in statistics or probability theory, or you're not a coder or don't have access to people who are coders, you are fooling yourself. To be a professional, it's all algorithm-driven right now."

Tony Bloom, the forty-seven-year-old poker pro and English football club owner, is a catalyst of that algo-driven world. He studied mathematics at Manchester University and dedicated himself to the numbers in sports betting, the pursuit of the total elimination of human emotion and persuasion. He is clandestine and rarely gives interviews about the gambling aspect of his life, but in Michael Atherton's *Gambling* he said he promised himself, in college, to become fiercely disciplined. "I wanted to gamble because I enjoyed it, therefore I needed to do it properly in order to win. I didn't want to lose my money."

He steered Mayfair's boutique quant investment world, according to *Business Insider,* into the "murky area of Asian bookmakers." He divided Starlizard's hundred and sixty employees into four independent operations, so one knows scant of what the other three are up to. The syndicate makes approximately twenty million, in U.S. dollars, a year just for the English football information it provides, and another sixty tax-free million or so, give or take forty million either way, in bets that it executes on behalf of Bloom and his associates.

Industry experts told *Insider* that Starlizard is one of about a dozen major professional gambling syndicates worldwide, but some of those are even murkier because they deal in match-fixing. That runs counter to Starlizard's model, which relies on "as clean a game as possible to let the statistics come good," wrote *Insider*'s Oscar Williams-Grut.

Breaking even, Roxborough says, should be a logical initial objective. Single bets, whether the side or total of a game, will require a 52.38–percent success rate—the juice, or eleven-to-ten odds, that the house makes to book the bet. So consider breaking even at about fifty-three percent.

"They think, 'I have to pick fifty-five-percent winners, right?' But I think the key thing is shopping different prices. Some lay minus-108. At others, you can lay minus-110 and get six and a half instead of six. Just get close to breaking even, first. That should be everybody's goal. It shouldn't be to go out there and pick fifty-six-percent winners, to grind out a living. You have to understand the prices to figure out how you can get the game down to as close to even as you can, then go from there."

At no time, Roxy insists, should anyone consider betting money that will be missed, much less follow through with such poor judgment. "Now you're in sort of the thrill-ride territory, not the professionalism," Roxy says. "Just to get a rush, right?"

These days, along with his consulting positions, he follows American baseball, the English Premiership and lower British football leagues, worldwide cricket, and Formula 1 racing. He doesn't bet on, or watch, individual games; he favors futures tickets, Overs and Unders, on season-victory totals. He tracks results daily, and will make corresponding bets on or against those total figures as he sees fit. He visits racetracks around the globe, and for one round of follow-up email inquiries, he had just returned from ten days of racing festivities at the Melbourne Cup in Australia.

As American sports betting expands, he envisions casino properties clashing for sports bettors the way they battle for big-time roulette or baccarat players. "Most of the big players are in baccarat, and there's a lot of competition to get the biggest baccarat players. I think you'll see a competitive period where sports books will compete for players, and maybe they'll give away too much, to the player's benefit. But now, in sports betting, it's hard to get free rooms because the edge is so small."

With all of the wealth that exists on the Eastern seaboard, in and around New York, New Jersey, and Pennsylvania, he believes it could be a given that that region will surpass Nevada in sports-betting handle, and soon.

"But that doesn't mean Nevada won't be a fun place to come to to watch the Final Four and football," Roxy says. "In the big scheme of life, sports betting is a niche market. It's never going to drive fantastic revenue for states. But it's an interesting niche market."

In his office in his Las Vegas home, Roxborough retains some select memorabilia. A Stardust logo catches his eye. "It's funny, when things are going on, we're all trying to make a living, we're working hard . . . maybe we didn't know we were sitting on top of fabulous events. We're just in it every day. But looking back on it, it's pretty spectacular."

# SEVEN

# Shrewd Instincts

PURDUE HAD NOT ONLY BEEN performing well, but the Boilermakers were playing football in an aggressive and entertaining style under Jeff Brohm, their daring second-year coach. The Boilers were just plain fun to watch, even without a buck on the outcome of their games or with zero ties to the program. Unlike so many coaches and teams that were so often flummoxed in basic time-management situations and down-distance strategy, Purdue operated cohesively and efficiently, reflecting Brohm's poise and precision.

Smart boss, smart team.

"Frankly, there are NFL coaches who could learn a lot from Brohm and Purdue," Matt Youmans says on "The Edge," his regular segment on the satellite Vegas Stats & Information Network, from the Fish Bowl in the center of the South Point in Las Vegas.

Second-ranked Ohio State was visiting Purdue, in West Lafayette, Indiana, in the middle of the 2018 season, and Youmans spoke highly of the Boilers' chances against the Buckeyes in the days before the game. In reality, he had been stalking this particular game for weeks.

The Buckeyes had gone four consecutive seasons without playing Purdue, and they had walloped the Boilers, 56–0, in their previous visit to West Lafayette, in 2013. However, Ohio State had not been so efficient of late. It had won its first seven games, but had failed to cover the spread in four of its previous five games.

And among the hobbled Buckeyes was defensive end Nick Bosa, who had been playing at a high level but whose abdominal surgery would end his collegiate career; he'd leave school early to prepare for the NFL draft.

Purdue, having reeled off four consecutive victories and covers, had been producing exactly what the demanding Brohm had been preaching.

Youmans is a Purdue graduate, but school spirit played zero role in his even, rational, robust assessment of both sides in the game. His only allegiance, always, is to his wallet, which makes him such an asset, broadcasting and writing, at VSiN. He not only favored Purdue, as a fourteen-point home underdog, but he recommended playing the Boilers on the money line, at roughly plus-400, depending on when and where customers shopped.

His customary formula in such a situation is to place seventy percent with the points, thirty percent on the money line, his seventy-thirty rule. Lem Banker, the longtime pro handicapper, nods his head in favor of that tactic. Banker will play the home underdog, taking the points, and lay a third of that figure on the money line, approximating Youmans's tack.

But, to Youmans, this one was different. This one stood out. He had been following specific aspects of both teams, for nearly a month, with the sole purpose of lowering the hammer on Purdue, on the points and the money line, if every single sign, on both sides, continued in the manner in which he believed they would. They did. He acted.

Anyone listening to Youmans dissect that game, praising Brohm on multiple occasions in the run-up to it, and was coaxed into laying money down on Purdue was rewarded. Toward the end of the first half, in a play that reinforced all the praise that Youmans had bestowed on Brohm, the Boilers had a fourth-and-short play deep in Ohio State territory. The typical vanilla coach would have attempted a field goal, to take a 10–3 lead. A secure decision, by the book, lacking any degree of imagination or assertiveness, that would have kept it a one-score difference.

The bold Brohm, though, instructed placekick holder Joe

Schopper to run with the ball. He scampered left for four yards and, by a couple of feet, secured a first down. Purdue scored on the ensuing play. Touchdowns, Brohm knew, trump field goals, and they are imperative if the objective, to upend one of the nation's top programs, is to be accomplished.

Youmans knew that Brohm knew.

Purdue rolled that enthusiasm and derring-do into a resounding 49–20 victory over the Buckeyes, the biggest Boilermakers football victory in several decades. A great performance, Brohm told reporters. "We came in and played aggressive, and I think you have to play aggressive against these guys."

"He proved to be a prophet," professional prognosticator Paul Stone, on a VSiN guest appearance, says of Youmans. Everything had pointed to handicapping perfection, so he amended his seventy-thirty rule to eighty-twenty; laying a healthy four-figure amount on the Boilers plus the points, with a mid-three-figure wager on the Boilers, which he had nabbed at a plus-500 money line, to win outright. It came in as if he had written the script, but Youmans did not gloat. A phenomenal coach, he wrote of Brohm on his Twitter feed when the result became inevitable. "You could see this coming."

Matt Youmans was destined for Las Vegas and the pilot seat of a groundbreaking satellite radio station, writing and talking about sports gambling, and employing a wealth of tools to the fine benefit of his bank account—and an eager audience. He had only been preparing for this spot, which he accepted near the end of 2016, all of his life.

He grew up in Sheridan, Indiana, north of Indianapolis. His uncle was an avid gambler and taught Matt, when he was in elementary school, to read the betting lines in the sports section. His father, Al, was a high school football coach and principal, and he'd take Matt to Purdue (in West Lafayette) and Notre Dame (in South Bend) football games. En route, Matt would circle the sides he liked in the paper that day, and he'd compare it to the results in Sunday morning's sports section.

However, he also picked up, from his father, the finer nuances of scouting players and teams as they watched the Boilers and Irish, not just on the field during games, but in warm-ups and on the sidelines. "He'd point out certain aspects about certain players, as we were sitting there. I consider myself a good talent evaluator of players, and that's part of handicapping."

He made his first big bet, of a hundred dollars, on the Chicago Bears in Super Bowl XX. He and some friends had a bookie. "And I was sweating bullets," Youmans says. The game, however, was never in doubt as the Bears, a ten-point favorite, won 46–10.

At Purdue, he ran a small book-making operation, with a betting limit of two hundred dollars, to guard against a bad day. About six-feet-four, with brawn, Youmans also played hoops alongside Glenn (Big Dog) Robinson, but not on the Boilermakers' varsity squad taking instruction from colorful coach Gene Keady. Big Dog was a casualty of the old Proposition 48 minimum-academic requirements his first academic year, so he ran on Youmans's intramural team.

They reached the final of the campus-wide tournament, but lost on a buzzer beater. For some reason, their two guards shot them out of the game with errant bomb after errant bomb in the first half. "Tried to play hero ball," says Youmans, who pronounces it "HE-row." Big Dog stormed out of the gym. Two years later, in 1994, he'd be the top pick in the NBA draft, and Robinson would earn more than eighty million dollars over ten-plus professional seasons.

A stint at the *Indianapolis Star* out of school led Youmans to the big time, covering the major Chicago sports teams for *The Times* of Northwest Indiana, in Hammond. That is where Youmans developed instinct and depth, gaining invaluable experience, for instance, writing about the Chicago Bulls and Michael Jordan when that franchise became the epitome of class and success.

"He covered great teams playing at the very highest level," says Patrick Everson. "So he has the thoroughness that a long-time journalist will bring to a story that's well-reported and doesn't have holes. He'll cover all the bases to present a balanced story, coming from a guy who's had to be a neutral, fact-based journalist. That helps his craft and really leads to interesting discussions and opinions."

A senior writer and videographer who provides tirelessly stellar content for the sports-betting website Covers.com, Everson, fifty, says he's powered by equal portions of French toast, Mr. Pibb, and Coffee Bean. Joking aside, he spent years on the inside, in layout and editing, of the *Review-Journal* when Youmans worked at that paper. Youmans's efforts to provide additional wagering material were often disregarded by superiors.

A report broke on Twitter, early the afternoon of Friday, November 16, 2018, stating definitively that Jimmy Vaccaro would be heading back home to Pennsylvania to work in the state's nascent sports-betting industry. "Jimmy Vaccaro is coming home . . . congratulations and welcome back," wrote Bert I. Osborne Jr., namesake son of one of those gaggle of sports-book personnel to bolt the Cradle of Bookies for Las Vegas. However, Youmans reported, Wait just a second. "Jimmy V might not be ready to talk about the report," he wrote. "Announcement on hold."

Late that afternoon on VSiN, Vaccaro appeared with Brent Musburger, and the topic was not even broached. Did Vaccaro not want to spoil, or jinx, ongoing negotiations? Possibly. Nothing to the report? A denial could have been quick and painless, and necessary since the news item—however firm or flimsy—had been publicized. But for a bona fide news-gathering organization, especially one with the incomparable Brent Musburger on its roster, it represented oversight of a timely topic involving one of its own.

(In December, Jimmy Vaccaro was still at the South Point, getting his weekly rubdown, releasing his missives to the *twix* universe. About that initial Jimmy's-coming-home report, Sonny Vaccaro tells me of his younger brother, "He has always wanted to go back home, but I don't think that [news item] is terribly true. He might, but he hasn't told me that. I do think both sides are trying to work something out." On the first of February, Rivers Casino in Pittsburgh announced its acquisition, in a part-time media-relations capacity, of Jimmy Vaccaro.)

Plenty of sports-talk radio is filled with yes-men, littered with incessantly agreeable sorts in a cocoon of mutual admiration. VSiN is guilty of some of that. Youmans is not. It can be an innocuous throw-away line, but if his co-host says something that he can't digest, Youmans will speak up. His manner isn't confrontational, but he does speak up.

"He definitely will push back on the air, if there's an opinion that he strongly disagrees with," says Everson, a Youmans co-host on occasion. "He will present the other side of that argument. That makes for great radio. Honestly, it's really good for the listener, or viewer, however you're consuming it. It's good for the public to get that dissenting opinion as they figure out how they want to play these games."

In 2000, Youmans arrived in Las Vegas with ten grand and designs on taking down the books, one by one.

"Thought I could make a killing," he says, laughing. "Then you learn some lessons the hard way. When you're young and dumb and you come to [Las Vegas], you think, 'I got this figured out.' I bet big on a couple of NFL games and lost. You start to see the bankroll wither away. Of course, it didn't help that I was going to strip clubs every night. Everyone has to get their butt kicked a couple of times to realize you're not doing things exactly the right way."

For a stretch we covered, for competing Las Vegas papers, the UNLV basketball team. Youmans would, at times, wear black-and-white Stacy Adams croc-lizard Gusto wing-tip Oxfords. Style. A nod to his Chicago days, I thought, of Al Capone and Prohibition? Nope. He just detests bland, basic dress shoes. When he would casually remark about having followed a specific potential bet for *weeks*—stalking another play, against UCLA—my own piker status was confirmed. Matt operated on a different, adroit level. He won that wager against UCLA.

His preparation and study sessions intensified. In a VIP booth at the Westgate SuperBook in late October 2018, VSiN colleague Pauly Howard inquires with Youmans about whom he'll be watching closely in college hoops as that season was about to begin. Youmans said he didn't know yet, but after *Sunday Night Football* the following evening he'd start digging into his hoops material. Howard asks him about a potential Oklahoma–Michigan football matchup. On a neutral field, who you got? Youmans pauses for a few seconds, then says, Wolverines. "Know why? Defense."

In a 2016 phone chat with his father, Youmans revealed his intention to leave the paper to focus solely on sports betting, writing and talking about it on a new satellite station involving the legendary broadcaster Brent Musburger to be headquartered at the South Point. "It's perfect," Youmans says as he recalls that talk with his dad. "Newspapers [are] a dead end. Basketball writers are a dime a dozen, and there are maybe three or four people in the country who can write about sports betting and know what the fuck they're talking about."

Youmans is in that select group, according to Roxy Roxborough. At the *Review-Journal,* Roxy says, Youmans translated the sometimes tricky world, and vernacular, of sports betting in an effective manner that the lay person could easily comprehend. "He has the ability to communicate with readers and audiences," Roxy says. "It was easy for him to adapt to a more sophisticated audience, as he already knew the game from the inside. Best of all, he has a great Las Vegas lifestyle."

Those countless hours of experience and research permeate his VSiN broadcasts. His delivery is even, conversational, laced with sports-betting insights. He possesses a dry wit that's always well-timed comic relief. He sees everything. When I joined him in the VIP SuperBook booth, the gum I had been chomping fell out of my pie hole, onto my long-sleeve black T-shirt. It was out for maybe three-tenths of a second. Youmans catches the gaffe and says, with a grin, "Might wanna put that gum back."

Moreover, he writes content for, and assists in editing, an impressive *Point Spread Weekly* online gambling guide produced by the VSiN staff, which is often triple digits in pages. Youmans has never counted the weekly hours he devotes to the position because it's his passion, but he also retains vivid memories of the auto assembly-line gig his father arranged for him one summer during college.

"It felt like you'd been doing something for an hour, and you'd look up at the clock and it had moved only ten minutes," he says. "That was the definition of hell. I'm convinced he got me that job to teach me a lesson, that you don't want to work at a blue-collar, nine-to-five job the rest of your life. It was the most mind-numbing job there is. I don't know how people do that for a living."

The test arrives right away. Youmans points out the opening line to the Houston–South Florida football game. The South Florida Bulls are not only the home team, and not only the lone unbeaten and lone ranked squad in this contest, but they are receiving seven and a half points.

He asks me about my thoughts on the game. All that in favor of the home team, I say, and if the Bulls lose by seven points they still cover? I fall right into his trap. That is exactly what the books want you to think, he says. You're falling right into their web. That hook sealed it, huh, he asks? I nod. A lot going in South Florida's favor.

Wrong. "The novice would say, 'Oh, I'm going to get seven and the hook, with a team that's undefeated. Are you serious?' The sharp guy looks at it and says, 'It's seven and a half for a reason. Houston is the correct side.' And Houston won by twenty-one points." Youmans, of course, had bet on Houston.

As a punter who leans toward situational handicapping, that fit what Youmans seeks in exploiting the game behind the game, as did that Purdue play over Ohio State, and what I had seen him concoct years ago with that UCLA basketball wager.

"I watch more games than anybody on the planet," he says. "I feel like my instincts are about as good as it gets, with games like Purdue–Ohio State. I had watched that for a month. I knew the Buckeyes had serious problems. I said, 'Someone will expose this team.' I had cashed four tickets against Ohio State before the Purdue game."

Just as sharply, those instincts told him to back off on the Boilermakers, who, against the spread, dropped three of their next five games. His timing had been perfect.

Those are the instincts he tapped when he watched the Los

Angeles Dodgers during the 2018 season, when he often scratched his head. He disagreed frequently with Dodgers manager Dave Roberts. "I don't think Dave Roberts has good instincts for when to make the right moves," Youmans says. "Some people have an instinct, knowing when to make the right moves, and other people just make all the wrong moves."

The forty-six-year-old Youmans bought a condo in the Las Vegas Country Club, across the winding street from the SuperBook, in October 2016. A jaunt to the east inside those confines, the length of one lap of a high-school track, is the former home of Lefty Rosenthal. It has original bulletproof doors and windows, ceiling mirrors supposedly from the Stardust, and was listed at seven hundred thousand dollars when it went on the market in 2017. In his second-story office, a bank of screens—high-tech stuff in the 1970s—enabled Lefty to constantly monitor action at the four casinos he'd eventually oversee.

For a hiccup in 1953 and '54, the country club was the site for the ill-fated Las Vegas Park, a thoroughbred race track where only twenty meets out of a scheduled one hundred and fifteen were held over that two-year window. Joe W. Brown Drive, named after a race-track investor who had been involved in the Vegas track, snakes between the Westgate and country club.

## THE SKINNY

Matt Youmans has witnessed many people making bad bets, and he cannot emphasize enough being able to handicap a game with no involvement of the heart. Must use the head and think, divorcing any loyalties or sentiment from the equation. "Guys who are big fans [of teams, and bet that way] are the worst gamblers," he says. "They do not have good instincts. They just want to bet whatever they see, whatever is fresh in their minds. The team that won last week, 42–7, they want to bet. Novice gamblers think like fans."

It was on that road, when we covered UNLV hoops, that Youmans came to the defense of a friend and paid for it. They'd been out, and, unbeknownst to Youmans, the friend had made some enemies, who tracked Youmans's truck back to the SuperBook in the wee hours. He was going to drop the buddy off, but wouldn't with trouble lurking. At a stoplight on Joe W., the goons pulled the buddy from Youmans's rig and whaled on him. Youmans jumped in, pulled his friend free, and got in some punches when he looked up. He barely raised a forearm in time to block a golf club that was zeroing in on his noggin; he wore a cast on that broken forearm for a few weeks.

As we watch no fewer than fifteen games before us, on the SuperBook's mammoth ultra-clear video board that's nearly a football field long, Youmans takes advantage of the five apps on his mobile phone regarding Iowa's game at Penn State. He had initially wagered on the Hawkeyes plus six and a half points, and when they take a 12–0 advantage he taps an app to get Penn State plus five and a half on a live wager, for half of the price of his Iowa ticket. He's hedging against a potential collapse by the Hawkeyes, with a shot at a middle. Penn State wins the game, 30–24, so the half-point hook with Iowa pays off and his dog ticket on the Nittany Lions cashes since they win outright—a successful middle for Youmans.

He wears a LAS VEGAS RAIDERS cap, adjustable-fit with stitched lettering, backward; when he caught a vendor selling them out of a truck for twenty-five bucks a pop, he bought ten knowing friends would be eager to own one. They went, fast, at cost. He recommends having fun with sports betting, not getting in too deep to where the consequences or ramifications could become serious.

"If you use your brain, you won't get stuck on the dark side," Youmans says. "Like when you see people playing video poker. How much money do some people piss away playing video poker? With sports betting, ninety-eight percent of the people I know do it for recreation. The two percent who try to make a living at it, the serious bettors, treat it like a business. Very few people can treat it like a business and be successful at it."

Youmans puts his opinion out there, and people can judge for themselves, on convincing evidence or a string of success, how they want to proceed. "They can make their own judgment: do they want to follow you or do they want to fade you?"

Before Youmans joined VSiN, as its first on-air talent hire, many had the benefit of following his track record, in the quality of his selections and caliber of his columns for the *Review-Journal*. He wrote of Leicester City's improbable run to winning the 2015–16 English Premier League. The Foxes had preseason odds of five thousand-to-one in the U.K. (where twenty-five punters had nabbed that number), twenty-five hundred-to-one in Las Vegas (three bettors had risked two dollars, five bucks, and a ten spot at William Hill books in the state). While Nevada lost about a million on the proposition, English books might have had fifteen times that exposure.

Brent Musburger became an ardent fan of Youmans and his work. Some inquire about buying select picks from him, but Youmans deflects those inquiries. One big-time gambler bet on every single college hoops play Youmans offered—three hundred seventy of them—a few years ago, via his two-dozen global "outs," or casinos to which he had access. The bettor fared well, netting five figures. After the season, he cut Youmans in on a percentage of the profits.

That, and the fear of those assembly-line memories, drives Youmans to always obtain the best, most pertinent, most accurate information to deliver to his listeners and readers.

"I don't try to hide anything," he says. "I try to be transparent. Sometimes, if I have a really, really big game that I love, I won't talk it up on the air like it's the biggest thing, 'a five-star play . . . got to hammer this!' I know I've got my ass on the line on that game and I don't want other people to go down with me, if I go down. I have a conscience about that. I don't want people to lose money based on what I recommend. I feel bad when people lose. If I say bet big, and it loses, I feel worse about other people losing their money than I do," losing his own money.

Everson knew exactly to what I referred when we discuss how Youmans has a penchant for stalking situations in games weeks away. If this team or these players keep going in this direction, and this other team and those players continue in that direction . . . when they meet, the opportunity to capitalize will be exceptional.

A week after that Ohio State–Purdue game, another one lurked for him when Arizona State played at Southern California. Youmans had been watching the circumstances, siding strongly with the ASU Sun Devils, for weeks. The Devils were getting three points, depending where and when a patron shopped and bought. ASU won the game, 38–35.

"I was really impressed," says Everson. "He nailed [it]. He gives out strong opinions, and they happen. Now, they don't hit all the time. Nobody is that good in this business. But when he gives out strong opinions, with a lot of strong research and opinion behind it, people have to listen."

# EIGHT

# The Grinder

LIKE HIS FATHER AND TWO OLDER BROTHERS, a young Ron Boyles believed—as Sonny and Jimmy Vaccaro might have, at times, in their youth—he was bound for the steel mills of Western Pennsylvania. The iron ore, the heat, the noise, the dangers, the drudgery. Through elementary school, junior high, and high school, Boyles watched the same old grubby, sooty, back-breaking story play out on an endless loop all around him.

Every neighborhood in and around New Castle, Pennsylvania—dubbed "Little Pittsburgh" for a while, due to its industriousness as an artery of U.S. Steel Corporation, the world's first billion-dollar company—and every family was the same. The father worked in the mill, mom was a homemaker. Boys grew into men and worked in the mills. College did not factor into the equation.

The Monday after Thanksgiving isn't a school day, Boyles says, because every boy would be out hunting deer with their fathers, uncles, or friends. Why bother? Daughters got married, started their own family, and those kids continued the loop. Divorce was never discussed.

For a window into that world, view *The Deer Hunter,* Michael Cimino's second directorial effort, a 1978 epic that starred Robert De Niro, Christopher Walken, Meryl Streep, and the magnificent John Cazale in his final role.

"It was the same all over Western Pennsylvania. In those small towns, that's the way it was," Boyles says. "You thought nothing of it."

The games, and the wagering on them, became more popular by the generation.

"That area is football crazy and gambling crazy," says Boyles. "You didn't have to look far, growing up, to find a bookmaker, a dice game, a poker game. On the weekends, all the clubs would have dice and poker. Bookies were everywhere. You'd go to the local newsstand if you wanted to make a bet. There was a culture."

Boyles recalls with dread the inevitability of getting sucked into the smelting whirlpool. He bucked against it, resisted it with every fiber. The mills started fading in the faltering economy in the late 1970s and early 1980s, but Boyles still might have fallen into its futureless vortex. "I wasn't thrilled about going to work there."

He caught the sports-betting bug when he was thirteen. An uncle would take him, a brother, and some of their friends to Pirates' games, about an hour drive southeast. En route, they'd make bets on fifteen different game propositions, a quarter a prop, from the number of foul balls hit into the stands, how many players would be used, to errors. "Everything," he says of the many options. "The winner kept all the money on each individual prop. My introduction to sports betting."

In February 1981, he escaped. He bought a west-bound ticket and boarded a Greyhound bus—whose stainless-steel alloy shell might have been mixed by his brothers, or neighbors, or other relatives, assisting his getaway—with sixty bucks in his pocket and one suitcase stuffed with clothes. At 2 A.M., Boyles alighted from the hulking gray coach, strolled out of the Las Vegas depot, and beheld the dazzling Fremont Street.

"I said, 'Wow!' Goosebumps," Boyles says. "I was fearless. Twenty-one years old. I wasn't scared. I loved it. I said, 'This is for me.' Adventure. Just great."

Today, Boyles nearly falls off his chair in the VIP section of the Westgate SuperBook when a young running back for the University of Maryland runs it in from fifty-four yards out in the final minute. The Terrapins, with a 56–33 lead, had been killing the clock against Illinois, a bad strategy for Boyles—but the correct call by Maryland—since he had made a wager on the halftime line, on Maryland giving five points. The Terps had led, 28–9, at the break, which plays no role in his wager because his ticket is based solely on the second half.

Maryland holds the ball in its own territory, with less than a minute remaining. It is winning the second half, 28–24. (Boyles's ticket, in real time, is a dud.) The Terps call running plays, intending to bleed the rest of the game time. Then, stunned, Boyles watches Chigoziem Okonkwo scamper fifty-four yards into the end zone with thirty-nine seconds left. Maryland wins the second half, 35–24. Boyles wins his bet.

"They were just running out the clock. I considered it a loser," he says with a wide smile that qualifies as boisterousness for the usually quiet, self-described loner. "This is like finding six hundred dollars on the floor!" Boyles had wagered three hundred and thirty dollars, to win three hundred, on that Maryland second-half wager.

His reserved manner requires no publicity, no acknowledgment, no back pats, which makes him an attractive subject. A mutual friend facilitates the connection, and Boyles agrees to discuss his exploits—including getting barred from a chain of casinos by a titan of the industry—as a professional bettor for more than thirty years. He is among a select group of pro handicappers most respected by its peers.

With Maryland, he had just experienced the other side of the "bad beats" label, which receives only one-sided coverage by Scott Van Pelt on ESPN. That other side—a stunning reversal or shocking score that benefits the bettor—goes largely unnoticed, and that's where Boyles is today.

It's where I was on October 19, 1996, when I had bet on Arizona State, giving eight or eight and a half points, at home to Southern California. It went to overtime. Giving more than a touchdown, in an overtime game that will most always be settled by seven, four, or three points, even one, I was certain my bet was toast. It went to a second overtime. The Sun Devils scored, and on the Trojans' turn quarterback Brad Otten threw what appeared to be an incomplete pass. However, officials did not whistle the play dead. ASU's Courtney Jackson scooped up the ball and ran it in for the game-ending touchdown, securing a 48–35 victory for the Devils.

As stunning of a betting triumph as could possibly be manufactured, and not easily forgotten. Boyles remembers that game. The next season, he says, the NCAA outlawed such a defensive TD in overtime. He laughs at the "bad beat" nomenclature because, over the long haul, he is certain the counted-as-out windfalls will equal the horrible defeats. Sometimes, they can make a person nearly fall off his chair.

Thirty-seven years after catching that Greyhound out of New Castle, Boyles has no regrets about his life-altering decision. "I was kind of happy to spread my wings, head out west, and see what I could do," he says. Dubbed "Skinny" by Jimmy Vaccaro, long ago, because of his slight build, Boyles has been a successful bettor for many years, but it did not happen overnight, the moment he stepped off that bus.

He immediately found weeklong accommodations for thirty-eight bucks and took a job in the laundry room of Jackie Gaughan's Union Plaza. He hung out in Vic Salerno's Leroy's turf club, the original one. "A little Damon Runyonesque hole in the wall," says Boyles, fifty-eight. One ticket-writer post in a sports book led to another one. "I just realized, as the years went by, that I could make more money on the other side of the counter."

It took a few years. When he was writing tickets those initial years, he was also betting. (Not at the same shop; it's a long-standing Vegas rule in which employees are forbidden from wagering where they work.) He'd get his paycheck and soon be broke. Zero discipline. "I'd make scores, but then I'd give it all back. It wasn't until I developed some serious discipline, approached it as a business and started shopping for numbers, betting both sides of games, that's when I started having success, experiencing really good success."

He frequented several turf clubs every day, looking to give four and a half points on Team A at one shop and take six or six and a half, with Team B, at another. He quit writing tickets to devote all of his time to betting on sports, tightening his tactics. Food and rent depended on winnings. He got married in 1987, and they had two sons. That made the winning ever more critical.

"When you got a wife and kids, and you don't have an income coming in," he says, "you better win. You better know what you're doing." Says one insider, "It's impressive what he's accomplished." We'll get to the nitty-gritty. At one point, he had at least twenty grand apiece in phone accounts at six different properties.

When he walked into the Mirage one day, to hang out, check the numbers, maybe make some wagers, sports-book director Jimmy Vaccaro approached him. Boyles's wife had worked for Vaccaro for a couple of years, so Vaccaro knew her. "Skinny," Vaccaro said, "I got some bad news for you. Your account is frozen."

Boyles ran all over town trying to make withdrawals. "But it was too late," he says. "They were frozen everywhere." His wife had hired a lawyer, who had filed court orders to freeze all of his sports-betting accounts in preparation for divorce proceedings, "so she would get half of everything," says Boyles. "It's very difficult staying married in this town, especially if you gamble for a living. Just impossible. Brutal."

Boyles enjoyed Las Vegas most from about 1986 through 1999. Many diehard veterans, on both sides of the counter, retain a degree of sentimentality about a certain city era they most favor. For Boyles, in that stretch the federal tax rate was chopped from two percent to a quarter percent, sports books were inside casinos and independent shops were still around, opportunity was aplenty.

Most amateur gamblers, he says, do not understand that beating the price is by far the most important aspect to a bottom line, and in that timeframe the bookies were bold. "Bookmakers had opinions," he says, "and they put those opinions into the lines. It was a shopper's paradise. We didn't realize how good we had it, too. We took it for granted."

Even when he had a wife and two kids to support, he had devised and polished pinpoint methods, so he rarely worried about the finances.

"I didn't sweat," Boyles says. "I *knew* I was going to win. Again, back then, with the numbers being the way they were, you could walk into one store and the game would be four. Walk across the street, and it would be five and a half, or six. I was betting both sides. I would stay high on the weak number, the off-market number, but I'd also have a bet with a built-in middle. And when you're betting that way, you basically can't lose. You're going to win money."

He enjoys betting on college sports the most, for many reasons, and especially favors college basketball. It's five months of many games a day, just about, which enables him to cover his living expenses, and then some, for the year.

Just for kicks, he highlights a mythical hoops game between Kentucky and Duke to illustrate how he goes about his business. Kentucky is listed as a four-point favorite at the Mirage. He doesn't just randomly name the Mirage, because doing this the proper way demands, also, that the pro bettor knows the sharp books from the square books. He talks about the Mirage, under Jimmy Vaccaro's leadership, as having been one of the sharpest shops in town.

"Because they dealt with all the wise guys, and Jimmy was sharp himself," Boyles says. "So the Mirage has this game at four. You go to a smaller place that you don't respect, you consider it a square book, and they've got the game at five and a half or six. Say six. There, you bet Duke plus six points, for a dime [a thousand bucks, the ten-percent vig being implied so he's actually doling out eleven hundred dollars]. You go to the Mirage, or Imperial Palace, and take Kentucky minus four points for a nickel [five hundred dollars, with the implied fifty-dollar vig making it five fifty]. You have four, five, and six working for you, but you're high on the side you want to be high on."

## THE SKINNY

When the situation presents itself, professional handicapper Ron Boyles pounces on number variances at different shops, placing the bigger bet—the "high side," he calls it—at the establishment that he least respects. If Team A is about a two-point hoops favorite at most places, and one has it at three and a half or four, he will make the biggest bet at that second shop, taking those points. That's where the value lies, he reasons. He will place about half that wager where he can give the two points.

If it lands on either of those numbers, that bet is a push and he wins the other. If it lands on three, he wins both. The worst-case scenario is Team A winning in a blowout. But even then, the big bet on Team B is tempered, halved, because of his wager on Team A. If Team B, the underdog, wins outright, he's still ahead for the game. It's how he has made a living for decades.

Duke plus six points is that high side, Boyles reiterates, because that's the square side, the number he obtained at the book he doesn't respect. With Jimmy Vaccaro then at the Mirage and Jay Kornegay then running the Imperial Palace, those are the smart numbers, the sharp numbers, and they very likely will match. Kentucky giving four points, probably at both joints, is the sharp action, at which he'd lay half the bet he put on the square side.

Kentucky wins by five points, he is in the money, a winner of both bets and roughly fifteen hundred dollars. If the Wildcats win by six, the dime bet on Duke plus six is a push and the Kentucky wager, minus four, would return five hundred dollars. If Kentucky wins by four, that nickel bet is a push and the Duke-plus-six garners a thousand dollars.

Should the Blue Devils win the game outright, that grand on Duke plus six is a winner, returning four hundred fifty bucks when that five hundred fifty "nickel" bet on Kentucky minus four points is factored into the equation. The only way Boyles loses money is if Kentucky wins by at least seven points; he had Duke plus six, which loses that eleven hundred, but at least he would have had five hundred fifty on Kentucky to win by four, which made five hundred. He's a net loser of six hundred in that scenario, which could have been worse had he not had that winner on Kentucky. His buffers are also called hedges.

Apologies, to whomever, for the simplicity of the above explanation, but its options deserve detail.

"And you're doing this on multiple games, every night," says Boyles. He could have action on ten or twelve games, often more, on any given evening. "You're not going to lose. You're going to get the money, and that's pretty much what I've done for many, many years."

College football, in his betting focus, runs a close second to college hoops. The emotion of the collegians provides the entertainment value. What's more, those passions provide Boyles with stellar opportunities in which to take advantage of situational mood swings, in players and teams. This is also the bedrock difference between him and many other professional handicappers, whom he divides into two camps. The situational players, like himself, and the numbers crunchers, the math-model guys concerned only about what their numbers tell them.

## THE SKINNY

Reducing a game to mere numbers, with no regard for injuries or rosters, or quality of substitutes or coaching ability, has its merits. Namely, it eliminates any degree of personal bias or favoritism, or dislike, for either side. The numbers rule. What the numbers say, the proper bet follows suit. I like to employ pure statistics, and nothing else, in certain baseball and hockey situations. With so many games being played, patterns and tendencies are more accurately reflected in aspects of these sports.

In baseball, after a month or so, I take a close look at 5-inning lines, with an emphasis on Overs. From my 2018 folder, I pluck, at random, Saturday, August 4. I'm seeking opposing starting pitchers who have been getting rocked of late, so I go directly to the "Last 5 (Pit.)" column on the reverse side of the sheets widely available in most books. I only care how starting pitchers are running of late, the colder the better, and this category reveals how the scheduled starting pitchers have performed in their past five outings.

And one game stands out: Lockett for the Padres starting against Hendricks of the Cubs. Their combined ERAs, over their past five starts, is 12.53. I divide that by nine, multiply that by five, and come up with 6.96 5-inning projection for this game on August 4. The five-inning total is 5½, so it meets my first parameter; the projected 5-inning total of those two pitchers must be at least one run greater than the listed total. Check. It comes at a minus-115 price, so a bet of $115 will return $215. My records show that that's exactly what I played, and after five innings the score was 5–3. Who was leading? Don't give a damn. Don't care who won. Only care that both teams combined to score eight runs over five innings.

(For the record, two other games that day would have warranted 5-inning Over wagers, and they would have split. For an outlay of $325, that return would have been $415, or a $90 gain. I played only the game with the greatest disparity between projected 5-inning total runs and the listed total on the sheet.)

One personal play did stand out in baseball in 2018—Tampa games Under on the 5-inning line in Blake Snell starts. In four of his first five starts, he allowed one run or fewer four times in his first five innings. And those were overall runs, not earned. I favored the 5-inning lines to eliminate bullpen headaches. That caught my eye, so I started taking Tampa 5-inning Unders in Snell starts.

The six-foot-four (and almost sickly looking) lefty did not disappoint, winning those 5-inning Unders regularly; from then on, he allowed two runs or fewer in twenty-three of his final twenty-six starts which included nine shutouts. Remember, this was over five innings. He either shut out a foe or allowed only one run in nine of his final eleven starts. His start on Saturday, August 4, was magnificent. The book adjusted, slicing Tampa's 5-inning Total to 3½, and at a minus-115 price against the White Sox. No matter. He'd been paying fantastic returns. I bit. After five innings, the score was 1–1. No wonder Snell won the American League Cy Young Award.

I hone in on game Totals in the NHL, seeking Overs, highlighting how teams have fared in their previous five games. Again, those are noted on the reverse side of the day's game sheet. (If they are not included, may I suggest shopping elsewhere?) Goals For (GF) and Goals Against (GA) are the main columns under "Last 5." I take both of those numbers for both teams, add them, divide by two; if that number is at least a goal higher than the total on the sheet, it's a play.

On Thursday, December 6, 2018, the one glaring game was Chicago at Vegas, with a projected total of 7.5. The total on the sheet was 6. That 1.5 difference warranted a play, since the difference was at least a goal, but that also represented the greatest disparity of the eleven games scheduled that day. So it represented my single wager of the day. The Over came at a minus-125 price, so it cost $125 to win $100. And the thrilling game ended in a 4–3 victory, for Vegas, which did not matter. Cashing that ticket is what mattered. And, for the record, three other games that day had a projected total of at least a goal higher than the sheet total, and two won.

Two nights later presented a sterling example of why I mainly disregard players—and favor Totals, primarily Over—in hockey. Golden Knights goalie Marc André-Fleury had been on a golden roll, having won eight of his previous nine games, heading into a game in L.A. against the league-bottom-feeding Kings on Saturday, December 8. An imposing challenge for the Kings, yes? No. L.A. won, 5–1. The odds, either way, didn't matter because I didn't play it. But an average bettor might have viewed those circumstances and believed the Knights would have rolled.

Those are some simple math models, in which keen analyses of the statistics can return rewards. Pay attention. Scan the box scores. But remember what former UCLA football coach Terry Donahue always liked to preach—Paralysis by Analysis. There's too much out there, so try to keep it simple. Poach and pick, and disregard, what best fits how you like to operate.

Many bettors might incorporate variations of both systems into their wagering actions, and flexibility has many merits. There is not one correct way to go about this, no one way that will ensure results. For our purposes, though, and again for simplicity, we'll address the two disparate methods, courtesy of someone who's done it for decades.

"I'm pretty much a situational handicapper," Boyles says. "I'm not a big numbers cruncher or math-modeler. I look for situations in college sports. [With] the kids [players], there's just more emotion, more flat spots, where teams don't show up. There are more spots where they really get excited, focused, and ready to play. If you have a feel for that, which teams are going to come ready to play and which teams might be a little flat, that's a pretty big edge."

He is pressed, explaining that the math-modelers do not pay any attention to the emotional value, highs or lows, of players or teams. This also removes their own biases and beliefs—head over heart. It's just what their numbers tell them, he says. "That's it. Their math model says Team A should be a seven-point favorite over Team B, and the number on the board is five. They're going to lay the five because their model says the game should be seven. It's all black and white with the math guys, the numbers guys.

"They're not concerned about whether a team had played a huge emotional game two nights earlier against an archrival and they might be flat for this game. They don't even take that into consideration. They don't care about the situational; it's strictly whatever the numbers tell them."

Boyles dislikes that strategy. He doesn't say it's senseless, but his tone implies it. He relishes betting *against* teams coming off emotional games and he savors betting *on* teams that are coming off a blowout loss, by twenty-five or thirty points.

"They got embarrassed," he says. "Especially if they got a little extra time to let that stew, and the coach has been all over them. They're going to come out that next game and be ready to play. You're going to get a big effort by a team that gets blown out by thirty, so I like betting *on* those kinds of teams.

"I like betting *against* teams that are coming off an emotional game against an archrival, and now they're a double-digit favorite against a team at the bottom of the standings. I want to bet *against* that kind of team. I'll take the bad team in last place getting double digits. I know the favorite won't be focused. They won't be ready to play. That's what I'm talking about when I talk about situational handicapping."

## THE SKINNY

An example of the situational type of handicapping that Ron Boyles likes to employ involves the aftermath of big victories or huge defeats in college basketball. He follows them religiously. A team that just lost by twenty-five or thirty points? He will take a very close look at playing it in its next game, believing that embarrassment—and choice words by the boss—will propel it to a cover. Could be a points imbalance in that next game, especially by those betting on what they just saw, a big loss, that team's no good . . . a value situation.

Conversely, with a team coming off an emotional triumph against an archrival, and it's a double-digit favorite against a lower team in the league standings in its next game? Boyles relishes taking those points against a team that likely will be full of itself.

He offers another fictional scenario, of the Lakers playing the Warriors and the game goes into overtime. The next evening, the Warriors play at Sacramento. Boyles would take a very close look at the Kings, especially since they're likely to be getting points, and more than a few. They're rested, haven't played in two or three days. "And this is their Super Bowl," he says. "Golden State could not care less about it, and they're coming off an emotional game. Again, it's situations I'm looking for pretty much in all sports."

Boyles cannot impress enough, to the amateur or weekend punter, the importance of getting the best number, even if it takes just a little bit of effort. Utmost care should be administered in getting optimal prices and point spreads. "But they don't care," he says. "They just want to be on the Packers or Steelers. They don't care what the line is. It could be six at their book, and they lay it. But had they walked across the street, they could have laid five. They are not price sensitive."

They are too sensitive, Boyles believes, about what they just saw, what just happened, and they roll with that. "Whatever they've last seen," he says. "Whatever is fresh in their minds, the week before or the game before. They generally want to bet on teams that looked good and they want to bet against the teams that looked terrible. It's just the way they're wired."

Today, Ron Boyles has seven apps on his smartphone. Like many playing this game seriously, he calls them "outs." He has not dealt with an offshore outlet in years. He does not keep stringent book-keeping notes, tracking wins or losses, or deal with a specific bankroll and bet a specific percentage, that serves as his unit, of that account. He keeps running and cumulative logs in his head, of which he always has accurate figures. At no time would he have ever been in danger of losing a big score with the mortgage, or weekly family grocery bill, on the line.

"Because I'm not a plunger," Boyles says. "I'm just a grinder, just grinding away, doing the same thing every day. There's no big bet where, I have to win *this* bet or I'm going to go broke. Pro gamblers aren't like that. They just know when they have something good and they have an advantage, and they look to exploit that advantage over time. It's not plunging.

"The bigger I think my advantage is, the more I'm going to bet on it. If I really love a game, I have a strong opinion on a game and I'm beating the price, I'm getting the best of the numbers, the market number is five and I can get six and a half—and I love the game, also—I'm going to bet more. My perceived edge will determine how much I bet."

He has been around Las Vegas long enough to have come across Lefty Rosenthal, but they were never introduced. As if it aired last night, Boyles vividly recalls KLAS-TV anchor Garry Waddell, in October 1982, leading off the 11 P.M. broadcast of the Channel 8 news with the report of the car bombing that nearly cost Lefty his life. "He *knew* they were out to get him," says Boyles.

Some have speculated that the Rosenthal car bomb had the fingerprints of the Milwaukee mob; boss Frank Balistrieri, after all, had been nicknamed "Mad Bomber." But South Point owner Michael Gaughan disagrees. He tells me, "It was the Chicago people. This was the gang that couldn't shoot straight. They put the bomb in the wrong spot."

Boyles did meet Tony (the Ant) Spilotro at the former Food Factory restaurant on Twain owned by Spilotro's brother, John, an introduction by a friend that the relative youngster from New Castle could have done without. "I shook his hand," Boyles says. "A scary guy to look at. Short, stocky. Just knew he was nasty. No good. I said, 'Hello.' That was it. Ordered my food."

Michael Gaughan also had an unceremonious run-in with Spilotro at the Las Vegas Country Club. The Ant had been turned down for membership. During one of his regular lunches, with Frank Toti and other friends in the club's coffee shop, Gaughan excused himself to use the gents. He's standing there. The door opens. The Ant had apparently used a backdoor to access the diner and facilities.

"I don't know him at all," Gaughan says. "A guy stands next to me and says, 'Hello, Michael.' I look over; it's Tony. I don't know Tony. How in the fuck does Tony know me by my first name? I talked to him. I went back to the table, and we left. He was a psychopath. I stopped going. I didn't want to run into this guy."

The Ant came to Las Vegas in 1971. Within six months, police investigated his potential role in no fewer than six homicides. He'd be linked to twenty-six murders, including fellow Chicago Outfit associate (Fat Jerry) Delman, who owned and ran the Saratoga turf club. The day before Thanksgiving 2018, Roxy Roxborough wrote a Twitter tribute to Delman, "my friend," on the forty-second anniversary of Delman's death. He was gunned down in a parking garage, forty thousand dollars left untouched in the trunk of his car. "So far," Roxy wrote, "the only legal Nevada bookie to have been murdered." Friends placed a newspaper ad awarding twenty grand to anyone who could provide information leading to the arrest and conviction of the murderer, but it remains unsolved.

Like Michael Gaughan, Boyles prefers to keep a low profile. But that was upended in late November 2002, when he made a bet of twenty-two hundred dollars on the Miami Heat plus eight and a half points, against Orlando, at the Green Valley Ranch, near his home in the Henderson foothills on the southeast rim of the Las Vegas Valley. He placed it about fifteen minutes before tipoff.

Shortly after the game started, sports-book manager Kelly Downey approached Boyles and, Boyles says, asked him to hand over the ticket; the casino had learned that Orlando starters Tracy McGrady and Grant Hill would not play. (The Magic would win, but only by two points. So Boyles's bet made him two grand.)

Boyles says Downey told him Art Manteris, the Station casinos' vice president of race and sports, was on the telephone line and had ordered his employee to retrieve the betting slip. Boyles refused to surrender the ticket to Downey. At the time, Boyles told reporters that if he had done anything nefarious, he would have made the bet and bolted from the property. Instead, he was hanging around, watching a couple of NFL games, nothing to hide or run from. Boyles had made two other bets, which he split.

Stations, at this writing, owns twenty-one casinos around town, mostly on the city's periphery where they cater to locals. Boyles went to Boulder Station a couple of days after the drama to cash his winning tickets and was told not to return, that he was barred from the company's properties. That episode was repeated when he visited Sunset Station. Manteris, at the time, said he was prohibited from discussing individual customers' wagers, but he did say Boyles had inaccuracies in his account of the incident.

Manteris has never shied away from barring a gambler from his workplace. In his *SuperBookie,* written when he was running the SuperBook for the Las Vegas Hilton, he wrote: "I throw a lot of people out of the SuperBook. On what grounds? My grounds . . . if I find a player with too much of an edge, I have the right to refuse his bet."

Asked if getting barred by Art Manteris represented a feather in his cap, Boyles laughs. "No. I don't like Manteris, he doesn't like me. I wish I could still bet in there, but it is what it is. Actually, it's helped me through the years; they have so many [casinos], I've been able to go into places where they don't know me and then make bets. So, even though I'm technically banned there, I've made plenty of bets [at Station properties] over the years."

# NINE

# The Astute Scribes

THE CUSTOMER HAD BEEN LOSING sports wagers. Badly. He had run up a tab of four thousand dollars to his bookie, in Orlando, Florida, and time came to settle the account. This is the dramatic gray area for both sides of the vast illicit gambling equation in the U.S.; the ensuing transaction can be fraught with danger, some trepidation for either party. So the grizzled bookie tapped the imposing muscle to make a personal-collections visit to this client. In this instance, Todd Dewey served as both bookmaker and enforcer.

Anyone who knows Dewey will recognize the ludicrous incongruity of those lines. In the city of Las Vegas, or in the newspaper field in general, it would be a tall task to engage a more mild-mannered and genuinely pleasant person than the sportswriter for the *Las Vegas Review-Journal* who covers sports gambling at ground zero of the industry.

So some astonishment accompanied the revelation that he was a campus bookie as an undergraduate student at the University of Central Florida. Adrenaline pumped through him, though, nerves a bit on edge, when he approached the apartment complex to collect that four grand. He kept telling himself that he would not, in any way, enter into anything physical, or make any degree of threat, to force this client, or these guys, to pay. He retraced his route into the building, to facilitate a rapid retreat. "Yeah," they told him in the open doorway, "we got the money. Can we have higher limits?"

All right, Dewey thought as he exhaled, this is a little out of control.

"But they paid it," he says. "I couldn't believe it. I'm like, 'Where are these kids getting this money? They're just college kids.' A friend of mine said a neighbor wanted to bet. I said, Okay. And they're betting five hundred dollars, even a thousand, a game! I was still putting in [for myself] twenty- or thirty-dollar parlays."

Case Keefer never flirted with making book while he attended Kansas University, but during ten years of writing about sports betting, for the *Las Vegas Sun,* he has honed a practical approach to handicapping football games. Of late, that sport has been his bailiwick. In 2017, he finished atop a select group of sixty national writers—from the *Boston Globe* to the *Washington Post* to the *Dallas Morning News*—in a pick'em contest, against the spread, run by NFLPickwatch.com.

He had been writing a weekly NFL pick'em column for the three previous seasons, and someone at the website took notice. Unbeknownst to Keefer, the Pickwatch folks entered his selections into their 2017 contest. A couple of months into the season, a colleague notified Keefer that he was high on that chart; he hadn't even known he was on it. And he won it.

In the regular season and playoffs, Keefer went 148–111–7, a rate of fifty-seven percent that would have pocketed about twenty-six units. With an average bet, or unit, of a hundred bucks, a punter would have made approximately twenty-six hundred dollars, just by blindly following his lead. *Sun* sports editor Ray Brewer called the achievement a testament to Keefer's "dedication to our readers and to his craft," adding that the paper is proud to provide to its audience "the nation's best betting analyst in mainstream media."

## THE SKINNY

Many bettors refer to their average-size wager as a "unit." This is part of a disciplined approach to the endeavor, related to the "bankroll." Many out to make a profit will do so by employing money separate from whatever account, or sources, is used to pay the rent or mortgage, and the rest of the bills necessary to everyday life. Not co-mingling those two sources can usually save many headaches, or more serious ailments.

Whatever the bankroll, the punter who sees this as more than just a hobby will devote one percent, sometimes two, to a single wager, and that will serve as his or her average bet in nearly every circumstance. If there is eagerness, and some trepidation, in testing the sports-betting waters, this might be a smart and healthy way to begin. Again, though, it's important to say that everybody is different. One very smart, and profitable, punter records nothing on paper, keeps no weekly charts on how he's faring. It's all up here, he says as he points to his noggin. But most players aren't like him—it's important to track your plays and have a record, to manage a bankroll wisely and to easily spot strengths and weaknesses.

When his newspaper ran an article to promote the achievement, Keefer insisted that his four-year accumulated record—of 550–493–24, a fifty-three-percent success rate that would have produced fewer than eight units of gain—be included, to illustrate the difficulty in trying to beat the book. For the proper long-haul perspective, he says. Professional handicappers have singled out Keefer, on Twitter, and recommended him as a smart connection to their followers. Dewey is a wise follow, too.

"I love sports betting, love being around it," says the genial Keefer. "I take it very seriously, and I found something that works for me. [In 2017], everything just really clicked. A breakthrough year. I think betting should be de-stigmatized, because I think a lot of the stigma around it is unfair."

In Las Vegas newspapers, Dewey and Keefer are the two insiders who provide regular coverage of the business whose growth could be exponential in coming years. They are tapped into the lines, movements, and those on both sides of the counter trying to stay a step ahead of each other, and their favorite teams are the ones that cover, that make them money. It's all reminiscent of an old adage—"Good teams win; great teams cover"—that Jay Kornegay trumpets in his shop.

Old Dominion, a 28½-point football underdog, had just defeated Virginia Tech outright, 49–35, at home. The next day the threadbare Buffalo Bills, as a seventeen-point underdog, went into Minnesota, which had been 1–0–1, and completely destroyed the Vikings, 27–6. At the Westgate, Minnesota had been a ten-to-one preseason shot—one of five teams at those odds or fewer—to win Super Bowl LIII. But that game exposed Minnesota, whose ensuing slide corresponded to a slip in championship odds, by early December, to fifty-to-one.

"My boys back east tell me, 'Gimme some winners. Help me out here. You're covering all this!'" says Todd Dewey, shaking his head over those fresh and freaky Old Dominion and Buffalo results. "But just because you cover it doesn't mean you have all the winners."

He knew of that weekend's carnage from the frontline. At the MGM, someone had bet a hundred and eighty grand on the Vikings on the money line, to win ten thousand. At the SuperBook, a customer had laid down nine thousand bucks to win four hundred and fifty. At a William Hill outlet, a patron risked eighteen thousand to win a grand.

"They all lost that one," Dewey says. "Whoever bets like that thinks it's free money. 'No *way* are the Vikings going to lose.' These guys probably have so much money it doesn't matter. I don't know. I try to ask who these people are; doctors, lawyers, just pros, rich guys?" As the veteran oddsmaker Jimmy Vaccaro has so eloquently stated, People always, *always,* want more.

While sports-book directors and managers are not bashful about dispensing monetary sums, of certain high-figure bettors that hit or miss, they are loath to reveal height, facial features, mannerisms, and idiosyncrasies of their clientele. Understandable, because the books want to retain that high-end business.

"Over the weekend, someone at CG Technology hit a three-hundred-and-sixty-six-dollar eight-teamer, for sixty-one thousand dollars," Dewey says. "When you hear 'three hundred and sixty-six dollars,' that's an odd amount. I just picture a guy at the window, like, 'Screw this. This is all I have left. Put it *all* on *this*.' A last-ditch shot, or maybe he had hit a bet and rolled it over. Just an insane amount. Very strange."

Someone else had bet four dollars and seventy-five cents on a two-team money-line underdog parlay, eschewing the points to tie the Tennessee Titans (a 9–6 winner over Jacksonville) to the Buffalo Bills (over the Vikings), and when both hit he or she pocketed two hundred and fifty-five dollars. "A great one, at fifty-five-to-one. A classic. You know that guy is a small bettor and it's all he's got left."

Dewey, fifty, savors the eccentric and odd industry scenes. They keep his job unique and interesting, a bottomless trove of subjects and topics to document. Like when downtown renovator emeritus Derek Stevens, live on VSiN, risked eleven grand on all thirty-two opening-round games in the NCAA basketball tournaments in 2017 and 2018. That first one did not go so well, as Stevens went 10–19–3, losing a hundred and nine thousand dollars. He had about ten seconds to make each selection. He netted sixteen grand the second time around—by going 17–14–2, which included an inadvertent, but triumphant, double pick on Loyola–Chicago—with more of a time cushion, and app selections, to make his picks.

In 2018, Stevens also made a twenty-five-grand futures bet, at forty-to-one odds at the Golden Nugget, on Michigan—his alma mater—to win the whole thing. When the Wolverines reached the championship game, Stevens hedged his action by putting three hundred thirty thousand dollars on Villanova on the money line, at a William Hill outlet, to beat Michigan and win a hundred grand. The Wildcats won, and Stevens netted twenty-three thousand bucks when other previous hedging action was taken into account.

The Michigander has two large, strategically placed slot machines, one trimmed in Michigan State green and the other in

Michigan maize and blue, at the front of The D, but the color of money induced him to make that sensible hedging bet on Villanova. In 2012, when replacement referees botched the end of a Green Bay–Seattle *Monday Night Football* game, gifting the Seahawks a victory, Stevens refunded losing wagers to those patrons.

The spirited Derek Stevens is part of an ever-expanding cast of characters that Dewey taps for interesting and insightful copy.

"It is [fun]," Dewey says of his beat. "I love it."

And he doesn't say *winners*. He says, *win-nahs* . . . as in, suburban Boston. Thankfully, Dewey never said *chowder* during our long meeting or boast about how New England teams had been spoiling him—his Twitter avatar is a mug of Larry Bird—for so long. He did say *wicked*. Once.

The family moved to Nashua, New Hampshire, when he was young. In the fourth grade, maybe due to an affinity for orange, he latched onto the Denver Broncos in Super Bowl XII. He drew Crayola pictures of players in bright orange uniforms and helmets, and before that big game against Dallas, he booked fifty-cent bets with schoolmates. After the Cowboys won, 27–10, he ran crying to his mother, Ann Marie, "*Mommmm*, I owe the whole school *thirteen* dollars!" I swear to god it felt like a grand back then. I should have known, then, not to bet."

The fun was just beginning. In high school, a buddy doled out black-market parlay cards. Dewey had never seen such temptation. He flipped it over, to scan the odds. Pick four games, bet ten bucks, win a hundred. So enticing. High school is a common introduction to parlay cards, from coast to coast, and that's when I first saw, in suburban Los Angeles, their multi-choice magnificence. The older brother somehow got into distributing them, and when the principal found stacks in his locker, a week-long suspension was meted out.

Those parlay cards served as Las Vegas lures as I matriculated to San Diego State, where making book—with scant bankroll and even less nerve—was never on the agenda. Way too much else going on, but inexperience with the spread made that a non-starter. I would make a "HammerLock" pick, in my weekly *Daily Aztec* sports column, but a semester's worth of books and tuition, even a round-trip spring-break flight to Mazatlan instead of a hellish twenty-four-hour train ride (each way), could have been garnered going against those selections. Otherwise, impromptu Vegas runs from the fraternity, with requisite "rest stops" at Zzyzx Road, were typical.

Dewey's friend also got popped for his parlay-card mischief.

No matter, because another friend, Little Pete, had a father, Big Pete, who was a bookie and would take bets, goof-around amounts, from Dewey, Little Pete, and all their friends. That association was critical because, at UCF, Dewey and his fellow bookie would have a convenient secondary resource in Big Pete.

"We'd lay some off to Big Pete," Dewey says. "We couldn't take all that action." If four grand had been taken in on the Miami Dolphins, with only a thousand on the other side, the duo could avoid trouble by calling in a wager of three thousand bucks with Big Pete. "That's when it really came to me, where I'm like, 'The *only* way you can win is if you're the bookie, if you're the house.'"

One customer routinely laid three hundred and sixty dollars on three-team teasers, playing with nine points in his favor on each game. "And he never collected. Not once. We thought he was guaranteed to win one of these, but he lost every time. Guy named Gene. Older guy. Felt bad for him, then."

During one rousing spring break in Daytona Beach, Dewey needed to lay off some bets, fast, to limit his exposure. He found a pay phone and quickly rang a number in New Hampshire. "Yeah, is Big Pete there?" he said. "No, but this is Little Ernie. Are you okay, Todd?" On the other line was a female, his mother. In his haste, he had dialed his home. Profuse apologies followed. Today, he can laugh about that episode.

Dewey took a part-time gig as a ticket writer at the jai alai fronton in Orlando, which gave his informal book another base of customers. He graduated, matriculated back to New Hampshire to do some writing and TV work. He cold-called an ad in the now-defunct *Editor & Publisher* and got a job at a tiny paper in Pahrump, an hour from Las Vegas. He made his way onto the

*Review-Journal,* and he took over the sports-gambling beat, in late 2016, when Matt Youmans shifted to the Vegas Stats & Information Network.

Married with a daughter, Dewey had settled, somewhat, in his betting activities before taking over the sports-betting beat. Now, his wife told him, you're not going to start betting all the time again, are you? "Like I'm 'Frank the Tank' or something," says a giggling Dewey of the comedian Will Ferrell's hilarious role as a born-again partier in the popular 2003 movie *Old School.* "I'm like, 'Of course not.'"

He might have been holding two entwined fingers behind his back. Dewey's first piece in his new capacity was about the barista who won the Westgate SuperBook's NFL pick'em SuperContest, in which contestants pick five games a week, sides only, against the spread. The entry fee is a thousand dollars, and the pot for that season was almost a million bucks. An Illinois soybean farmer, who told Dewey he had barely watched any games because he had to be outside, harvesting the crops, finished second.

Anyone can win this thing, Dewey told his better half. Maybe I should give this a shot? "She looked at me like, 'Oh no, what have I gotten into here?' I have not joined that contest, but I have placed some bets."

It comes with the territory, lends validity to his writing, makes him credible. The sourness of a bad beat often seeps into his columns, to which every loyal reader can relate. Unfortunately, for his many buddies back home, Dewey has not unlocked the keys to pummeling the point spreads.

"It just seems like when you go with every sharp pick, that's when the public will win," he says. "It's just how it is. But even the sharpest guys in the world, they don't even hit sixty percent, right? If they're lucky. I wish [writing about sports betting] would help [handicapping] a lot more."

One former player is conspicuous in his wagering career. In 2004, he had nabbed Connecticut giving two and a half points to Duke in a national semifinal basketball game in San Antonio. A late twelve-point run by the Huskies put Dewey in fine shape, up

78–75 with 3.2 seconds remaining and UConn's Emeka Okafor going to the line. Dewey hoped Okafor would hit the first free throw, giving him extra cushion, and miss the second, starting the clock and making it that much more difficult for Duke to connect on some sort of a prayer.

Dewey had put a hundred bucks on a three-team parlay, and the first two hit. Connecticut was the final piece to that puzzle. He nets about six hundred bucks if it covers. Okafor misses the first freebie, hits the second. UConn leads by four, but the clock does not start until the Blue Devils inbound the ball. Chris Duhon drills a one-legged forty-footer at the buzzer. Duke loses, 79–78. Dewey loses.

"The Duke Bad Beat," he says with melancholy. "And he banked it in! Totally meaningless, except for the spread and the seven hundred I had been counting on." He laughs. "Brutal." Dewey chronicled that betting drama in a piece for his paper, culminating it with broadcaster Jim Nantz's fateful words—"It doesn't matter!"—about Duhon's shot.

Longtime Las Vegas sports-radio personality Mitch Moss, now at VSiN, bought himself an extra half-point; instead of giving a point and a half (at eleven hundred bucks) with UConn, he only gave a point, at an extra ten percent (at minus-120, so it cost twelve hundred dollars). The biggest bet of his life, at that point. "Thank God I had the push," he told Dewey. "But if I was smart enough, I would have had [UConn] on the money line and had the win."

Moss should not have felt so bad. He had the wisdom to buy himself out of what would have been a loss, getting his money back. Roxy Roxborough, in the 1998 book *Sports Book Management* he penned with Mike Rhoden, determined that such an extra half-point can increase a bettor's chance of winning—not losing, from Moss's angle—by four percent.

One offshore book reported winning a sizeable six-figure sum, which it would have lost had Duhon not nailed that prayer.

"There are so many bad beats, an endless string," Dewey says. "We can all relate to them. But for every bad beat, there's a miracle cover, too." He laughs. "One guy told me about a football game ending with fans rushing the field, tearing down the goal post, so they couldn't kick the extra point. And it affected the spread! THAT sounds like one of the worst."

The few legitimate professionals that Dewey has met, he says, do what Las Vegas legend Lem Banker typically did, by playing different numbers at different casinos against each other to guarantee either a push or narrow victory, a slim loss or a handsome return. To fund a nice night on the town, Banker would execute two three-thousand-dollar wagers that might net a couple of hundred bucks. Maybe, today, that type of bettor would lay two thirty-grand bets to win two thousand. Maybe more. The books know who they are, though, and can refuse their patronage, even bar those players—or anyone—for any reason.

"The arbitrage game, or scalping," Dewey says. "In college football, they'll take advantage of different prices on the same team season-win totals." If one book, say, has a team at a plus price on under seven and a half, and another book has a plus price at over seven and a half on that same team, the same amount wagered on both guarantees that the action will pay off.

They scour odds daily and put down big money. I heard someone had put one hundred thousand dollars on the Golden Knights *not* to win the Stanley Cup [in 2017–18], which offset their Knights *to win* the Cup ticket, just to guarantee a thousand-dollar win. Guaranteed wins.

"It also sounds to me," says Dewey, "like there are a lot more guys playing the middle, going for the middle and trying to play the numbers, than just guys handicapping the games—as in, 'This is the team I like, and I'm betting big on it.' The guys playing with those numbers, like a stock market, it seems those are the professionals."

## THE SKINNY

Arbitrage bettors, or scalpers, often put five figures on both sides of a wager, at different casinos, a move especially rewarding—and rare—when a plus price can be had on each bet. That guarantees a profit, but it can require a lot of shopping and perfect timing. Plus, bookmakers are scanning the landscape with just as much gusto to prevent such a scenario, making the window of such an opportunity a narrow one that can close quickly. Watch the fingers.

Middlers want it all. If they can take 3½ at one book and give 2½ at another, they are in hog heaven, knowing the common occurrence of three-point victory margins in football. Taking 4½ at one shop and giving 2½ at another is a most-dreamy scenario, too, because they cover those magic three- and four-point spreads. The same could be said regarding six- and seven-point margins; if you favor, say, an underdog getting 6½ points but can find that side plus 7½ points elsewhere, the obvious smart maneuver would be to nab the 7½. You have that seven-point defeat covered.

A case in point was Wynn sports-book director Johnny Avello opening Navy as a 13½-point favorite on the road against Southern Methodist early in the 2018 season. Avello, before he moved to DraftKings, was known for displaying the first college-football lines, at about three o'clock every Sunday. (Caesars might now own the claim.) Some offshores opened with Navy minus seven points. "Everyone hammered SMU getting thirteen and a half points at the Wynn," Dewey says, "and they took Navy on the offshore, hoping to get the middle."

Not accounting for line moves at either shop, a Navy victory by eight to thirteen points constituted that "middle," a two-way payoff. SMU—off a twenty-five-point defeat at Michigan, in which it covered as a thirty-seven-point underdog—defeated Navy, 31–30.

"The thing with middles, it's so tough to hit those," Dewey says. We drift into the absolute importance of discipline, in betting and managing money, to make a profit and not turn around and lose it in the flip of an eyelid. "Most guys don't have it. You got action junkies, every Monday night there's a game on and you want action on it. Plus, when you visit a book, there are all the casino games, like video poker, roulette, blackjack. Like [the late legendary poker player] Stu Ungar; he had drug issues, bet huge on sports. Had he just stuck with poker, coulda made a fortune."

Ungar did make a fortune, of approximately thirty million dollars. He is one of two people to have won the World Series of Poker Main Event, featuring Texas Hold'em, three times. In 1998, forty-five and essentially broke, he died of a heart condition, exacerbated by years of cocaine abuse, in a room at the Oasis Motel, still doing business on Las Vegas Boulevard near the Stratosphere.

He was not, and is not, alone. Many successful bettors have what's called a "leak"—whether that's losing at the horses or feeding video-poker machines, or doing drugs—something that distracts them from their core competence; no matter how successful they might be in one endeavor there's always something else holding them back, drawing them down.

Dewey respects, among others, pro handicapper Steve Fezzik, retired police officer Doug Fitz (whose analyses and free picks are available at SystemPlays.com), and BetLabsSports.com (which joined The Action Network in October 2017); for a fee, a database of more than four hundred BetLab filters can be accessed to investigate trends and patterns, creating proprietary betting systems.

In a Dewey column, Fezzik hesitated to reveal the wisdom of taking the Under in NBA games featuring two teams that both win at least sixty percent of the time, which pro bettor Van Smith had known about, and played, but had reinforced by seeing Fezzik's comments in ink. "Some people don't want stuff out in the public, and he was the same way," Dewey says of Fezzik. "He didn't know if he wanted to share it, exactly. But I want to try to give people some tips, and I'm glad I had a good one there. I'm glad [Van Smith] had good things to say."

We drift back to discipline, money management, getting the best numbers early, and shopping thoroughly. When we discuss the mantra, spoken by many professionals, of avoiding parlays and teasers as if they were dark alleys echoed by loud barking, Dewey breaks into more laughter.

"All the things I don't follow," he says. "I think I'm like a lot of people; we know all the things not to do, but you just can't help yourself sometimes. Most people do not have a hundred bucks to put on games, on straight bets. They'd rather put thirty, forty, fifty on a three-team [parlay], to try to win three hundred, instead of putting three hundred and thirty bucks to win three hundred, or three hundred-and-ten-dollar [side, or straight] bets. Everyone wants to bet a little to win a lot. Probably the only way you can win, in the long run, is by doing straight bets."

Soon after Case Keefer landed in Las Vegas, in 2009, he took a seat at the end of a big oval table, covered in green felt, a space to store chips, a hole for drinks. Quiet anyway, he did not say much. Gambling, however, pulsates in his bloodlines, as generations of Keefers have been involved in thoroughbred and greyhound racing.

This Texas Hold'em deal, though, was something new. It was half possible to see the gears clicking inside his noggin, trying to compute not only probabilities but those around him, these new characters, the odd tells and tendencies; a lot to digest.

Then, it was over. I was there. Specific hands can't be recalled, but he most definitely was a non-factor neophyte. To Keefer's credit, he is also a very quick study, which he displayed a week later when, deftly using his innate earnestness against his foes, he won the tournament that served as a weekly gathering among colleagues. He has since won nearly fifteen thousand dollars in an online event, before they were shuttered, and nearly seven grand for cashing in one of the many undercard events in the World Series of Poker.

"I had no idea what was going on," says Keefer, thirty-one, of that maiden poker voyage among new friends. "That second time, it was like a drug. I won maybe two hundred dollars. But at that time, it was a ton. I was an intern making nothing. It was such a huge thing to me. After I won that second game, I dove so much into it."

Sports betting would match that interest, curiosity, and exhilaration, which is why his columns attract national attention and interest from professional bettors. His coup of besting so many peers in that Pickwatch contest is even more impressive when portioned into his categories.

He qualifies a pick on each game as either Play, Lean, or Guess. Pickwatch used all of them, of course, for its contest. But if a reader focused solely on Play, Keefer's choice selections, he would have gone 36–17, a winning percentage of 67.9; a delivery of more than seventeen units of profit within five months at the end of 2017.

He knows the lunacy of betting on every NFL game on every weekend. "As anyone who's ever been to Las Vegas knows, you'll go broke doing that." That is what precipitated the three categories, emphasizing a Play when the information he has culled warrants action, reaching for the wallet.

Like Lem Banker, Keefer relies on power ratings, numbers gathered from reliable outlets that he then tweaks, depending upon injuries, patterns, weather, site, and other factors that he deems integral to the outcome of a game. In his *Changing the Game,* Wall Street analyst William O. Hall III relies on seven areas, including rushing and passing figures, and turnovers, to compute a team's rating, to compare to other teams. Those are common ingredients in power ratings used by many professionals.

(Hall mentor Bob Kahn told stories of how Greek philosopher Diogenes was obsessed with discovering truths, and how a securities analyst requires that same fanatical persistence and passion, all of which—Hall hypothesizes, between the lines—is applicable to the sports bettor out to make more money than he loses.)

The ratings are impersonal, reducing human variables to impersonal symbols. Head over heart, Keefer says. Sentiment is completely extracted from the thought process of picking a winner against the spread. His go-to source is FootballOutsiders.com, a site edited by Bill Connelly that analyzes a range of NFL and NCAA football computations.

His S&P+ college ratings delve into every play on both sides of the line. As this is being written, Alabama is at the top of the overall list. No surprise. Offensively, however, Oklahoma is tops, with a 50.1 rating; the Crimson Tide is second at 47.0. Defensively, Michigan is first at 12.6, the lower the rating the better; the Tide checked in at twentieth, at 20.2. It's a deep dive into various aspects of a team's performance, which does not require Keefer to sift through many, if any, other resources.

"Possession data, drive and yardage data," Keefer says. "I'm always looking at those. I got way into analytics in college, from a football perspective. But, since I'm doing this for fun and not trying to do it professionally, I didn't necessarily want to just throw a bunch of numbers in and spit it out. I try to monitor all that, moving parts up and down, as I see fit. It's a marriage of the two worlds, because I also think there's merit to the old-school approach as well."

He rarely alters home-field advantages in the NFL, where three points is the standard, Keefer says. College is different. "There are some places where home field is worth more than others, like Auburn playing at home probably means more than if Vanderbilt is playing at home, but it's minuscule. Half a point? But there are such small margins, those half-points add up after a long time."

In the previous eight bowl seasons, before the 2018 regular season, Keefer went 168–129–5, a success rate of 56.5 percent. And in the 2018 NFL campaign, through the first seven weeks, Keefer went 58–42–8, a profitable success rate of 57.4 percent. (However, the season would soon nosedive on him.)

Keefer has apps on his mobile phone for three casino sports books, but on the eve of the 2018 season he had not injected money into any of them. He constantly reviews their point spreads and odds. He lives across the street from Green Valley Ranch, so it's a stroll to the casino. Early Sunday mornings, he'll make that jaunt in long-sleeve T-shirt, blue sweats, white athletic socks, and flip-flops, to observe last-second line movements. The apps, he knows, are sometimes a convenience and a curse, maybe making it too easy to place a wager. He'd rather shop in person, anyway, to feel the excitement of the crowd, to actually be given, and hold, a betting ticket.

He sticks with a certain bankroll in his mind, ensuring that he does not tap into his and his wife's living expenses. He also keeps a level head, no matter the situation, whether someone flips a full boat to beat his flush or a terrible series of events leads to his twenty-point favorite yielding a last-second touchdown to only win by seventeen.

"I don't go on *tilt* and get angry, go, 'I'm going to bet five times my unit,'" he says. "I stick to my unit. I know the math. I know *this* is how much I can lose and be fine. I don't deviate. I think a reason people might lose a lot is because a game or two will go against them, then they'll fire away beyond their means. I look at it like a long process, so I don't ever change how much I'm going to bet."

All of which ties into a main goal, of having fun. Simmering over a gambling loss, maybe tossing a pillow or two, would defeat the purpose. Such an act would be very uncharacteristic of Keefer, anyway.

The Vegas Golden Knights tested him, he admits. Like many who believed an expansion team would get pounded, early and often, he fired away against them from the start of their first season. All of those punters paid for the misdiagnosis, as the energetic squad sprinted all the way to the Stanley Cup Final before showing fatigue. One book had pegged Vegas with a regular-season points total of fewer than seventy, and the Knights finished with triple digits. Keefer quit betting hockey by the All-Star break and doesn't envision returning to it.

"I don't think I have a winning formula for hockey," he says. "I was busting my ass trying to bet it. I put in so many hours without getting anything in return. It was not fun, trying to figure out hockey plays. I decided to just leave hockey, focus on football. I don't need to be betting on hockey."

Again, fun. Keefer stresses not betting money that will be missed, a recurring theme among many subjects that bears being repeated. Entertainment value should be a priority for people who walk into a sports book or seek some extra excitement when viewing a sporting event on television at home or out with friends.

"I think that's what people sometimes lose sight of, one of

the more important things that isn't going to be in any gambling guidebook. But if you look at it like I love football and I'm going to have fun by coming down and betting on some games, you can lose a couple hundred dollars. It can be hard, but you have to be positive, like, I really love doing it and that was really fun, having some rooting interest in those games."

The time he's logged at poker tables, among those who play it for a living, reinforced maintaining perspective. Seeing someone drop two hundred grand and not be affected by that consequence resonated with Keefer.

"If they didn't play wrong, they're not going to be slamming the door or punching the table. You have to take emotion out of it. You can't beat yourself up. 'Oh my god, I just lost a thousand dollars. I could have bought a new couch!' Can't think like that. You have to separate it, more like keeping score for a year, the long run."

Soon after Case won the Pickwatch championship, a rumor floated about a ring. Visiting from Georgia, Kip Keefer, Case's father, sat in the Green Valley Ranch race book—in the far-left section, with the rest of the horse players—and beamed as he told a friend, on his mobile phone, about his son's big triumph in this national contest. Might get a ring, too, said Kip, who happens to be connected to one of the storied pooches in greyhound history—called "Keefer."

In 1981, owner Keith Dillon had a thrilling racer, named Perceive. Kip Keefer raved about that dog, in greyhound magazine articles and at Southland Park, in West Memphis, Arkansas, where he served as publicity director and announcer. Kip made a huge production of every one of his starts, and Perceive would earn Hall of Fame status. Dillon was so grateful to Kip for the steady attention, he promised to name a pup—"the best looking one"—from Perceive's first litter after him. Dillon sent Kip a Polaroid photo of his young daughter, in the snow, holding the adorable little dog.

Keefer, the greyhound, eventually appeared at Southland "and was an absolute monster," Kip writes me, via his son, of his name-sake canine that overcame many setbacks to become celebrated for impossibly late charges, and victories. He was named the best distance greyhound of 1986. A year later, Kip's wife Cathie was four months pregnant with Case when the couple went to Derby Lane, in St. Petersburg, Florida—where Keefer (the man) had trained Keefer (the dog) on occasion—to watch the four-legged blur win the $100,000 Distance Classic for a second consecutive year.

En route to the hospital to give birth to Case, Cathie wore a pink KEEFER T-shirt bearing the dog's mug. He was featured in a front-page article in *The Wall Street Journal,* had a book (*Keefer: The People's Choice*) written about him in 2007, and has his own Facebook page and bobblehead—tan body, red silks bearing No. 1 on each side, wide toothy grin.

(Syndicate kingpin Tony (The Lizard) Bloom owes his gambling nature to a grandfather, Harry Bloom, who owned greyhounds. "He was a small-time gambler and probably a loser, as ninety-nine percent of people are," The Lizard said in *Gambling.* "But he loved it, and the losing never became out of control.")

Case Keefer has no bobblehead, at least not yet. No ring, either. He reports that there will be no need for a sizing ceremony. And that's just as well, because the 2018 football season has started. He cannot emphasize enough the mentality and work ethic that the quest demands.

"You have to figure out a process that works for you over the long term," Keefer says. "You have to believe you have an edge that will bear out. I can lose a game and not be disappointed about it, if I know that I bet *this* on Tuesday and I got the best number by two and a half points. You make those bets long enough, in the long run you'll come out a winner. But if you think you can make a living off sports gambling, I hope you're ready to work harder than you've ever worked in your life, times two. It just takes so many hours and so much manpower. You have to be wired a certain way, too."

As the legendary (Amarillo Slim) Preston used to say about

poker, which just might apply to sports betting, too—"It's a tough way to make an easy living."

The GVR sports book, on this early afternoon, erupts at times, reflecting a touchdown or a turnover, action that just might make some of the tickets among the maw worth something. The trial-and-error of trying to help some of those people make a buck or two, for Case Keefer, is taxing but gratifying, when everything clicks. Like Kip Keefer's namesake greyhound that delivered so regularly to a reverent public thirsting for a winner, his son tries to satiate his own base of devotees.

# TEN

# A Frameable Ticket

THE GUY HELD A TWO-HUNDRED-DOLLAR TICKET on the Vegas Golden Knights to win the Stanley Cup Final, at three hundred-to-one odds. If the Knights went all the way, he'd win sixty thousand dollars.

In the championship round, against Washington, the Knights had just lost Game 3 to trail in the series, two games to one. It did not take a hockey expert, someone who had been following the sport for decades or an avid lifer, to note that the Capitals were the faster, stronger, better team.

Yet, at that very moment, when a potential PropSwap buyer offered eighteen thousand dollars for that ticket—grossing the bearer seventeen thousand eight hundred bucks—its holder laughed in the trite technological manner of the day.

"He writes 'LOL,'" says PropSwap co-founder Ian Epstein. "Wouldn't even consider. It wasn't even like, 'I'll counter at twenty-five grand.' Just, 'LOL, get the fuck outta here. I would rather bet thirty grand on the Capitals than take [eighteen thousand for that futures ducat].' Well, one, a thirty-grand bet on the Capitals [at that point] would have netted him thirteen grand. Two, if he bet two hundred bucks, he probably doesn't have thirty grand lying around to go make that sports wager."

Ahh, the maths. Epstein and business partner Luke Pergande deal with those type of equations many times daily as co-founders of the lone secondary-market outlet for futures bettors to hedge against potential loss.

It was poignant that the Golden Knights' tanks started running dry during the penultimate series of their season, their glass skates falling off in a most dramatic way, just when so much of their rabid new fan base was convinced of unheard-of expansion-season glory.

The smug holder of that futures ticket was left with a somewhat expensive bookmark—just another "coaster," VSiN's Pauly Howard likes to say—not long after turning down such profit, as the Capitals won the next two games to close out the series and lift the cup.

For the record, in the aforementioned deal the seller would have received sixteen thousand two hundred dollars, for Epstein and Pergande retain ten percent—in that case, eighteen hundred bucks—of the sale as their cut for transacting the business. Minus the two hundred that the ticket cost, the seller would have netted sixteen grand. The buyer would have been responsible for a three-percent deposit fee, or five hundred and forty bucks. Pergande and Epstein would have made twenty-three hundred and forty dollars on the single transaction.

Epstein endured a similar ordeal a couple of years earlier, when somebody who had paid a hundred dollars for a futures ticket on Syracuse basketball to win it all, at five hundred-to-one odds, balked when offers started coming in. He hung onto it, losing all the way around. Epstein talks about the basic education and wisdom of turning a profit on something that could so soon be so worthless.

"When we first started, people were, 'I'd never sell my bet. That's dumb.' Now it's, 'I'd sell, but the money has to be right.' The final stage is having people who will sell their bet and be reasonable about it. The bidding will become more mature. We're getting there."

At several sports-betting conferences in 2017, Quinton Singleton, then a vice president for the digital-software giant NYX Gaming Group Limited, mentioned PropSwap in relation to the future of the industry. At that two-day sports-betting seminar I attended at the UNLV International Center for Gaming Regulation in the summer of 2018, Singleton was a featured speaker; and he highlighted PropSwap.

Through so many hurdles, those references represented significant victories to Epstein and Pergande. "He's a sharp guy," Epstein says of Singleton. "PropSwap made the slide [presentation], about where sports betting is headed. A small thing, but that was cool. There have been some rough patches, but I wouldn't change anything."

Epstein, twenty-nine, and Pergande, thirty, are both Chicago natives, but they first met, in passing, in Tucson at the Eller College of Management, the University of Arizona's business school. The summer between their junior and senior years, they'd meet again in Asia, where both were partaking in internship programs.

Pergande, with a finance emphasis, was in Nanjing, on mainland China. Epstein, with a focus on management, was in Hong Kong. Epstein and his group were responsible for organizing a "Hed Kandi Pool Party" at the Venetian Macao, in Macau, that would also serve as its going-away bash. Epstein's roommate could not attend, so he suggested that Pergande attend in his place. Epstein rang. Pergande confirmed.

Pergande and his group had landed in Hong Kong, preparing to fly back to the States, when he left them to take a ferry ride of thirty miles or so, across the South China Sea, to Macau. Mobile service was horrible, but Epstein's directions were spot-on because they found each other poolside at the Venetian.

The deejay played techno house music, something new to Pergande and Epstein. Splishing and splashing, board shorts and bikinis. Big rubber ducks and beach balls. They had a cabana. The festivities drifted from day into night, the former Portuguese colony serving as the exotic backdrop.

"Super glitzy," Pergande says. "I had gotten sick of China; it was hot, humid, dumplings for breakfast. Then, at this party, European girls are walking around. Super cool. We were drinking and hitting on girls till four in the morning. A total blast. Tsingtao beer, champagne; whatever was on their trays as they walked by, 'Yeah, I'll take one.' We got to know each other as we hit on chicks from France. We got along."

Both were twenty-one, and the mingling never seemed to cease. It all flowed into an unforgettable episode that both might have taken for granted at the time. It cemented an initial bond that would morph into a friendship and form a partnership that is on the cutting edge of a thriving industry.

"It was one of those things that you don't appreciate until after the fact," Epstein says. "When you're that young and that naïve, given that opportunity, you don't know what to make of it at the time. As an intern, so much work went into organizing that party; you want to enjoy yourself."

The genesis of PropSwap.

"If Luke doesn't like my style, maybe he doesn't call me in 2013," Epstein says. "And if I didn't like his style, maybe I don't decide to team up with him. We didn't know it at the time, but we were feeling each other out. It wasn't like we had been best friends and we were going to enjoy this [party]. We weren't even buddies. We were barely acquaintances."

They went their separate ways, Pergande to San Francisco to take a job with Bloomberg selling—what else?—hedge funds. Epstein went home to Evanston, Illinois, booked a flight to Las Vegas *before* arranging an interview with Cantor Gaming, convinced them to create a position for him, flew back home, and drove back to Las Vegas in February 2012.

For Cantor, he'd scope casinos that used the company's lines and odds, and reported what he saw. A strong lack of branding was apparent everywhere, but he hadn't known that was written into its contract with each individual property. He talked his way into assisting with the company's risk-management operations on weekends, which would become his full-time post.

"Bets were coming in, and you'd see your 'P' and 'L' [price and liability] for the game," Epstein says. "You're looking at what every other sports book has; 'Yeah, okay, should we move that line to take a bet on the other side?' I do remember thinking, 'Holy shit, this is a lot of money.' You make one little mistake . . . it isn't my money, but, damn. You mess up, it's a fifty-thousand-dollar fuck-up. They never let me be in charge of major, major things. I was very low, down low in experience."

Epstein clarifies that he began working in Cantor's risk room after Michael Colbert, a former risk-management director, had violated the company's internal-compliance policies, as well as state and federal laws. The sordid episode ended with Colbert getting sentenced to five years in prison.

Another part of Epstein's responsibilities at Cantor casts a relatively unknown light on leagues' and conferences' integrity issues. Professional and collegiate entities have maintained mutual-protection relationships with Las Vegas, as a check on anything that might constitute unusual behavior, for years. That does not get reported much—like the trip Jay Kornegay and Kenny White made to Indianapolis in 2004—but executives of professional sports leagues often insist on discretion. Same with commissioners of collegiate conferences and NCAA executives.

That activity is so under the radar, Epstein asked to keep it that way in relation to an event that occurred in a college football game in the mid-2010s. He'd provide details, only if the specific schools and conference, and year, were kept anonymous. He was responsible for spotting any potential issues, after the fact. He would compare a game's final result with odd or unusual pre-game betting movements, backtracking for information that might explain any questions or incongruity. "Really cool stuff," he says.

A blip appeared on that radar. For our purposes, let's say it involved "State" at "University." State won the early-season game, 24–13. A month earlier, State had been the favored side by twenty-four points, but by kickoff it had been shaved to seventeen. A lot of money was being bet on University. Seven points is a big swing, drawing attention to the shift.

"A huge move," Epstein says. "And it dropped three points the day of the game. Why did the line move?" He discovered that State's veteran center did not play. When was that known? He had been injured in training camp, but the coach said he'd be fine. Unlike professional sports, college has no players' association that requires, theoretically, accurate and concise injury reports. In fact, federal HIPAA regulations guard collegians' privacy in such matters.

"They don't have to say shit about injuries," Epstein says. So the veteran center is in uniform, and he stretches before the game. He doesn't play. The backup had never started a collegiate game. State's offensive line was a sieve, and it only won the game because of the gross inefficiency of University's quarterback. State's backup center told a reporter he knew he would play the Wednesday before the game.

Valuable information for anyone possessing it. Epstein and his colleagues conducted further research. The Cantor team, per its contract, notified State and the conference to which it belongs that there might be a leak.

Nothing came of it.

"I'm not saying someone is on the take, or whatever," Epstein says. "But maybe someone is in the barber shop and says something, and it just leaks out. The point is, we let them know. The coach says, 'All right, what do you want me to do? Release my injuries? I'm not doing that, because nobody else will.'"

LeBronGate, involving the Cleveland Cavaliers' failure to disclose the player's hand injury over the final three games of the 2018 NBA Finals, is part of that discussion, too. "Should the team get fined for not releasing that? I don't know," Epstein says. "But it's the cool stuff I was working on."

When he visited Las Vegas in 2013 to partake in Labor Day festivities, with Epstein and others, Pergande placed a futures bet on the New Orleans Saints to win the ensuing Super Bowl, at fifty-to-one odds. A month later, those odds had fallen to fifteen-to-one. He rang Epstein to inquire if any avenue existed that would allow him to peddle that ticket early, at a beneficial price to both him and an interested third party.

"No," Epstein said. "There is not."

"Why not?"

"Honestly, I have no idea why not."

"Well, if I make the bet and it wins, and I give you the ticket, can you cash it?"

"Yeah. Whoever walks up with the ticket gets paid."

"These things are transferrable?"

"Yeah. We should look into this."

Eureka! That sprouted PropSwap. From there to here, though, it becomes complicated. Epstein is sort of a pessimist, Pergande an optimist. That dynamic might have helped them propel the endeavor through many legal hurdles and headaches.

"I had this idea in my head, but it always seemed like a big undertaking," Epstein says. "Maybe when I'm older, I thought, I'll get back to it." Pergande was gung-ho. His determination registered with Epstein, to where Epstein believed Pergande was going to power through with it, to whatever conclusion, with or without him. "So I jumped on," says Epstein.

Macau made the difference, according to Pergande. They got along, sipping bubbly, maybe trying a word or two of Portuguese, meeting so many people poolside at the Venetian. That's why Pergande pitched Epstein when he could have contacted several other connections. Pergande confirms that he has a sunnier outlook than Epstein, but that neither is perfect and they do complement each other well.

"There are times that I can be super optimistic," Pergande says. "This is going to work! And he's thinking of ways it could fail. One is thinking how everything is rose-colored and, 'We're going to have really big projections.' The other is, 'Maybe we won't, for these reasons.' If we both were, 'Everything is rosy!' no one would say, 'Here's how you fail,' and 'Have you thought how this could collapse?' There's no more of an up-and-down lifestyle than being an entrepreneur. If you have a good month, it pays that month's rent. Literally, if we don't have a good month, we can't pay the rent."

They submitted a business plan with the Nevada Gaming Control Board, believing that would be an obvious place to begin. They received a very formal letter from the Nevada Attorney General's office, the GCB legal wing. A business like PropSwap, the letter read, would not be allowed, and here are the four reasons why. Potential money laundering and messenger betting were among them.

Pergande and Epstein wrote back, disagreeing with every point. Money laundering isn't an issue, they wrote, "because we pay out in checks; we're pretty sure no money launderer wants to get paid by check or wants to buy with a credit card." (When initiating business with PropSwap, the submission of such collateral is required from both parties.)

They finally made phone contact with an actual person at the GCB, and she said, "It's not going to happen." She yielded. The only way it might happen would be if Epstein and Pergande hired a lawyer "who has a good relationship with the board."

Epstein admittedly freaked out, to Pergande, saying, It's not going to happen. Pergande remained calm. That's great, he told his business partner. "There is a way." But fifteen lawyers declined to take their case. The lowest point, Epstein says, was when one of them wrote a very lengthy rebuttal explaining why this business proposal was preposterous. Pergande scoffed at that email and every barrister that had declined their invitation. They have not given me a good reason, Pergande said. "We're going to keep going until someone takes this case."

Ultimately, they found Dan Reaser, a gaming and regulatory affairs attorney for the Fennemore Craig law firm, with offices in Arizona, Colorado, and Nevada. Having represented both the Nevada Gaming Commission and the GCB, Reaser possessed the vital experience and contacts Pergande and Epstein had been seeking. He told them they have a case. "These tickets are bare paper, property just like title to a loan." Reaser finagled an April 2015 meeting with GCB officials, and he walked out of it with spirits soaring. That entity had determined that PropSwap did not fall into their jurisdiction because it did not constitute gambling.

Pergande quit his job at Bloomberg and moved to Las Vegas that July. Epstein followed suit, leaving Cantor a few weeks later to pursue PropSwap LLC full time. They opened their business doors, kind of, that September 1. They developed a website and set up shop at Sporting Life Bar, on Jones and Robindale, in southwest Las Vegas. There was a podium and a table; customers had to visit the bar to drop off, or purchase, a ticket. The seller would have to return to retrieve his money.

"It was a start," Epstein says. "But we quickly realized it wasn't scalable. We had to move it online. It was a very slow progression."

GCB officials have since been pleasant and supportive. And in a poetic scene, at least to Pergande, the Venetian in Las Vegas was the first casino to allow them into its sports book—run by CG Technology, the successor to Cantor Gaming—to market and extol PropSwap's virtues.

"Our first meeting was having fun in Asia at the Venetian Macao," Pergande says, "and that's the property where we launched in Las Vegas. They let us put up signage, and we had two chairs in front of the sports book. I really don't think PropSwap would be here had we not had such a good time in Macau."

I tapped PropSwap midway through the 2018 baseball season. That January, after the Milwaukee Brewers had acquired the exceptional outfielders Lorenzo Cain and Christian Yelich, I bought futures tickets on Milwaukee to win the National League pennant, at twenty-to-one odds, and the World Series, at forty-to-one. It hovered near the top of its division, but I had grown weary of their shaky bullpen and manager Craig Counsell's constant and questionable tinkering with lineups and those unreliable relievers.

A Milwaukee native, the haymaker from St. Louis, in the 1982 World Series against the Brewers, was still fresh on my cranium. To avoid adding to my collection of bookmarks, or coasters, and baseball headaches, I submitted the two tickets on the PropSwap site. Also, it was a head-over-heart play. Just wanted to break even, at worst, and that's what transpired. "Bet like a banker," a Twitter follower called "QuantCoach" messaged me. "A bet is a loan to the bookmaker. PropSwap protects your principal."

The Brewers would lose Game 7 of the National League Championship Series to the Los Angeles Dodgers. I did not watch a single pitch, of the entire series, because of the constant meddling of Counsell and Dodgers manager Dave Roberts. Four-hour baseball? No, grazie.

Of most significance is my status as a betting minnow. Yet, Epstein and Pergande treated me as if I were a whale. They informed me of interest in the tickets via text message and followed up with emails. They were quite professional handling a transaction that would make them peanuts. It's a business I will certainly use again. (The other facet of the operation, regarding transactions, is that money can be transferred from a customer's PropSwap account to a PayPal "wallet" once a month, for free. Subsequent transfers, within that month, cost ten bucks a pop.)

## THE SKINNY

PropSwap can be a convenient hedge for a betting ticket. For example, a hundred bucks is wagered on Team A to win its championship, at 50-to-1 odds. That's a potential payoff of five grand. It has a solid season, reaching the playoffs. By then, its odds have dropped to 10–1; $100 will return $1,100 (a grand plus the principal). If the ticket bearer doesn't want to take a chance on that team losing in the playoffs, and winning nothing, he could post the ducat on PropSwap at a price that is attractive to both him and a suitor.

This is the art of negotiation. A potential buyer would not offer $500 for it, because, at 10–1, he could make that wager by himself to nab that five grand. To him, an offer of $250 might be reasonable—he'd be getting 20–1 odds instead of the current going rate of 10–1, so he'd be doubling his potential value. The ticket holder had paid $100, so at $250 he's a bit more than doubling his money. An actual transaction might start out with the potential buyer offering $200, to test the waters. The seller might go to $300, and a counter of $250 might be accepted.

This is to what Ian Epstein refers when he speaks of "mature bidding." Should the seller want $500, he'd draw laughter because that's what anyone could get at the going rate. The buyer will be the source of giggles if he were to offer, say, $150; the seller will aim to at least double his money for the effort. That common middle ground, at times, isn't so common or sensible.

"Eventually, we'll get customers doing this so often that there won't be as much personal contact," Epstein says on the eve of the 2018 football season. "I know it's cheaper to maintain a customer than it is to get a new customer, and word of mouth will be huge; you'll tell three friends, and so on."

They're battling curious psychology. Someone else bet on the Brewers to win it all at those same forty-to-one odds that I had nabbed, but in a much bolder way. This person had eight separate tickets, in various but large denominations, at those odds. The morning of that Game 7 against the Dodgers, Pergande says, the ticket-holder could have accepted a transaction of a hundred thousand dollars for all eight tickets. He declined, instead becoming the owner of eight very expensive bookmarks in several hours.

Both Epstein and Pergande spoke about Regret Avoidance as if they had majored in human behavior instead of business. People think their wagers cannot lose, they say, that selling them at a reduced price—even though they will make money in the transaction—is a sign of giving in, of capitulation.

"People have this inflated idea: they value what they own more than what they don't. It isn't rocket science. It isn't a collectible. People aren't framing this. It's worth a finite number," Epstein says. Nobody wants to be the person to sell a winner, says Pergande. He mentions a study in which people who had bought a lottery ticket for a dollar in New York were offered five bucks for their tickets. The overwhelming majority declined, even though they could earn four hundred percent profit right then and there, and go buy more lottery tickets.

"Obviously, that's the stupidest thing ever," Pergande says. "No one wants to be the person to sell a Kansas City Chiefs [futures] ticket in November." The Chiefs were one of the NFL's élite teams halfway through the 2018 season, but they also owned a long history of strong starts and bitter playoff endings, usually on their home stage. Once again, that came to fruition when New England defeated Kansas City in the Chiefs' Arrowhead Stadium in the 2018 AFC title game. "In reality," Pergande says of the merits of pocketing an early profit on a futures ticket, "you can make ten times your investment, and move on to your next play."

They have had some issues partnering with casinos, much of which can be attributed to old-school mentalities. One veteran bookmaker hemmed and hawed when Epstein explained the service. He said he might come onboard if Epstein struck a deal with another sports book. And get a gaming license, the guy added, while you're at it.

"He was making it all up now," says Epstein, who suggested the man call the Gaming Control Board, who would inform him that they don't need a license. "Those guys have operated so long no one can tell them how to book a game, no one can tell them their domain. That's what we're dealing with. But I want to get into sports books, that's the primary objective. I guarantee people will start making bets with us in mind: 'Well, the Cardinals are a hundred-to-one to win it all. I don't think they'll win the Super Bowl, but I think there will be value.'"

They drummed up a GO FOR TWO campaign, in which a punter buys not one but two of the same futures ticket. Let's say the Cubs are fifteen-to-one to win the 2019 World Series. Buy two tickets, at a hundred bucks apiece. If the Cubs begin well, by mid-season maybe one of those tickets could be sold for two hundred fifty or three hundred dollars. A profit will have been made on the combined purchases, and one remains alive for the ultimate cash-out. That's business, making money by using your head, instead of betting with your heart and wondering why the wallet is empty.

"And why would a sports book NOT want that?" Epstein says. "They make double the amount of bets, and [in that Cubs scenario] you'd be free rolling," having already made a profit while still owning a live ticket.

A Westgate SuperBook compliance officer has raised some issues, something to do with a third party cashing a ticket he or she did not originally buy, but book director Jay Kornegay has been amenable. During its SuperContest sign-up period in the summer of 2018, Kornegay had no issues with Epstein being on property to conduct official business.

The business has its many challenges, but one the duo has not had to deal with, yet, is competition. As this is being put to bed, a second purveyor in the secondary-betting market has not emerged. That surprises Epstein, but he and Pergande would not shy away from such a battle.

"On one hand, it's great to have the entire market share," Epstein says. "I have a lot of issues I deal with, every day. One of them isn't, 'How are we going to beat the competition?' On the other hand, it might validate the business. We walk into meetings with investors, and they're looking for comparables. People want to bet on a horse who will win the race. But when there's only one horse; you need another horse to have a race.

"Am I nervous that someone will come along and drop three million dollars in a company and blow us out of the water? Well, that validates the business. It would prove that this industry is worth millions. That's nuts, but we've got the name. I feel pretty good. People at the Westgate said, 'I know PropSwap.' Yeah, I said, but you never used it. They know we exist. They say, 'Cool, but I'd never sell a bet.' Well, no. You should."

Quinton Singleton—now the COO of Bet.Works, which handles all facets of start-up operations for entities, like tribal casinos, that want to enter the sports-betting market—mentions PropSwap in industry conferences for a reason. "It's a derivative market, like the securities market," he says, "and I think there's a lot of room for it. Those types of innovative companies and products will grow and be more available as interest grows."

Brian Musburger, Brent's nephew who has spearheaded the VSiN business operations at the South Point, has boosted PropSwap, allowing Epstein and Pergande on the air to promote the company. In mid-2018, Pergande moved to Atlantic City to give PropSwap an East Coast presence, and he has been a guest in VSiN's studio in New Jersey.

The duo also made their first hire, a part-timer in Florida responsible for what is expected to be fertile gambling turf in Mississippi and, eventually, other Southern hotspots. At press time, they had been granted permission to conduct business in twelve states—remember, they are not involved in betting, just the exchange of property for money.

Both Pergande and Epstein confirm that demand outweighs supply, that a yen exists in those dozen states for tickets. "I sleep well at night knowing the economics of this makes sense," Pergande says. "In certain scenarios, it's important to hedge to guarantee a profit."

During the 2018 baseball playoffs, PropSwap recorded its biggest sale, to date, when it found a buyer for a $1,200 eight-leg parlay that would collect $71,860 if the Red Sox won the World Series. It was sold for $41,700. The seller of the ticket made a profit of $36,330; the $41,700 minus $4,170 (the company's ten percent charge) and minus the original $1,200 for the ticket. When the Red Sox won the title, the buyer earned $30,160. PropSwap netted $5,421, the ten percent ($4,170) from the seller and three ($1,251) from the buyer's deposit.

As this is being typed, a thousand-dollar ticket on the Milwaukee Bucks to win the Eastern Conference, at twenty-two-to-one odds, had just sold for $2,875; the seller nearly tripled his money, the buyer received a much better potential return than the current four-to-one odds, and Pergande and Epstein earned about three hundred fifty bucks for their efforts.

A solid few weeks, they acknowledge, but they're on a hamster wheel in which good months must be followed by better months. They have to pay a lawyer and a developer, there are advertising and marketing costs, that new part-timer is on the roster. The big sale on that Red Sox ticket will pay bills and, they hope, enhance pitches to investors by showing PropSwap's cash flow. As word spreads about their service, they hope they're on the road to sustainability, to averting the need to dip into savings that have been dwindling.

Epstein harbors grand visions of becoming the StubHub, a

multi-billion-dollar company, of sports betting. That secondary ticket-exchange company was founded in 2000 and sold, to eBay for a reported three hundred ten million dollars, in January 2007. It logged record revenue of two hundred seventy-nine million dollars in the fourth quarter of 2017.

Pergande strives to remain sanguine, even though he liquidated his entire 401(k) account—money that has been exhausted—to help fund PropSwap. Every time he glances out the window of his apartment complex in Atlantic City, he is reminded of the business of business. Right there is the former Revel Casino Hotel, which cost two billion four hundred million dollars to build and opened in April 2012. It shuttered in September 2014, eventually selling for just eighty-two million bucks. In June 2018 it re-opened, after additional financial maneuverings, as the Ocean Resort Casino.

"The largest, biggest loss in the history of American real estate," Pergande says as he peers out his window on a cold, gray November day. The irony isn't lost on him; a piece of property was purchased by someone for a fraction of what it might one day be worth. Pergande still has that futures ticket on the New Orleans Saints. If only PropSwap had existed a few years ago.

"At this point, I probably should frame it."

# ELEVEN
# Kelly in Vegas

SHE COULD NOT HAVE KNOWN its ramifications, but Kelly Stewart assembled the three-team money-line parlay of her life the third week of September 2012. Operating in that vague ether between amateur and professional handicapper, she had the financial wherewithal, courtesy of working in bottle service (Vegas slang for slinging cocktails) at some of the Strip's high-end clubs that earned her six figures annually, to score big when the information and evidence tipped the scales a certain way. And she had the courage to make those scores with impressive wagers.

That's no plebe. Las Vegas shreds rookies before dawn, barely burping before seeking more chum. A pizza maker who had just moved here from Vail, Colorado, tells me, "Man, *Vail* chews people up." I laugh. As I walk away, I tell pizza boy we can discuss this further in six months, if he's still around. Stewart would exhibit patience, polish her discipline, and soon earn some publicity that would propel her in an industry that is an ocean of testosterone.

Her career arch would alter September 22, 2012, a Saturday. Since moving to Las Vegas in 2007, she had come to value underdogs, getting the points but also drilling them as money-line plays, extracting the house juice to provide a more attractive return, especially when connecting two or three of them in a parlay.

For that particular Saturday, she had earmarked Oregon State (plus seven points) to win at UCLA, Rutgers (plus nine) to win at

Arkansas, and Kansas State (plus sixteen) to win at Oklahoma. She slapped a hundred dollars on that money-line three-teamer, eliminating the additional points in each game, and they all won outright—the Beavers beat UCLA, 27–20; the Scarlet Knights beat Arkansas, 35–26; the Wildcats beat Oklahoma, 24–19.

That hundred bucks became eight grand, a sweet return of approximately eighty-to-one odds.

Matt Youmans, then writing about sports gambling for the *Las Vegas Review-Journal,* noticed her tweet, a photograph of the winning ticket. He wrote about it, promoted her discernment, others took notice, and—among other opportunities—she began making weekly picks against the spread, on a select *Review-Journal* panel, in 2014. That launched her on a trajectory in which, today, she is a dynamo, executing her many responsibilities in the world of sports betting.

Stewart deserved the early attention. She has run with it, focusing on underdogs. "Her instincts are good," Youmans says. "Most chicks play favorites. She's an underdog player with attitude, too; when guys give her shit, she'll fire it right back."

Pondering an inquiry about that particular three-teamer and its ramifications on her life, she pauses, as if she had not thought about it. She says, "If the 'Kelly in Vegas' thing hadn't come to fruition . . .'" It's possible, she says, that she'd be working some meaningless job at a hotel, making forty grand a year, "and hating my life."

Stewart has been booted from a couple of properties, she had just made a score betting against the football team at her beloved Kansas State, her alma mater, and, in early November 2018, she's still connecting on money-line three-team parlays—one recently paid twenty-eight-to-one odds, another thirty-eight-to-one.

She suffered a stunning defeat on February 12, 2019, after LSU and Penn State, underdogs with a straight-up return of better than three-to-one odds, won. A third, though, flamed out in spectacular fashion when Louisville let a second-half advantage of twenty-three points slip away in a home loss to Duke. Her hundred bucks would have returned $7,668.31. WTF, she wrote on her Twitter feed. "I hate everyone right now." ESPN showed just how big of a deal sports betting had become by highlighting Stewart's bad beat, with a snapshot of the wager she had posted on Twitter, on a SportsCenter segment.

"People say, 'She loves parlays.' I don't love parlays, it's just what I look for, those underdogs that have a shot to win outright," she says. "It's a hundred bucks. If they hit, they're profitable. If they don't, you're only out a hundred bucks. It gives you something to cheer for. North Carolina cost me one a couple of weeks ago because it couldn't gain *five* yards. That was pretty brutal."

Women have held prominent positions in Las Vegas's lifeblood industry for decades, it's just been an incredibly spotty history. Mayme Stocker (casino partner soon after gambling was legalized in 1931), Judy Bayley (first woman to own and operate a casino), Sarann Knight Preddy (first black woman to receive a gaming license), and Jeanne Hood, voted by the Hyatt board to run its Nevada operations upon her husband's death, all had major impacts on the business, as has—and likely will—Elaine Wynn.

Jan Jones Blackhurst served two terms as mayor, paving the way for current mayor Carolyn Goodman, wife of the former mayor Oscar Goodman. Herroner just might be a better gambler than Hizzoner, too, as he related, in *Being Oscar,* about a long-ago weekend break from college in Atlantic City. With friends in a poker game, he was down more than he had in his pockets. In pajamas and robe, she re-entered the game and soon recaptured lost chips. She counted cards in her youth, he wrote, and fared very well at single-deck blackjack, which would probably, today, get her barred from casinos.

Patricia Becker became the first woman to serve on the Nevada Gaming Control Board. And on the players' side, Annie Duke and Jennifer Harman are among a few women who have made impressive poker scores, while Alice Walker and Eleanor DuMont are known figures in the blackjack community.

Still, it registers as a novelty to find a woman in certain positions of power in Las Vegas. A couple of years ago, I was given a potential story idea for a magazine feature on women in executive positions in the hotel-casino business. My first call was to a friend of a friend who is positioned somewhat in the hierarchy of one of the four Fortune 500 companies that dominate the Strip. No way, she said, would she talk. It had taken her this long, she said, winning more battles than she had lost, just to attain her position, that she wasn't about to jeopardize it by speaking on the record about that climb.

Sports betting? Women, of course, do bet on sporting events, and they are prevalent behind the counter at some shops, like the South Point, for many reasons. But distaff entries are extremely under-represented in the handicapping arena. The site Vegas-Insider currently has a roster of forty-one experts, or insiders, that can be tapped for picks; not one is female. During the NFL season, the respected weekly *Gaming Today* runs a pick'em contest, called "Bookies Battle," involving book directors, managers, or employees from fifty-six properties. Eight are women, with Donna Stoneback (Park MGM) in a tie for third place as this is being typed. When I asked one professional bettor, who is not young, how many times in his life he had heeded female advice in determining a sporting wager, he said, "Zero," before I had even finished the inquiry.

Currently there is one female handicapper of consequence—Kelly Stewart. In April 2018, the SportsHandle site concocted a list of the fifty-nine most important industry voices, to follow on Twitter, and it included a single woman—Kelly Stewart. The endless drone of the fast-growing sports-betting business is interrupted, thankfully, by a different voice, someone who knows very well what she's talking about.

She knows it does not hurt her brand, image, or allure that she is easy on the eyes, no other way to put it. The petite thirty-four-year-old native of Manhattan, Kansas, has blonde-streaked brunette hair, a tan complexion, dimples . . . let's say she's camera friendly. And she knows it.

"Obviously, sex sells," Stewart says. "And sex is a driving

force, let's be honest. If I was a guy, I'd be a nobody. And if I was an ugly girl, I wouldn't be who I am. There are a couple of other girls [doing this] out there, but they don't get the [same] publicity or hype. I try to stay humble about it, but it's just the honest-to-god truth."

When Matt Youmans discovered Kelly Stewart, in her oval Twitter avatar she had situated a photograph of herself wearing a Kansas State football jersey, full eye black, a fetching countenance—her costume from her first Halloween in Las Vegas, sure to attract a male follower or two, or two thousand. Then maybe they'd catch her keen handicapping of a game or two, and loyalty would follow. Today, the page-wide top strip of that Twitter page is K-State purple, embossed with the thin, white letters of her marque, KIV. The photo has been replaced by one of her wearing a purple blazer over a black top, very businesslike. Professional. No eye black.

"That [uniform pic] became attached to me," she says. "I left it there for so long. Then I hit thirty and thought, Okay, I should probably do other stuff, try to get away from that."

From sports book floors, she will produce video spots, detailing certain plays and factors that are making her lean a certain way in a certain game, in a tight black sleeveless top. Her mother, of course, favors the ones in which she wears a high-neck dress.

"Thanks, mom, I look like I'm forty," she says. "Of course, that's my mom. Hey, I work my ass off. I go to the gym. I am not always going to be in this great of shape. Even at fifty, some things, gravity-wise, just aren't ever going to be the same. You're right, of course; you want to show off what you've got and enjoy it, but I try to keep it fairly classy. You want to accentuate stuff like that, to an extent. It's a balance. Let's leave it at that."

Stewart has always been a tomboy. At six or seven, she was given a bike, with training wheels, as a Christmas present from her father, John, a Vietnam War veteran who has some lingering issues having been exposed to Agent Orange. His friends pestered her to remove those extra wheels at once, and she complied. Scars on her elbows and knees are evidence of her learning the hard way.

She learned another hard lesson when she rode that bike to the bar, a block away, to see John and those pals playing poker. She wanted to learn. Go get your money, they said, and we'll teach you. She returned with all of her allowance money, in a purple Crown Royal bag, and lost it all.

Okay, she whimpered, you guys are gonna give me back my money, right?

Nope, they said. Not how it works. "You wanted to play, and this is what happens."

In recalling that episode, she seems to be making a much grander statement when she says, "Gambling is a total bitch."

Stewart arrived in Las Vegas armed with a business degree, with an emphasis in sports marketing, from Kansas State, which did not get her far in Kansas when the economy started tanking. An internship with the Denver Broncos seemed exciting, until she discovered it paid nothing. A girlfriend had decided to come to Las Vegas and tend bar, and Stewart came along for the ride. Serving cocktails at some exclusive clubs would pay very well for a few days and allow her to have her own fun most of the week.

A friend was a bookie, so she became interested in sports betting. She had many questions, and he'd have her place his bets. She quickly picked up the vernacular and nuances, and she asked more questions, expanding her scope beyond the Big-12 Conference and Denver Broncos.

When that big three-team money-line parlay led to exposure by Matt Youmans, others noticed. People at the Don Best sports-handicapping service inquired about adding her to their roster, taking her out to a lavish lunch to make their pitch. She hesitated, because she never saw herself as a peddler of picks, a *tout*.

"I'm making a hundred grand slinging bottles, and they're saying, 'We can pay you an extra twenty grand a year to sell picks.' I told them I didn't care, that I really didn't want to do that," Stewart says. "At lunch, they said, 'Listen, you have something we can definitely market here. If you would just listen to us. Let us help you.' I said, Okay."

She and her picks were featured, but she knew it would not be a long-term arrangement. She did enjoy the people with whom she worked and she did learn; they made her a better handicapper, sharper, polished her administration of a bankroll and units. Still, she was a tout, something she loathed. The ones who are transparent and professional, who own up to their defeats as well as their victories, get a bad label because of the questionable tactics and dishonesty employed by the many dirt bags who dominate the field.

"Scum bags," Stewart says. "There's a way around it in this industry, to not be that scum-bag guy. I'd say more than half are scum-bag guys. Everyone was like, 'Selling picks is great!' When you're winning, selling picks is great. But when you're losing, selling picks makes it worse because not only are you losing, yourself, but you're losing for your clients. It's just a lot. If you go 8–0 in college football and you turn around and sell a lot of weekly packages for the next week, you're going, Grrrrreat. You *know* the regression is coming, you just don't know when."

In April 2018, her career had not been taking shape the way she had envisioned. She entertained an offer to join Sports Book Review, an establishment in Costa Rica that scrutinizes hundreds of online sports books and betting sites. It seemed to be an exciting, adventurous option.

Then the Bradley Act, that barred states from pursuing any ideas about sports betting, got quashed in May 2018. That might open up some options, she figured, and that's what happened. Stewart, a partner for the past couple of years in a proxy firm that submits weekly SuperContest and SuperContestGold picks to the Westgate SuperBook for out-of-state clients, accepted an offer to become media director for WagerTalk, for which she posts videos about the business and selects games. And she makes her regular weekly picks for the *Review-Journal,* for which she also participates in video shoots.

On a near-daily basis, Stewart appears on CBS, either its na-tional radio outlet or on its CBS Sports HQ sports-betting Internet platform, and she does promotional and industry video work for SugarHouse Casino, in Philadelphia. Moreover, she has partici-pated, with other pro handicappers, in premier betting seminars on the East Coast; one was scheduled for the Meadowlands, in New Jersey, in early 2019. We've probably missed something, and by the time this comes out Stewart might very well have added more to her responsibilities.

Somehow, through all of that, she makes her betting picks, on one or a few of her seven apps.

Stewart does more than place a C-note on a few three-team money-line parlays and cross her fingers. She's always research-ing, exploring situations to exploit underdogs, tapping various sources across the country to capitalize on advantages and avoid-ing the juice that helps the house pay its electrical bill every month.

A shining example had just occurred, and it was close to her heart. Kansas State had just been trounced, 51–14, at Oklahoma. She knew that the Wildcats had covered seventeen of their previ-ous eighteen games after sustaining a double-digit defeat. In its next game, five days before I met with Stewart, K-State was an eight-point underdog at TCU. She fired on the Cats, which lost 14–13. They covered. She won.

"The market went against us, so I was a little nervous," she says of that play. "You have certain things to look at, and sometimes trends put you over the edge; sometimes they don't."

For good reason, Stewart almost always has an opinion about Kansas State. She has well-placed eyes and ears all over. And some of her best sources are right there in the Little Apple, where her connections are many. "I have people in the locker room at K-State, I have people in the athletic-training department, people in the media," she says, "that I can text and say, 'Hey, what's go-ing on?'"

In the upcoming weekend, Kansas State is at home giving eleven and a half points to rival Kansas. The Wildcats are on a strong run against the Jayhawks, but KU is playing better and

Stewart has some concerns, like longtime K-State coach Bill Snyder calling out individual players for their foul-ups. "I wouldn't bet Kansas State minus eleven and a half with *your* money," says Stewart, with a laugh. She didn't like Kansas, either. It moved to Wildcats minus nine and a half, but they only won by a 21–17 margin.

Her situational guidelines involve letdown spots, key injuries, and motivation, "which team has more [incentive]," she says, which is highly subjective. Stewart detests giving huge points, in nearly any situation, but something developed that demanded her attention. The chatter was about Florida State and Willie Taggert, who was an underwhelming 4–3 in his first seven games as the Seminoles' coach. Clemson, an outstanding team, was laying eighteen points at Florida State in Tallahassee, Florida. "I was all over Clemson," she says. "With Florida State, why? Where's the motivation?" She didn't like how the Seminoles failed to cover four of their first five games, losing two of those outright as the favorite.

Clemson beat Florida State, 59–10.

"Sure enough, Willie Taggert called them out at the end of the game, 'You guys quit.' Well, yeah, they have quit. We saw them quit weeks ago."

Another sterling example arrived on a Thursday night NFL game, when the Oakland Raiders, a favorite by about a point and a half, played at the San Francisco 49ers. Niners starting quarterback Jimmy Garoppolo was injured and out for the season. His backup C. J. Beathard had played well on brief notice, but he, too, was injured and wouldn't play. Nick Mullens was essentially the San Francisco third-stringer who would get that nod versus Oakland.

Stewart was perplexed. The Niners had opened as an approximate three-point favorite at many shops, but tidal waves of money on Oakland over forty-eight hours had made the Raiders the favorite in the hours before kickoff.

It did not make sense to Stewart. That point-spread movement represented a story that Stewart believed to be pure fiction. She sent a text message to Kenny White, a former Don Best colleague and confidant. Stewart rarely computes her own power ratings, because she so trusts those that are produced by White, Andy Iskoe, and Ralph Michaels, all former or current co-workers who provide such strong numbers, often available on their Twitter feeds or websites.

## THE SKINNY
Power ratings are essential to peg an outcome of a game. This can be achieved several ways, and can be very taxing and time-consuming. Pro handicapper Kelly Stewart suggests another avenue: using what Kenny White, Andy Iskoe, or Ralph Michaels concoct. They provide a valuable public service by making their power ratings available on a regular basis. Visit them on their Twitter feeds or websites, and at least toy with the numbers and matchups. Thank them online for their talents.

She had information, the line movement and the Mullens-Beathard difference, to vet through White. We know a little bit about Nick Mullens, she wrote White, but we don't have a lot of evidence. He is confident. White wrote, "Kelly, there's about a half-point difference between" Mullens and Beathard, meaning the overall effect on the San Francisco power rating would be nominal. Hence, the reason for such a big point-spread movement was questionable if not baseless.

I'm going to play it, she wrote of taking the point and a half with the Niners. Yeah, why wouldn't you? White wrote. "You're getting four and a half points of value." San Francisco thrashed Oakland, 33–3. Looking back, bettors were too nervous, she says, too focused about C. J. Beathard's absence, which clouded the true nature of how far Oakland had slipped.

"Everyone failed to recognize how bad the Raiders are, how bad the Raiders' defense is, how banged up the Raiders are," she says. "Speaking of tanking teams, they kind of are."

It took moxie for Kelly Stewart to smoke out the true story of that line movement and grit to go against a tsunami of sharp and square opinion, and cash, fattening her purple Crown Royal bag in the process.

The professional punter Ron Boyles got in on that action, too, turning twenty-two hundred dollars into forty-two hundred bucks. In professional and collegiate football, especially, such a line move poises him to eventually get the very best value in relation to the opening number.

"College hoops is a little bit different because I respect those line moves much more; generally, it's almost all smart money that's moving those games," Boyles says. "In pro football, I'll go against it in a heartbeat. Doesn't faze me one bit. That's value. In pro football, when the line crosses and the other team becomes the favorite and you take the original team [that was giving the points and is now getting them], you'll win more often than not. The sharps bet in, then the followers—the steam chasers—push it up even higher. That's what happens in those kinds of games. Generally speaking, I want to be on the other side of those games. That's one of my favorite angles in all of sports [betting]."

Kelly Stewart is intrigued by the Kansas City Chiefs' upcoming home game against Arizona, another league bottom-feeder. Against the Cardinals, Kansas City had opened as a favorite of approximately seventeen points, and that line settled around fifteen and a half. The Chiefs were one of the league's best teams and had just won, 37–21, at Cleveland.

Astonishingly, Stewart says, ninety-one percent of the tickets wagered on that Browns game were on the Chiefs, as an eight-point favorite. "And [the Chiefs] didn't even bat an eye, they just absolutely rolled" the Browns, she says. "That's something to think about. And now they have to get past Arizona [laying a lot of points], then they go face the Rams. There aren't really look-ahead spots in the NFL, like we see in college, but you have to wonder. Is there motivation for Kansas City? Now, I'm not rushing to the window to bet Arizona, but I'm definitely not laying the big number with Kansas City."

Kansas City defeated Arizona, 26–14. Her instincts, to pass on a play, were splendid. She admits that she was not so spot on in diagnosing Louisiana State's game against Alabama. She'd been trumpeting LSU quarterback Joe Burrow Jr., the game was played in Baton Rouge, and the Bayou Bengals were getting fourteen and a half points. (That half-point hook, window dressing that could be easily misconstrued, made me ponder what Matt Youmans had pointed out about that Houston–South Florida game.)

Alabama flexed its way to a resounding 29–0 victory.

She had paid for stepping onto the rails of that Tide train, but she insists that all of the points 'Bama had been giving would catch up to it. "I have stepped in front of that train a few times this year," Stewart says. "Listen, Alabama is overvalued a lot." They'd been covering first-half numbers, but then reserves would play in the second halves and, up by a lot, a human tendency to maybe lay up would enter the picture, too. Alabama would lose second-half lines, and game sides, as frequently as it won those first halves.

Against Arkansas, she was with friends watching the game and knew they were holding tickets on Alabama when Tide coach Nick Saban put third-stringers into the fray in the fourth quarter and, well, she tells the tale best.

"I KNEW that everybody holding an Alabama ticket next to me was a loser," she says. "I just sat there and laughed, and Arkansas punched it in with twelve seconds left. I just had the biggest smile on my face. Everyone was like, 'I HATE you so much!' I'm like, You *have* to watch. They did the same thing against Texas A&M, and the same thing the following week."

She knows venom, like when a casino app with a five-hundred-dollar limit only allows her to wager three hundred. When a William Hill representative called to say her patronage would no longer be welcomed, on its apps or in its books, she wanted a single good reason why. "Other than, 'You win money,' I wanted a legitimate reason why they booted me, and they couldn't do it," she says. "That was frustrating. Something about, 'Your IP address . . . you can't be on WiFi when you do it.' So what? I can't log into my boyfriend's iPad to place a bet, versus my own iPad, iPhone, or someone else's iPhone? So my iPhone is dead. I log into the app on a friend's phone, but I can't do that? That's basically what they were telling me.

"Everybody in the industry has been booted from those same places. Goes along with what people say, that they just don't want anybody that isn't betting five-dollar thirty-team [parlays]. They don't want people betting bad lines or who will win money."

We've highlighted some insights, some clever victories, for Kelly Stewart, but she is quick to remark that she has no Midas touch, nobody does. Had a good week? A bad one is around the corner. A bad one? Keep that head up and keep working hard, damn hard, because a great one is just around the bend. Like most, she tries to accumulate the best information to make a smart decision, to make more money than she loses. She does pretty well.

She isn't peerless, and that's why she enjoys what she does for WagerTalk. She works with people she respects, they all work hard, and her picks are free. She can rest easy at night knowing that, while a selection might have gone down in flames, costing her money and anyone who went along with her reasoning, at least that other person did not lose additional money by paying for the selection.

Complimentary or not, transparency is vital to her business. She is unique in the industry for her gender, alone, but her honesty also separates her in a market rife with buffoons, charlatans, and egomaniacs. She makes her selection, explains why, it will win or lose, she will review it, and let's move on to the next game or next day.

Stewart is still learning, every day, and that's imperative, she says, for anyone participating in sports betting; you never know it all, and the moment you allow hubris to rule the day, well, hopefully the padding is sufficient for the hard fall that is imminent.

Super Bowl XLIX still irks her. Had Seattle coach Pete Carroll only called that most important play of the game to go to Marshawn Lynch, a bull of a runner who needed only a yard to give the Seahawks the late lead and probable victory over

New England, she would not need to still be answering questions about her handicapping of the game.

It arose again recently, when someone inquired about her analysis, which, he prospected, had something to do with fading the public, going one way when the overwhelming trend had been pointing the other way.

## THE SKINNY

Betting a game just to bet it? Kelly Stewart says, Think otherwise. Your favorite team is in the Super Bowl and you want some action? You have money you won't miss and want a reason to view the big game? Fine and dandy, she says. Valid reasons, she says. But to have a bankroll, an aim to make sports betting a worthwhile and profitable endeavor, part of the discipline must be knowing when to pass, when the deciphering of how the game might play out is pretty damn even, one side not so different, or better or worse, from the other; then the best advice is to pull a Dionne Warwick—just walk on by.

"It had nothing to do with fading the public, or this or that," she says. "It's how I handicapped the game, and it all came down to a last-minute play. That's why I don't really bet a ton of money on the Super Bowl anymore. I kind of learned my lesson, as far as bankroll-management goes." She added, "You cannot just go put a bunch of money on a game just because it's the Super Bowl. Stupid."

She is happy to report that, in an industry that is so heavily male influenced, many of the people with whom she has come in contact have been professional, cordial, and just plain nice. She says, "It's been really awesome."

However, and of course, having such a public profile in such a keyboard-assassin era attracts miscreants. In 2014, SuperBook maestro Jay Kornegay brought Stewart to the attention of Vice Sports, which profiled her. She then had a Twitter following of about fifteen thousand. Today, that's about doubled, which isn't necessarily positive. Some have crossed the line with her. But as

Matt Youmans alluded, Stewart can deflect flies and rodents. One clown did get sacked from his job for his crude comments to her, when his incensed boss established that that would not be how his company would be represented.

She's all for diagnosing a matchup and discussing the merits of one team against another, just consider yourself on alert if she refers to you as "bro." Clean up your act or language, or prepare for an imminent block. Her many blocks could build a prison for such louses. In late December 2018, someone wrote, *sorry i may be a male chauvinist but i'm not taking a females picks on sports i do quite well Lol.* To which Stewart responded, *Thanks for following,* accompanied by that little yellow smiling pie-face wearing shades.

"It's always up for discussion, whether or not I should be myself on Twitter," Stewart says. "I've been more of a lady, lately. It's definitely been brought up. Not saying I shouldn't [fight fire with a bazooka], but when people do talk a lot of trash, I can handle some things, for sure."

A previous boyfriend relished her winning days, but when she suffered inevitable losses he would suggest that maybe this gambling thing has run its course. She moved on. A current beau is in the business, but her complete opposite. He digs into the numbers, the percentages, and she'd be surprised if he could name five players on the Houston Texans. Gets interesting, she says half-gloomily, when they're on opposite sides of the same game. "Not too fun."

Just the other day, he paused and told her she must have just dropped six f-bombs in her previous ten sentences. In such a male-dominated environment, which describes nearly every moment of every working day for Stewart, the lingo hardly elevates beyond the average dugout or clubhouse. He said he wished she would act more feminine, at times.

"I told him, Uh, that's not going to happen. But we already knew that, from the beginning, that that's not who I am. I've always been a tomboy, always been one of the boys growing up. That's just who I was and who I always wanted to be. Doesn't

bother me. I actually get along better with men. I know that's usually what women say who are usually the bitchy ones. I have quite
a few girlfriends, but they're usually the alpha females.

"I just don't get along with the meek, ditzy people of the world,
whether they're male or female. I get along well with strong personalities and people who are genuine."

# TWELVE
# Brussels Sprouts

THE THIRD RAIL OF SPORTS BETTING is an area dominated by scoundrels, cheats, and blowhards, out to snooker customers from their hard-earned bees and honey—er, money—with every breath. That's more Cockney rhyming slang, from the East End of London, of which we can't get enough. In and out? (Snout.) Rats and mice? (Dice.) Lump of ice? (Advice.)

A bit of levity is necessary here, due to the preponderance of arrogance, deceit, and misinformation—ads of arm-crossed, jaw-clenched jackals dispensing a thousand-yard stare at anyone daring to glance at the photo and ring the 1–800 number—that fuels so much of this raffish business. "Scamdicappers," as the masses of reprobates are known. Unless "selling" Team A plus the points to half the clientele and Team B minus the points to the other half, to hook the group that wins into ringing again for another pick, doesn't qualify as questionable activity in anyone's book.

The marketing gimmicks employed by these carneys rankle VSiN's Matt Youmans as much as the self-promoters and outright cheats themselves, the dregs of the business. One alleged "expert," who supposedly does not fall into that gray area of tout deceit, suggests that it is never wise for a bettor to wager half of the bankroll on a single play. Half? So, to hazard a third of all he hath is acceptable? A quarter? Ten percent? Utter irresponsibility, say many successful pros who strongly advise against ever putting more than two or three *percent* of that bankroll on a single game.

Consider such an irresponsible statement an indictment, and gravitate toward figures who are more trustworthy, who come with a solid combination of credentials and references. Devote some time to it, and it will be invaluable to the endeavor.

Even at companies with which he has been associated, Dave Cokin has steamed at some of the ploys, like "Ten-Star Picks," and "Five-Unit Plays" and "Ten-Unit Plays." "That is so fucked up," he says. "You cannot win doing that."

Dave Cokin and Tom Barton, in their own ways, are swimming upstream against a strong current as they try to stem that tide of dishonesty, to bring some degree of decency, fairness, and transparency to the overwhelming shadiness of a dubious business.

"If someone does not have the time or inclination to handicap properly themselves and they want to make bets, paying for advice can be profitable," Cokin says a day after he nailed all four plays he released. "It depends on what level you're playing, how disciplined you are, all those factors. Most people who pay for picks probably [otherwise] lose. They go hunting for big gains. They want the locks. You're not going to win doing that.

"But there are definitely people in this business who win consistently. If you follow their advice, and follow it with discipline, you can win."


Dave Cokin sauntered into the Rhode Island Auditorium and knew, just knew, his Providence Reds were going to win this minor-league hockey game. He was so confident, he found a bookie and wagered all he had on the Reds winning this one by the puck line, yielding a goal and a half. He sidestepped paying the juice, or vig, and went for the plus-price puck line to enhance his return.

He was six years old. He put down five dollars.

"Didn't have to pay to get in," Cokin says. "Lived a block from the arena. I laid the goal and a half, and the Reds lost, five to three. Don't know who the opponent was, but I still remember that score. Bookies were all over. They stood there in the aisles and handed you a piece of paper with your bet on it. If you won, you showed up afterward with your ticket to get your money. That was a lesson, because I couldn't buy baseball cards or candy for a month. I wasn't getting more than a dollar a week for my allowance."

Cokin, who has supported himself his entire life through sports gambling, left Rhode Island for Las Vegas in 1987. He is sixty-five, short with a trimmed beard, and he often wears a signature flat cap. Wrap-around black sunglasses are customary, too, to protect a vision issue that is steadily keeping him from driving his elegant Mercedes-Benz.

His most distinctive characteristic, however, is a gravelly, raspy voice that sounds like decades of bourbon and cigars. Cigarettes, he says, a lifetime habit. He's loyal to no brand (except Mercedes-Benz) and, in fact, uses the habit in a novel way on his SMOKIN' DAVE COKIN website, with requisite smoky wisps on his main page, whose blog he updates daily.

He has been a regular presence on Las Vegas radio since he got a start in that medium from the late Lee Pete, the sports-betting radio icon who began the Stardust Line in 1981. Cokin owes the blossoming of his career to those radio appearances at the Dust—how some Las Vegas veterans refer to Lefty Rosenthal's popular sports book. But Cokin owes so much more to Pete, avuncular in his delivery and demeanor.

"He taught me a lot of lessons," Cokin says. "He was not a broadcaster. He'd be the first to tell you. He'd sit there and talk, and that's kind of what I do. And he never had any pretense that he had any idea on the gambling front, which is why he had guys on who either sold picks or had good reputations around town. He never talked negatively, about casinos or people. It'd be easy to burn a bridge. And don't talk bad about the competition, as in, 'So and so, oh boy, that guy stinks!' Keep it to yourself. Just be concerned with what you do and not with what anybody else does.

"I had that philosophy, it just became more chiseled into my psyche with Lee. I really looked up to Lee. Everybody loved Lee Pete. We were doing something nobody anywhere in the country was doing, which was talking about [sports] gambling on the radio."

I had heard Cokin on the radio during my Las Vegas baptism of about twenty months or so when I finally got the opportunity to speak with him, in detail, for a feature on Hawaii's funky 2004 football season, which showed the raw beauty and intrigue of the Vegas numbers. I noticed the wild mood swings early. I tracked how Hawaii exhibited such a virulent home-road dichotomy.

The Rainbow Warriors would lose by twelve points on the road as a single-digit favorite, return to Honolulu as an eleven-point favorite to win by twenty-eight, lose by thirty-one as a three-point dog away from home, win by eighteen on the island but fail to cover as a twenty-two-point favorite, lose by sixty-six as a twenty-three-point dog on the road, lose two weeks later as a twenty-one-point dog by fifty-six, cover as a twenty-one-point favorite with a victory by thirty-one points.

Baylor and Oregon, that season, were the only other teams that had received at least twenty points as an underdog and given at least twenty as a favorite in consecutive games. In final scores of back-to-back games, adding the scoring margins of a defeat and a victory, no team recorded such a split personality—forty-nine combined points, fifty-three, seventy-seven, eighty-four—as Hawaii. A good portion of that dichotomy concerned the Warriors leaving the island, and traveling so far to weather conditions of which they might not be fond, and holiday-minded opponents coming to Oahu.

A huge disadvantage for those visitors, Cokin told me in 2004. Fellow gambler Jay Ginsbach said that disparity is worth noting, even though he played Hawaii games rarely that year. "But I think there are many who like to bet that late game."

Back then, Bob Scucci oversaw the sports book at the Stardust, which was razed in 2007. He confirmed that Hawaii presented a puzzle to all the book directors in town. "I don't think we, as oddsmakers, have gotten a very good hold on [the Warriors]," Scucci told me. "There's so much disparity from how they play at home and how they play on the road. You can't get a proper reading on them."

Injury issues on both lines, and June Jones's penchant for pulling talented-but-erratic quarterback Timmy Chang in the second quarter, only to start him in the second half, would frequently confound Scucci and his crew; they'd post a Hawaii number only to yank it back down, and Warriors games were often the last one posted during the week.

A close friend with wagering in his blood, as the son of an inveterate punter, bet often then. He and an associate had, through a bookie in an efficient underground system that thrives in Southern California and in many pockets of the country, risked four figures on Hawaii in an early-season home game against Nevada. They had the Warriors giving eighteen and a half points. The game was on TV. It eked past midnight. My buddy delayed his, ahem, wife's advances to watch it all. Hawaii's 48–26 victory was not secured until the clock read 00:00.

I recently showed him that feature—headlined SATURDAY NIGHT LIVE, it won an award of some sort—and he could not recall the last time he had made a bet. "Memory lane," he laughs of that specific Hawaii–Nevada outcome. "I don't miss that stress."

The Warriors capped their regular season by winning outright, as six-point home dogs, against both Northwestern and Michigan State. As a four-point favorite, on their own turf in the Hawaii Bowl, the Warriors belted Alabama–Birmingham, 59–40.

There was more to that Hawaii season than the slapstick nature of the high-scoring games. Every Honolulu game was on Las Vegas television, and broadcast partners Jim Leahey and Doug Vaioleti wore leis and tropical shirts, their voices "Mai Tai-smooth," I wrote then. The definition of exotic, but it was more than that. As the last game on a long day's docket of college football offerings, when Hawaii plays at home it still, today, offers gamblers unique late-night appeal in either padding an already-successful wagering day or, with a day in the red, an opportunity to get even, or close to it.

Industry veterans, not admiringly, call it a Bail-Out Special, or Get-Out Game.

"If Hawaii were playing in the middle of the day, with all the other games, it wouldn't draw near as much action," said Scucci, now the director of race and sports for Boyd Gaming Corp. "Because of the fact that it stands out by itself, at nine o'clock [kickoff, Pacific time] all the time, it becomes a much higher profile game."

That is what adds to the stress level of Hawaii home games. If, Scucci said, someone has an informed opinion on a game regardless of its start time, then follow suit and play it. If no lean exists, however, it would not be prudent to bet on a game just because it's either on TV or the last game on the card.

Professional handicapper Ted Sevransky dispensed money-management advice in 2004 that rings true today and can be attributed to any late game, or final sporting event of a given day. "Dangerous," he said then. "Many bettors think, 'Oh, I've lost today. I'd better double-or-nothing on the last game.' That's a strategy that's doomed to failure. That's ignorant and irresponsible."

## THE SKINNY

The Late-Night Hawaii Home Game Extravaganza, most commonly known to pro gamblers as The Bail-Out Special, should be avoided at all costs if the intent is irrational, says professional handicapper Dave Cokin. By that he means, you're up for the day and you want to double your profits, in one fell swoop, on the final game of the day? Or, it's been a stinker of a day, and this is the avenue to getting even in one fell swoop.

No way, says Cokin. That would be a major breach of discipline. Curtailing losses is a major part of a disciplined approach to betting on sports. That goes for *Sunday Night Football* and *Monday Night Football,* too. Even the Super Bowl, to an extent. If it's purely for fun, a hobby, with disposable income that will not be missed, partake, and Good on Ya. But if it's anything more, involving a bankroll and a specific unit of wager, a quasi-business with records and charts, betting on a game just because it's on the big board can have disastrous consequences. Formulate a plan, do the work, and if all signs point to a pass, then pass.

Sevransky goes by Teddy Covers, in his handicapping role, and he is a regular guest on Cokin's daily afternoon Las Vegas radio show. Cokin remembers those late-night Hawaii home games with some sentiment, since his work was over and he could sit back and relax.

He laughs à la the Marlboro Man. "It was absolute clockwork. I'm at home, done for the day at that point. I would roll a joint, kick back, and watch the Hawaii football game, and just wish it would never end. Jim Leahey had such a melodious voice, those Hawaiian names just rolled off his and [Vaioleti's] tongues."

Hawaii football games are no longer distributed to Las Vegas, known as the Ninth Island due to a heavy influx of Hawaiian transplants. No matter, because the point is about any late game, be it Sunday or Monday or Thursday, that might serve as a double-up or get-even opportunity.

"That's just bad gambling," Cokin says. "If the world were made up of smart gamblers, bookmakers wouldn't exist. Their edge isn't that much to begin with. It's thanks to people betting stupidly that I'm in business. They do very bad things, in terms of money management. That's something I've never had a problem with, except when I was six years old and betting my entire allowance."

Exhibiting extreme discipline, Dave Cokin says there is nothing flashy about how he operates. His picks can be purchased at VegasInsider—the Air Force–New Mexico game on November 10 had a $49.95 price tag attached to it—or on his website—weekly picks for two hundred fifty dollars, among the various selections. He has a bankroll, separate from his living expenses, and his normal wager is between one and three percent. He can't figure out the NBA regular season, so he doesn't even attempt to diagnose it anymore.

I close my eyes and nod in utter agreement with Cokin. During the 2017–18 NBA season, while running errands I stopped at a book to peruse the numbers. Sixers minus a point and a half at Milwaukee, a loser of four in a row and five of its past six, blinked at me. Philly was the better team. I laid my money down. When Philly took a 40–21 lead, I left. Could collect another time.

Wrong. The Sixers led 81–62 in the third when they collapsed like Bitcoin. The Bucks scored fifty of the next sixty-seven points. Philly committed a season-high twenty-six turnovers. Bucks win by eight. (I'd disown pro roundball, but that Under play in a game featuring two teams with winning percentages of at least sixty appeared to have some validity.)

"I'm always looking for new things that work," Cokin says. "Certain things, say, with college football come to mind. I am a matchup guy in college football. I definitely spend more time on college football than any other sport. Not into trends and angles; they're fifty-fifty deals, for the most part. I know the personnel, and I want to find the strengths and weaknesses. I know what I'm looking at, I know the teams, I know the coaches, and I think I have the advantage."

There are about a hundred and thirty teams, and games are once a week. That gives Cokin, he believes, enough of a cushion for due-diligent research that will yield advantages. He adjusts his own power ratings, makes his own lines, compares them to what's out there.

The books "can be dead on, in terms of sharpness, in every game," Cokin says, "and I'm still going to have advantages, either in a matchup or a scheduling dynamic, or a situational edge." Over his many years, he has settled on a combination of numbers and situations that is best for him. "If you can combine the two, you've got a bigger edge."

A case in point is North Carolina's football game at Duke on Saturday, November 10. Cokin has earmarked Duke as a fraud, having "out-stat'ed" only one FBS program all season; Army, in the season opener, by a paltry eleven yards. In the Atlantic Coast Conference, Blue Devils' foes have out-rushed Duke by a margin of better than two to one. At 1–7, Cokin says, Carolina has nothing to play for except pride, especially versus rivals Duke— against whom the Tar Heels are catching ten and a half points— and North Carolina State.

"I think North Carolina shows up," says Cokin, whose casino apps number in the double digits. The Tar Heels would cover in their 42–35 defeat in Durham against the Blue Devils. Moreover, as seven-point dogs, the Heels would cover the number, again, in a 34–28 defeat to North Carolina State.

Dave Cokin has a fine feel for underdogs and rivals.

He was also considering Maryland, plus three and a half points, at Indiana. The Terrapins had been besieged with controversy, since the tragic passing of player Jordan McNair, to heatstroke in an August practice, and the October ouster of coach D. J. Durkin. Cokin believes playing on the road might have a unifying effect on Maryland. The Terps would lose, 34–32, but cover Cokin's early number.

In college basketball, he does not get serious until teams are in the second go-round in their conferences. Identities have been established, patterns formed. In baseball, he's flexible, looking for openings. St. Louis gave him one when it dumped manager Mike Matheny, giving Mike Shildt the interim tag, in mid-July. The Cardinals muddled around for seventeen games, but Cokin had noted a difference. When they won sixteen of their next nineteen, Cokin rode an abundance of that wave.

"Boy, there was way more energy with this team than there was before," he says. "[Shildt] was very proactive, in terms of his lineup configuration, in-game changes, stuff like that, as opposed to Matheny, who was completely reactive. I just started playing the Cardinals in every game. Eventually, it stopped. But I had a run, just blindly betting them every game. It's nice when that happens. Those things don't happen that often. When they do, go ahead and ride them out."

My high point of baseball, in 2018, was latching on to Tampa starter Blake Snell on that five-inning Under line. He showed his excellence early, and the five-inning line eliminated his bullpen from blowing a fantastic start, at least when it came to my money, and costing me a game side. Cokin had somewhat similar results with Colorado starter Kyle Freeland, another lefty who produced solid numbers within his first five innings, especially his first three. Again, he recommends spotting something like that early and playing it until it loses is nothing but a bonus.

Like a two-by-four to his skull, Tom Barton entered the grocery store and was faced with a stark realization: he had only enough money to buy milk for himself or a can of dog food for Bogey, the three-month-old Shepherd-Chow mix that he and his girlfriend had rescued from a box by the side of the road in Cary, North Carolina.

He could not purchase both.

Barton had played the string out of a handicapping run that had started on the radio in Long Island, New York, to a boiler-room operation that had become too heated and dishonest, to a private offer in Cary that eventually proved to be far too good to be true, to that grocery store.

He bought the Puppy Chow.

Barton called his sister, in Long Island, for help. She invited him in, letting him sleep on her couch for a summer to allow him to get back on his feet. He called handicapping customers who had been jilted. Most surprising to him, many stuck with him, aware of the unfortunate circumstances that he had been dealt by unscrupulous forces.

Now, he has a big home, he married that girlfriend in a sixty-thousand-dollar wedding, they have two children, they drive nice, new cars, and he bought a sports bar. With the May 2018 SCOTUS ruling that unleashed the possibility of sports betting spreading like the spring ivy at Wrigley Field, he has capitalized with some increased exposure on an East Coast radio network.

Barton became the first person to make a legal, straight bet on a sports game, outside of Nevada, in Delaware—a thousand-dollar bet on the Yankees, at ten-to-one odds, to win it all in 2018. That didn't pan out, but the publicity (*The Wall Street Journal* was one of several media outlets to document his action) was fantastic. After Julius Erving and a state official, he became the first non-celebrity to make a similar bet in New Jersey, too.

"The *Thoroughbred Racing News* wrote an article, and I loved it," he says. "They wrote, 'Some guy named Tom Barton made gambling history . . .' That's cool. They took a shot at me cuz I'm nobody, in their minds. I don't care. Gambling history! The first outside Nevada to make a straight bet, legally. I don't give a shit if you think I'm nobody."

Maybe twenty years ago, he'd roam the Four Corners—around the MGM, Tropicana, Luxor, and Excalibur—and wait for the return of associates, who had ducked into each sports book for certain lines and odds. He'd weigh the differences, then dispatch each, with thousands of dollars, back to those properties to capitalize on the best numbers. "The MGM always gave bad lines," he says. "The line was different everywhere."

Now, Barton has a regular weekend late-night radio show in Las Vegas, five hours of total studio time for which he pays a nominal sum. (He has a co-host in the Las Vegas studio, and he chats from his home in New York.) Get just two sponsors, I've been told, and that can be a push. It can be difficult to tell whether it's a sports-handicapping or sports-talk show. With no notes, Barton's recall and attention to detail are impressive, even if the Chicago Bears fan's constant rebuke of Green Bay quarterback Aaron Rodgers might have grown stale, oh, years ago. Must be retaliating at the way Rodgers has absolutely destroyed the Bears over the seasons.

That droning aside, the forty-two-year-old Barton, via some extremely hard lessons, set out to alter the tout business, beam the spotlight on its shadiness and scampering cockroaches. For a month's service, he charges ninety-nine bucks. No frills. No extras. No special twenty-star diamond-jubilee selections with a much-higher fee. He never calls his clients; he doesn't employ a call center. He operates via email. If they like it, if they do well and make money, then, he says, let's do it for another month. Completely up to them.

He registers all of his plays online, on his website, which is decorated with different badges of excellence won from independent monitoring services. *Gaming Today* has called him a handicapper with integrity. When we talk, in the summer of 2018, he says he has had thirteen losing months over nine-plus years.

"I was on a pilgrimage to change the business," he says, "and I still believe that I am. I believe if I continue to pound the dirt . . . well, I don't care. This is how I do it. I've been in this business nearly ten years. I still think this can be a clean business. Reason and logic, you hope, eventually win. I think it will."

He was raised in Levittown, New York, the post–WWII subdivision of white picket fences and green lawns, whose affordable homes could often be assembled, in twenty-seven steps, in one day. *Time* magazine included creator William Levitt on its list of the one hundred most influential people of the twentieth century, but the progenitor of utter cookie-cutter housing monotony has more than a few detractors.

Barton is not one of them. He recalls near-idyll, kind neighbors, good friends, and a baseball hotbed, which stocked its two rival high schools (MacArthur and Division Avenue) with sufficient talent to make them well-known, even feared, in the Empire State. "I knew of the Levittown legacy, from a *Sports Illustrated* story," he says. "Looking back, [the original tract-housing subdivision] is how people know Levittown. But growing up, everything was dwarfed by baseball."

Ten years after getting accepted to Harvard, after getting sidetracked by his father's illness and business curveballs, he obtained a degree in history, with an emphasis on American history, from the esteemed institution's extension school. "Wanted to prove a point," says Barton, the Harvard grad. "Not the traditional path, but I got it done."

Mining value where others do not tread is an integral part of Barton's game plan. Belmont basketball, for instance, has paid fine dividends over the years as a mainstay pick. The Bruins, heading into the 2018–19 season, had recorded an incredible 100–8 record (92.6 percent success rate) at home over their eight previous seasons. That all arrived after their last season with three home defeats, in 2009–10. Including that 10–3 campaign at home and its four previous seasons (a 41–7 clip), Belmont is a resounding 151–18 (89.3 winning percentage) at home over the thirteen seasons before 2018–19. And the Bruins began the 2018–19 campaign by winning its first two home games, comfortably covering both favorite spreads.

## THE SKINNY

Professional handicapper Tom Barton has made a very nice living by looking where others don't, and part of his selection process includes Belmont basketball, the small school in Nashville, Tennessee, that is a member of the Ohio Valley Conference. In the eight seasons preceding 2018–19, the Bruins registered a 100–8 record at home, an amazing winning percentage of 92.6. Adding its previous five seasons, Belmont was an astounding 151–18 (.893) in its own building. A statistic like that is a gem to the wise bettor, a money-line option that can pay dividends, not just on a single wager for it to win, but as an addition to money-line parlays that are becoming more popular by the year.

Key stars aligned on Saturday, December 15, when the philosophies of Matt Youmans and Tom Barton collided, for me. Belmont played at UCLA, a clash of two Bruins squads that more than hinted at the home team not exactly knowing what was heading its way. An underdog getting only six and a half points, Belmont could have been figured to receive double digits, playing inside vaunted Pauley Pavilion. Instead, as Youmans has noted, that line in itself told the story. I had been tracking Belmont. It's precise and deliberate, something that has troubled always-athletic UCLA for decades. And Belmont backdoored its way to a 74–72 victory. I had the points, a money line of about two-to-one, and a teaser with an extra cushion tied to other legs that won. Yes, a very good day.

Barton has been on a bunch of those victories. Even as a favorite, as a money-line home play with that record, profitable returns have been inevitable. And using Belmont as a play in two- or three-team parlays, for those interested in such options and variety, enhances the payout.

"Anytime there is a money line [on Belmont], I'm going to jump on it," he says. "I don't mind paying for a trend like that. Who the fuck knows Belmont? I like Belmont. Might be the biggest game I ever played." He doesn't discuss the monetary figure. Bookmakers know of its success at home, so Belmont can be expected to be favored on its own court often, with some added juice—in points and maybe price—due to that success. That's what Barton refers to when he says "paying for" such a superb trend. Books might not even offer a money line on Belmont, but when they do Barton hones in on it.

He once made a big football score on Stony Brook, officially the State University of New York at Stony Brook, or more commonly SUNY-Stony Brook. You read that correctly. He was getting ten and a half points, but he disregarded that safety net; he put a bundle on the Seawolves on the money line, and they won, 23–3.

"Nobody had Stony Brook," he says. "People were like, 'I don't even know that team.' They won't bet it. I love small schools. Almost all of my successes come with small schools. You'll be hard pressed to see me betting on a Saturday night LSU-Auburn game. I'm probably not going to bet on that. If I do, it'll be a small play. I've made more money on Ivy League basketball in the past ten years than anybody out there. Why? Because nobody gives a shit about Ivy League basketball.

"I like to bet baseball. Why? Because I make money at it. For me, it's knowing the situations, knowing the trends—that's everything. I'm a giant trend bettor, but I break just about every rule that handicappers say not to break. I bet favorites. I don't care. Doesn't matter to me."

He, like Dave Cokin, played many of Colorado pitcher Kyle Freeland's home starts on the five-inning Under line, a winner in twenty-seven of thirty games over two seasons. Barton and I discuss Hawaii's crazy 2004 season, and the uniqueness of its Saturday home games, the last on the card, a chance to double up or get even. He agrees that it must be considered like any NFL game on Sunday or Monday evening.

"Put those games next to your card on a Saturday," he says. "Would you make the same bet? Would it be on your Saturday afternoon card? Would the *Monday Night Football* game be on your Sunday card? If not, then pull off it. No way you can touch that game. That is one of the soap boxes I stand on. People have too much of a problem NOT taking a play on those games. Sometimes, the best bet you make is the bet you don't make. I would much rather [customers] be mad at me because I didn't win them enough money as opposed to I lost them money."

We dig deeper into Hawaii football, its game at Army early in the 2018 season. The islanders' body clocks would tell them it's about seven o'clock in the morning at kickoff. Army had been pegged as a seven-point favorite, but it would be bet down to six in most books, five and a half in a few; many liked Hawaii and were paying for it. I favored taking Army, partly based on the visitors playing six time zones from home. Barton says that's valid.

"That is absolutely key," he says. "One hundred percent. There are statistics about West Coast teams going to the East Coast; East Coast to the West Coast doesn't mean a thing. West to East, even in the NFL; there are numbers that are massively in favor of the Eastern team, and you could just blindly bet on them. Army is a physical team, a running team, and Hawaii will be a little more tired, more jet-lagged, a little more out of their element, and now you have to go up against a team that will be pushing you around all day. And the whole country loves Hawaii."

On September 15, 2018, the Black Knights of Army defeated Hawaii, 28–21. I had teased Army down to a slim underdog, for more comfort room, parlaying that to some other winners. My sole goal is to cash tickets, nothing more. I aim to prove nothing, to pay no bills via my wagering exploits. It is just pure entertainment, always with money I will never miss. Risk a hundred on a two-team teaser, in which I get six points in my favor in both contests, to net eighty-three dollars and fifty cents?

Any day, with many perceived edges on my side.

Basically, the spread is too tough, on a weekly, monthly, and yearly basis, so I don't kid myself that I can beat it. I need that extra aid, and it often helps. I will come to call all such teaser parlays Roxy Specials, because if such an eminent figure condones it—albeit mostly on NFL home teams—I require no more golden stamp of approval.

Barton says he retains four or five clients who do not even watch sports, who view their relationship with him as investment endeavors. That's what Teddy Sevransky told me years ago; this is all about investment, no different than real estate, stocks, mutual funds, or a 401(k). Barton says he has an initial conversation with every potential client, to determine goals, what they want to accomplish.

"Having a goal is massive," he says. "I ask them, 'What are we trying to do here? What are you looking to do? What is the number you're comfortable with?' At that point, I can tell them how long it might take. One guy said he had just bought a new car, and its payment was three hundred bucks a month. 'I'd like to cover that,' he said. I said, 'It shouldn't be a problem, at a hundred bucks a game I should easily be able to get you up three units a month.' We were able to do that."

Barton has grown numb to the stigma of the tout industry, that so many are dirt-bag blowhards. He knows that, in fact, is the case. In a Saturday morning paid-ad Las Vegas radio spot, listeners are begged to call the toll-free line for a free play, which normally costs, says the annoying radio voice, twenty-five hundred dollars. The Vegas audience warrants such special attention? "Platinum-club plays, by the way, have gone 5–0, 4–1, and 4–1 over the past three weeks!" Another voice guarantees a winner in the Arizona State–UCLA football game, "whose line is off by fourteen points!" No worries if it loses, says the irritating voice, because then the rest of the college football season is free. Another declares, "I'm 19–0! That's one hundred percent!" A genuine math professor. "I'm on fire!"

Make the mistake of calling and your number is in the system. You will hear from these rakes so frequently you'll want to change your mobile number.

It's up to Barton, he says, to operate with proper decorum.

"If people didn't have a perception of this business and I walked up to someone and said, Here's my ten-year record of hitting over sixty percent, I'm part of monitoring sites, I've got championships . . . if you didn't know about the business, you would go, 'Oh, I'm one hundred percent in.' But the minute you hear about the business, people just assume that it's some kind of scam."

Anyone, he says, can do this, review notes and churn the proper research and watch games with a discerning eye, spotting what the commentators miss that is pertinent to a team and the outcome of the game. It's so ingrained into the fabric of his life, he posted a video of that day's selections outside the church, minutes before his wedding.

However, Barton advises that those with such an interest in "doing this" had best be prepared to do nothing else for the next ten years. Nothing. Else. "No job other than this. You won't have a life, generally, other than this. Be ready to tell your wife and kids 'I have to go downstairs and watch the game, because I'm working, looking at numbers, statistics.' It's a business. In a lot of ways, it can take the fun out of sports."

# THIRTEEN
# Against the Wind

PAUL STONE'S FATHER, RICHARD STONE SR., was irked and miffed, to put it mildly, when he discovered that his offspring had not just been gambling, but had been betting frequently, on sports. "Son," said the patriarch-lawyer, "there is no easy money to be made in sports gambling."

Decades later, the son has learned that no truer words have been spoken, unless Bob Seger is thrown into the mix.

"Dad was right," Paul says. "He was not too happy about it, but he was exactly right. And he *knew* he was right."

Doug Fitz can attest to the elder Stone's wisdom, too, especially in relation to a certain sport. In the middle two months of the 2018 baseball season, anyone in Las Vegas, or a neighboring state, who heard yet another ghastly howl just might have been experiencing the latest bullpen meltdown that affected yet another recommended play by Fitz.

In reality, the former police officer is far too congenial to let the outcome of a sporting event affect him in such an adverse, and public, manner. Stone and Fitz are similarly low-key, easy-going, and level-headed, attributes that no doubt aid their attempts to unlock the mysteries of making money at sports betting. They are touts, but they aren't, in their own unique ways.

\* \* \*

In thirty years as a police officer, in Cleveland and North Las Vegas, Doug Fitz had to draw his weapon so many times he could not possibly fathom an approximate figure.

Never, however, did Fitz have to fire the handgun.

"Lucky," he says as he slowly shakes his head. "Been shot at, too. But never hit. Just lucky."

So, someone wants to take a social-media shot at Doug Fitz for handicapping a baseball game incorrectly, for failing to recognize that the Brewers' bullpen was on the verge of yet another collapse? He will laugh for two reasons. First and foremost, he handicaps and releases plays for free. That's correct. Log on to his SystemPlays, and everything is gratis. His seasonal record in each sport is right there for the world to review. No charge. That, he admits, allows him to sleep like a puppy. He might err how he visualizes a game playing out, but nobody will lose an additional penny by having purchased that selection.

Which leads to his second reason.

"I just don't want to deal with" those who might buy an errant pick and fume to him about it. "I've dealt with crap, being a cop, from people. I've seen the bad side, the negative side, of people for thirty years, before I retired, and that's all I saw. I just don't need to deal with that."

By the way, Fitz can pick winners. He stands out as an anti-tout because of his benevolence, which he admits is driven by ego, but his work has drawn the attention of some important Las Vegas figures. The key connection was with Matt Youmans, who dubs Fitz "The Sheriff."

Five years after Fitz dialed up his interest in sports betting, he started his website, in 2006. Youmans was covering sports betting, among his various responsibilities, for the *Las Vegas Review-Journal* when he noticed Fitz's work two years later. Youmans was so impressed, he wrote about The Sheriff. He invited Fitz onto a daily radio show he co-hosted with Dave Cokin, with whom Fitz would eventually, at times, aid as a co-host, too. That led to Fitz being invited on the *Review-Journal*'s select pick'em panel during the NFL season, for which he's been a regular for most of ten years: he's won it twice, placing three times. He won the paper's 2017 college football bowl contest, when fourteen of his twenty selections covered.

A humble, good guy is how Youmans describes Fitz, who relies on systems and numbers, and was worthy of a shot. "I would give anybody a shot who isn't a fast talker or bullshitter, and Doug is not a bullshitter," Youmans says. "One thing in Vegas, you get real tired of people who are full of shit."

The sixty-seven-year-old Fitz is of average height, cropped gray hair, rose-gold wire-rimmed spectacles. Close your eyes and you'd swear you're hearing the calm, even delivery of Tom Brokaw, although he admits he has uttered "you know" too much, on the airwaves, in the past. His wife tries to convince him that he's only talking to Cokin (or Youmans, or her). Nerves, says Fitz. He has polished his delivery, but he has never promoted himself as a broadcasting veteran or a handicapping expert, rare authenticity in such a pompous business. He logs the immense work to be of some assistance to those who are interested in betting but do not have sufficient research time that is demanding and imperative.

He might have the connections to pursue an avenue in which he could peddle his picks, but that doesn't appeal to him for several reasons, the very top one being that, he assesses, ninety percent of that field is manure.

"Look, I'm a regular guy," Fitz says. "I want to try to impart knowledge and, maybe, some decent information to other regular people. I'm not claiming to have any more knowledge than anybody else, but there are some things that I've used that, I think at least, give me an edge, primarily from situational factors."

He moved from Cleveland to Las Vegas in 1985, and began dabbling in sports betting in a vague, uncertain way, like most residents. Hell, like most people. Fitz became more serious, though, and tracked his plays, sticking with what worked, discarding the fluff and fodder, outlining everything. He still does that today. He hands me four stapled sheets that serve as his guidelines, then rings me within a day to have me scratch two off that list; they hadn't passed recent muster, and he now considered them passé.

"Whatever the hell you're using," he says, "you oughta have something to back that damn play up, rather than saying, 'Oh, I just have *a feeling*.' And you better have some kind of sensible money management. In fact, probably more important than your ability to actually pick the games is your ability to manage your money. You should be betting the same amount on each game, per your bankroll."

This is so important it's an unwritten rule, superseding all other rules, a given for many bettors and critical for newcomers. Bet a hundred bucks a game, and you're 4–0 going into Monday night, and you feel so good about a side of that game "you bet a nickel," says Fitz, of five hundred dollars. "And you lose. Okay, so good for you. You went 4–1 on the weekend and you dropped money. See what I mean?"

## THE SKINNY

Another major rule, a given that many in this tome do not even mention, is when visiting a casino, have all the cash you will need already in your wallet, purse, or pockets. Tapping a casino ATM is as verboten an act as, well, doubling down on eighteen. In a locals shop, I found two discarded receipts from the same customer, eighteen hours apart from each other, with a fee of $3.75 attached to both. That's on top of what the person's banking institution will charge for not using one of its machines.

On the Strip, fees can be higher, much higher; I've seen one for more than $10. It's been documented that those fees make those ATMs fatter cash cows for the house than some slot machines. Beware. That first aforementioned receipt recorded a withdrawal of $300, the second $400, which reduced the patron's account balance to $55.27. Yikes, indeed.

Among Fitz's nineteen main rules, not playing a side and total in the same game is paramount. That would be tantamount to partaking in a parlay, and to anyone who is serious about making a long-term profit that is forbidden. (He is not against parlays and teasers, per se, but they are strictly reserved for recreational play—that's Rule Number Two on his list.) He won't wager on a game that has conflicting systems, and those systems must have simple, obvious advantages, few parameters with strong historical results and consistency.

"Consider both teams' relevant situational circumstances," is his sixth rule, and in number seven, "Pay attention to teams' tendencies and personality." Avoiding over-analyses (the Terry Donahue Rule), never laying minus-150 or higher on a money line, and never tapping into a system with less than a full season of results are high on the list, too.

## THE SKINNY

Handicapper Doug Fitz, the retired police officer and anti-tout who provides his selections for free on his SystemPlays site, has four pages of guidelines to which he strictly adheres. A site he most relies on is BetLabs, at which visitors can input specific game situations and have immediate feedback on the past performances; he will not wager on any play with less than an "A" grade. Moreover, he goes to BetLabs and StatFox for power ratings and statistics.

When a system's all-time winning percentage exceeds money-line or odds win-probability percentage, he strikes. If a play, say, has a long history of occurring half the time, and its odds are a plus price this time around, it's an obvious strike situation. If the true odds are fifty-fifty, it should be an even play, bet a hundred to win a hundred. Wager a hundred to win more than a hundred, when actual odds are dead even? Simple math, but the point is when such a value play can be had it must be played strictly on principle. They are rare.

Do this long enough and such a situation will blink like that famous sign at the south end of Las Vegas Boulevard at midnight.

In the NFL, Fitz will not lay double digits. In college hoops, he likes underdogs in the NCAA Tournament that sport at least a three-point power-rating differential in their favor compared to the spread. In baseball, in May and June, he targets home teams on the run line, getting a run and a half, with the spread between plus-102 and plus-115. The frenetic performances of bullpens in 2018 hardened his fourth rule—Don't Play Totals.

Upon his retirement in 2006, his hobby became his vocation. Now, if only he could pull the trigger more frequently when gifts present themselves to him with bows, wrapping paper, invitations, and steam whistles.

When Green Bay played in Detroit in December 2015, the Packers had soiled themselves for thirty-seven minutes and trailed, 20–0. The game went to commercial. Fitz was sitting in a sports book when he saw its in-game flash spread favor Detroit by nineteen and a half points. The Packers plus almost twenty points, with Aaron Rodgers, who had a sterling reputation as a comeback wizard? By the time Fitz had convinced himself to do something with that line, the game had resumed. That line had evaporated. The Packers would win, 27–23, on a bomb by Rodgers with no time remaining. Fitz did not recall the money-line odds on the Packers, during that particular timeout, to outright win the game.

"I figured Rodgers would come back," he says. "I didn't think he'd come back and win straight up."

In a more recent gaffe, Fitz pegged Virginia Tech football as the play getting six and a half points at home, in Blacksburg, Virginia, against Notre Dame. But it was no contest as Notre Dame won, 45–23. The Irish looked very good from the start, making Fitz consider taking the Irish and giving thirteen and a half points, during another in-game opportunity, to retain most of his bet.

"If you were watching, you *knew* your bet [on Virginia Tech] was lost. It was hopeless," he says. "It was pathetic. The Hokies didn't have a prayer of sticking with Notre Dame. I should have bought off on my bet, at least maybe losing a little bit of juice, in essence breaking even."

Can't be a wet chicken, Grandma's keen term, in Dostoevsky's *The Gambler,* for the group that just stood around the table as she won eighty thousand rubles at the wheel in Roulettenburg. The in-game nature of his operation requires some polish, but Fitz doesn't normally watch games in a book. He has apps for three casinos, but a part of him enjoys watching games at home and not searching for line movements, tapping away at his mobile phone every other minute.

Besides, he does most of his work days before the games, and that deliberation is what gets his full attention and money. Anything else is impetuous, even if a little voice might be whispering something to him between commercials. He's working on that aspect of his repertoire.

Fitz gives the NBA minimal attention during the regular season, and the playoffs only get a little bit of his action. Recently, he took heed to an angle that Youmans championed, betting on a team returning home—to win the first quarter and first half—in a series in which it dropped the first two games on the road. "I did a little research and, yeah, it was right on," Fitz says. Kiddingly, he told Youmans that he shouldn't have revealed the nugget on his Las Vegas Sportsline radio show, the one he did with Cokin before devoting the bulk of his waking hours to VSiN.

"The oddsmakers picked up on it. They claimed, Oh, we've known about that angle for a long time," Fitz says. "Well, okay. Maybe you did and maybe you didn't . . . they didn't! And I'll tell you why. The previous year, a six-point favorite was giving a reasonable three, or three and a half, for the first half. Well, in the [2018] playoffs, just as bookmakers said they'd known about that play all along, they adjusted it. That six-point favorite, for the game, was now giving *five* for the first half! In one game, the Wizards' first-half number was higher than their game number!

"And guess what? It *still* worked."

UNLV's football game at San Jose State offered another example of how Fitz operates. Two very bad football teams, and during the week an influx of money flipped the number, from the Rebels as slim favorites to the Spartans getting that attention. Over five-plus seasons, San Jose had covered fifteen of twenty-two games as a favorite, and three of those covers came against UNLV.

That's an "angle," Fitz says. He wants more information, a larger sample size that directs him to one side or another, a "system." I was on San Jose State, a favorite by two and a half points, which beat the Rebels, 50–37, but that was beside the point for Fitz. Too team-specific, too small of a sample size, he says. "I don't prefer those." Plus, he stays away from bad college football teams as if they were bubonic-plague carriers, so that weighed heavy on the aforementioned contest between very bad teams.

What he does prefer is a pattern that has played out over the years and is, say, 85–36 against the spread. He pays no attention to the Sharps-Squares, or Pros-Joes, debate. How, he says, can you tell? By size of wager? By who makes the bet? "A bunch of garbage," Fitz says. "Break down a hundred games; if you think one side is the sharp side and the other side is the public, or square, side, I would bet you over the long run it's about a fifty-fifty proposition."

Fitz's bottom line on 2018 would be something near a push if not for baseball, which lost nearly twenty-nine units over the course of the season, with a negative return on investment of nearly eleven percent. Specifically, June and July were wipeouts. Even more specifically, the sordid state of bullpens and managers' constant manipulations, the incessant usage of relievers, were mid-summer crushers.

"Motherfucking bullpens ruined my totals, and my run lines," says Fitz, getting salty for the only time in our extended conversations. "I include my team, the Indians. That used to be their strength. Just awful. Awful."

Run lines are a favored play of his because they remove the vig and their payoffs are much sweeter, even though they can turn sour with such shoddy back-end pitchers. And he will never, ever play a run line at a negative price, only even and, most commonly, an attractive plus price. "It's the amount of money you're saving on the juice," Fitz says. "I can't tell you how [minus–145] favorites I played on the run line; thanks to me doing that, I only lost a hundred instead of a hundred and forty-five. They lose straight-up all the time."

He has access to apps for the Westgate, and Boyd and Stations properties, because their MIOMI software, he says, allows a patron to make wagers on slips before logging into those sites. He likes the theory of Roxy Roxborough's two-team NFL home teaser parlay, but he's hesitant because the books are always making tweaks to safeguard their positions. Like the edge that the author John Ferguson, whose pen name is Stanford Wong, devised about teasing favorites of, say, eight points under those magic numbers of seven, six, four, and three; and doing the reverse when staking a claim on underdogs of two points, for example, to secure the three, four, six, and seven.

"They start gradually picking up on" plays like that, Fitz says, "and it goes into the line. It doesn't take them long to figure out, 'Hey, maybe we didn't think this was that crucial three years ago. But guess what? It's getting crucial, so we're factoring that into the line.' If you're not willing to adjust or adapt, you're doing yourself a big disservice. It will leave you behind."

Fitz is impressed by Cokin and other touts who receive remuneration for their sports picks. Not so much by their winning percentages or triumphant streaks, but by their thick skin. Inevitably, they will get one wrong. That's being kind. But they must forge forward. He has asked them, How do you deal with that b.s.? You're charging them money, and you can give them twelve straight winners, but if you lose two in a row, they'll be sending you emails—*You bum! What am I paying you for? You suck!*

"[Cokin] tells me, 'It's just part of doing business.' They ignore it. What else can they do? I believe that is the right way to go about it. I guess that's supply and demand. If you suck and you're giving out terrible plays and you're constantly losing. Well, I guess the market will adjust. People will say, Screw this guy."

Paul Stone admits that he lost money as a young man, betting on sports. "A *lot* of money," he says. "There's a learning curve. I have periods, now, where I lose money, too. You're not going to win month in and month out, year after year. I've used all those experiences. You have to hit some low points to be good at anything."

He is big on corollaries, which might be the artistic side of him, owed to his twenty-five years or so in the fourth estate. He spent as much time as a sports writer as he did scribing for the news division of papers in Tyler and Palastine, in Texas, and Fort Smith, Arkansas. The full-time journalism career closed about seven years ago. He and his wife have two side businesses, steady income that never requires Wisconsin to cover against Northwestern to pay the utility or grocery bill.

That would be too much pressure. He knows people who survive solely on sports betting, a roller-coaster existence that makes Stone cringe. However, having other forms of income does not make him immune from experiencing certain side effects common when placing hard-earned money on the Aggies to cover the number. Stone will endure bouts of sleeplessness, thinking about his selections, how he's determining them, and rain, sleet, snow, or wind. That damn wind. But the line is fine. Ultimately, he aims for an even, calm demeanor. He wants people to look at him and not be able to decipher whether he had just won or dropped a million dollars.

On a recent trip to Las Vegas, a friend had hinted that a buddy, a pro sports bettor, of his might join them watching games at the SuperBook. The man never made it. "He wouldn't leave his apartment," Stone says. "He was just looking at his computer screen, like a damn zombie, waiting on something to happen, a price to come up, a spread to change—and he'd tap in a big bet. Sports betting can affect a person's relationships, not only spousal but any type of socializing. Bettors can be isolated, detached, just consumed with their art so much that they don't participate in normal activities. I try to be more mainstream. You have to have a balance, the proper perspective and mental health to succeed in it long term."

In *The Odds,* the late handicapper Dave Malinsky said gamblers are by nature antisocial. "We'd rather not talk to anybody about what we do. In fact, it's kind of stupid for us to try and do what we do. So we don't want to tell anyone who may think we are stupid."

Stone talks about sports betting being a grind, how it's vital to know how to take a punch. He eases into an anecdote about Muhammad Ali.

"In his prime, with the rope-a-dope, he'd sit there and basically park himself against the ropes, especially in that Foreman fight," Stone says of 1974's Rumble in the Jungle. "He'd take punches, keep his head moving, absorb blows, and try to stay on his feet to fight another round. That's kind of what you have to do in sports betting. You have to be able to take a punch. You can't be short-sighted. And you're going to get knocked down several times."

Stone, fifty-six, began dabbling in sports betting when he started writing about football, collegiate and professional, in the early 1980s. In conservative Tyler, he aced masquerading the handicapping of a game as a thorough analysis of the strengths and weaknesses of two teams. In 1984, when he planned his first venture to Las Vegas, a friend told him there was only one destination to wager on sports—the Stardust.

He would visit several times a year, until the legendary property was leveled in 2007. Stone was no mere tourist, however. He often partook in its famous Sunday lottery; the Dust released the first college football spreads for the following weekend, and the lottery determined who'd get the first cracks at those numbers. Those in line, who were handed a playing card to determine the ultimate order, had to commit to at least a four-figure wager, eleven hundred dollars to win a grand. A dozen to twenty people would line up for the lottery on any given Sunday.

Stone has settled into the Westgate SuperBook since the Dust bit the dust, but he's known all over town. In March 2018, he rang Golden Nugget race and sports director Tony Miller to inquire if that establishment had posted a line on the summer's Ryder Cup golf tournament outside Paris, pitting Europe against the U.S. Miller had not established a number, but he vowed to have one up within two hours.

It was Europe plus-130, which Stone hammered. He aimed to keep betting the Euros at a plus price, knowing how the squad with the home-course advantage had been so dominant in that competition for so long. He figured the number would flop eventually, and then he would hammer the U.S. at a plus price, guaranteeing that he would make money.

The Euros, however, remained at an underdog price, through the start of the tournament, and Stone had kept laying money on the home side for the duration. "That turned out well," he says. "Europe dominated and won easily." Europe regained the trophy by winning seventeen and a half points to ten and a half.

Stone is anything but anonymous in Las Vegas, since he won college football handicapping contests at the former Leroy's, in 2011, and the Golden Nugget, in 2013. Heading into the thirteenth week of the 2018 college football slate, Stone, at 36–23–1, had a two-game lead (over Wes Reynolds) in a select ten-person panel of the *Review-Journal*'s College Football Challenge. He has participated in two-thirds of that paper's challenges over the past fifteen years. In a Golden Nugget college football contest, he had been leading most of the season until the Thanksgiving weekend, but he came out of it trailing first place by only a half game.

He had participated in the Westgate SuperBook SuperContest until 2013, when his success rate of sixty percent was rewarded with . . . nothing. He felt as if he had done all he could do, and he still finished a game or two out of the money. He says, "I was just making a donation." A record 3,123 entered that contest in 2018.

The Sports Monitor of Oklahoma, one of the few truly independent monitoring services, had recorded Stone as nailing ten of the previous eleven selections he had released to his clients at this writing. All of those plays pertained to college football, his wheelhouse; his specialty within that specialty is totals, and in that narrow window he had hit nine of his previous eleven releases, ten on Under.

He is a tout, but he isn't. Like many on all sides of the industry, he despises that word. "The word is a dirty word, and with good reason," Stone says. "Most people in the sports-service industry are unscrupulous. They lie."

He pays to have The Sports Monitor review his work. He is a regular VSiN guest; in his patient East Texas drawl, he disseminates games like a professor. However, as much as he's in demand by that innovative sports-gambling station and several newspapers, he is no marketing or promotions guru. In fact, it can be difficult to get ahold of him. He serves a select clientele, does not operate a website, does not pester his customers with unwanted phone calls, and he does not take credit cards; those customers can send him a cashier's check or money order, for his services, when they get around to it.

"Most are repeat clients, with long-term experience with me," Stone says. "I tell them the truth. This will be a grind. The Sports Monitor puts my release into their computer, and their system shows lines from seven major properties. You're graded, and you can't buy your record. Some think you can buy your record. With most touts, so-called touts, they make up their own monitoring agencies. No legitimacy to it at all. It's sickening.

"There are very few people in the industry who are on the up and up, who are honest, who provide a legitimate service. I hope I'm one of those small, small percentage of people."

Overall, on The Sports Monitor, Stone was 51–39–2, for a 2018 winning percentage of 56.57. Of those on the site who had made at least ninety selections, only two were faring better at this writing. Fifty handicappers were ranked below Stone in success rate. In five of the previous seven college football seasons, Stone registered a winning percentage better than the magical 52.38 required to show a profit, and three of those were better than fifty-seven percent; 60.67 in 2015, 58.89 in 2011, 57.28 in 2016.

"So if you hit fifty-two percent, over a large sample size—more than half—you will eventually land in the poor house," Stone says. "However, if you can take that fifty-two and raise it just two percent, to fifty-four percent, if you have a high enough volume of bets, and if you have a large enough unit size, you might eventually wind up in the penthouse. The difference between two percent, fifty-two and fifty-four, is being a prince or a pauper."

Veteran bettor Lem Banker has calculated the odds of being correct fifty-five percent of the time at six-to-one against the player.

"There are not too many people who will hit better than fifty-five percent, over time," Stone says. "In individual seasons, it can be accomplished. But over time, hitting fifty-five or fifty-six percent in a sport, you are, by every imaginable standard, an expert."

College football is Paul Stone's forte. Using a dull No. 2 pencil, a Big Chief eight-by-twelve writing tablet, and reams of printout paper, filled with statistics and references, and other materials, he works on his handicapping for a few hours most every morning. He digests at least one piece of information directly related to college football, whether from a website or magazine or other resource, every single day, year-round. At least once a year, he and his wife will visit a new collegiate stadium, even if it's the offseason and a janitor sneaks them in through a service door.

Stone is an amalgam of fundamental, situational, and technical approaches, picking and choosing what best fits certain scenarios, trusting his feel and experience to rank what matters most.

Weather is critical to his prognostication methods, something many others have not highlighted. Not long ago, he tracked the path of hurricanes, knowing the sloppy conditions they would produce in a time when those threats often would not lead to cancellations. That is different today, which he is not judging. But it was something on which he could once capitalize.

When the season deepens, and winter weather looms, he tracks snow and rain forecasts five or six days out. He also believes wind can be the most critical weather element. And his go-to source for such forecasts is Weather.com, with no other weather site—to him—deserving of mention. "The best there is," Stone says of Weather.com. "It's very, very accurate. I've used it for years now, and I feel very strongly about it."

## THE SKINNY

Handicapper Paul Stone should have been a meteorologist. He treats weather as importantly in a football game as the abilities of the two teams that will be taking the field. Rain and snow can dramatically alter performances, but, more than those two factors, wind is the dastardliest of equalizers, he says, and must

be included as a major component to the game. He will scout
weather days in advance, even in the hours before kickoff, and
pull the corresponding trigger on a game when he is certain of
his information. And for those details he only reviews forecasts
at Weather.com. Over many years, he has found it to be the
most reliable source for what Mother Nature is concocting for
a three-hour football game.

For Stone, prognosticating perfection arrived Thanksgiving
weekend, when Washington visited the Palouse to play Washington State in the Apple Cup. Stone knew days in advance of a
seventy-percent chance of rain turning to snow, with twenty-mph
winds. He followed the conditions, betting on the Under as the
forecast was reinforced by fact, right up to kickoff

The total of the game opened around forty-nine, most everywhere, and rose inexplicably to about fifty or fifty-one, depending
where customers shopped. The Huskies won, 28–15. Stone, whose
usual wager is between five hundred dollars and a grand, was all
over that Under.

"It hit on the money," he says. "That's when you feel like you
know what's going on, when something like that happens; it plays
out exactly as you had envisioned. That doesn't happen all the
time."

A week earlier, on VSiN, he had laid out a deliberate plan why
Iowa State's game at Texas would be a solid candidate for a first-
half Under, at twenty-three and a half points. Cyclones running
back David Montgomery would serve a first-half suspension, for
his extra-curricular antics from a week earlier, so a methodical
Iowa State offense would be even more plodding, Stone surmised,
to bleed the clock in the first thirty minutes, resulting in fewer
overall snaps, getting to halftime as quickly as possible and, hopefully, being in position to win it in the second half, with Montgomery.

The Longhorns led, 17–3, at the half, and they won the game
24–10.

Stone also pegged ten-point favorite Notre Dame to cover

against an overrated Syracuse squad (the Irish won, 36–3, at Yankee Stadium), Boise State plus two and a half points at home against Fresno State (the Broncos won, 24–17), and Ohio State in a very unusual position as a home underdog in its rivalry clash against Michigan.

"That was more situational and technical," says Stone. "Michigan, by every standard of measurement, had been perfect through its first eleven games. A person would have to pick Michigan. But in college football, more than professional, a team goes on the road and isn't the same. You are more likely to face adversity on the road, a tough situation; you get compromised a little bit. Things can snowball. I certainly didn't expect Ohio State to score more than sixty points, but you want to buy low and sell high, and Ohio State didn't have a whole lot of people lining up to buy them."

Before the season, many books release "Games of the Year" selections. The Buckeyes were favored by a touchdown, at least, over Michigan on those sheets. And after the first week of the season, the Westgate SuperBook had Ohio State listed as a nine-point favorite over the Wolverines. Now, in the run-up to the game, Michigan was favored by four points, in many shops, and that number just got bigger as kickoff neared. With Ohio State, that represented about thirteen points of value.

Ohio State won, 62–39.

"You want to get a bargain price," says Stone, who viewed that differential as immense value. "People were talking about how bad Ohio State's defense was, how bad its offensive line was, and [coach] Urban Meyer 'looks weathered, like he's going to quit coaching' . . . and everyone was saying Michigan is one of the best four teams in the nation, and they'll make it in the college football playoff. One team's getting pumped up, the other team is getting beaten down.

"Sometimes, it comes out differently than a lot of people think."

Another case in point, of nobody knowing anything, might have been Indianapolis's game at Jacksonville in the thirteenth week of the NFL season. At the SuperBook, ninety-nine percent of the money wagered on the game was on the Colts. *Ninety-nine percent.* The Jaguars won, 6–0. That wasn't Joes or Pros, but both, and both looked like chumps by sundown.

And sometimes, a solid historical trend just keeps rolling as a technically sound play. Stone mentions Kansas State under Bill Snyder. As an underdog under that longtime leader, the Wildcats were one of the best blind wagers in sports betting. In nine previous seasons, in Snyder's second go-round in the Little Apple, K-State covered thirty-four of forty-eight games as an underdog. In 2018, the Wildcats covered six of nine games as an underdog.

"That's over a long period of time," Stone says. "That's not just concentrated on a few in a row to start a season. As an underdog, it basically makes money every year. You take a step back, make judgments, and there's substance to that trend. They're a team, because of their status in college football's pecking order, that won't get as much respect as more notable programs, so they are constantly and consistently under-valued."

That gimme might have been altered on the second day of December 2018, when Snyder announced, after nineteen bowl games and twenty-three seasons coaching in Manhattan, his retirement plans.

Those were some exceptional calls by Paul Stone, but do not think that he is a sports-capping soothsayer. He only connotes such a statement when he is with a dear friend, and they're perusing the numbers at the SuperBook. Over those final few weeks of the college football season, he erred on Southern Methodist, getting seven and a half points, to win outright versus Memphis (the Tigers won, 28–18), San Diego State to cover a twenty-four-point spread at home against UNLV (the Rebels won, 27–24), and three-point underdog West Virginia to win outright at home against Oklahoma (the Sooners won a carnival affair, 59–56).

Stone reveals more when he talks about a friend who is in the Navy, serving on Catalina Island, and visits him when he comes to Las Vegas. "Other than me," Stone tells Jim, "if you don't think you're the smartest guy in here, you shouldn't be in here." Stone likes to joust with his pal, but even though it was said in semi-jest, there's some truth to that statement.

"You have to be confident," Stone tells me. "I don't know if it's eighty, eighty-five, ninety, or ninety-eight percent, but you will lose. You'd better be able to figure out how much you're willing to lose, for the enjoyment of it and the pursuit of it, the hobby of it. Or what are you going to do to be one of the rare winners?

"A lot of people get the numbers, the statistics, and don't know how to apply them. You have to know what to do with it once you figure out what's relevant, what's part of the process. You have to pick at it, study it, look at it inside out, turn it on its head, empty it out . . . you have to look at it from a bunch of different angles."

He suggests specializing in one sport, an area that has been of particular interest for years, and following it closer than ever, reading and watching everything that can be consumed. "It has to be a labor of love," Stone says. Comprehend the betting markets and the numbers, the fluctuations of the odds, what triggers those movements. "It's hard work. It's dedication. It's devotion."

To expand betting horizons, and the wallet, rely on others who are better-versed at other sports. Not people who you hope are good or talk a good game, he says, but people who are experts. "I have a guy for the Canadian Football League, the NHL, and other sports," Stone says. "I know very little about soccer. People say, 'I didn't even know you follow soccer.' Heck, I don't. But I know people who know it inside and out, and I've seen their results."

Respect the bankroll, the money, or suffer drastic consequences. A friend had taken two college football seasons to eke his profits up to two grand. For some reason, he felt the need to hazard it all on Notre Dame, a favorite by about fourteen points, over USC in November 2018; the Irish won by seven. Not a big deal, because his retirement cash-flow streams are many. It's a hobby. He does it for kicks. Still, it smarted.

"Don't get in over your head," Stone says. "The financial consequences can be dire." He links it to driving a Formula-1 race car, whose spark plugs must be clean, aerodynamics expertly en-

SPORTS BETTING FOR WINNERS 253

gineered, proper tire inflation, and the machine still must be piloted, around and around a track, at two hundred miles per hour.

"A misstep can have disastrous consequences," says Stone. "That's kind of like the sports-handicapping puzzle. Everything has got to be just right to be successful over a period of time. Mix it all up, and what some people consider I don't consider, what I consider some people don't consider. But both of us can be successful, or we both will be unsuccessful. There are so many ways to approach it."

In this new Golden Age, as technology appears to fuel every angle at hyper-speed, baristas and soybean farmers can still prove themselves as worthy sports bettors, playing the numbers like a concert pianist, making so-called professionals and self-styled experts resemble wet chickens, without even watching the games. Remember, the difference between a prince and a pauper—the penthouse and the outhouse—can be a gnat's ass, so check that vagus nerve, double-check those numbers, bet softly and carry a bankroll, the bigger the better. Heed the Bombay Sapphire–laced words of the fabulously popular former Las Vegas mayor, the ex-barrister to the mob—signage on his downtown steakhouse reads OSCAR'S BEEF BOOZE BROADS—who, like many, just hopes to figure out a winning system.

Stone segues to Bob Seger, a favored entertainer, and a certain line from a certain song that Stone believes sums up the sports-betting industry efficiently and succinctly. "In 'Against the Wind,' to which I've always referred as a newspaper writer and a sports bettor, there are deadlines and commitments, what to leave in and what to leave out. That is what it's about."

# ACKNOWLEDGMENTS

Since moving to Las Vegas in October 2002, with increasing curiosity I pondered how professional bettors operate, how they navigate and manipulate those tricky lines to pay the bills, what the nerves are like with the mortgage in the balance on the outcome of the Sooners–Mountaineers football game, and how the rest of the punting public just tries to turn a buck into two with anything remotely close to consistency? Finally, a hefty project provided entrée into that world. Fortunately, I had compiled enough credible contacts to begin that deep dive, which led to other insiders and experts, on both sides of the counter. At Kensington Publishing Corp., editor Michaela Hamilton championed this production, her support was unwavering, her enthusiasm and affinity for books relentlessly contagious, her colleagues model professionals. Every author should be so fortunate. Frank Scatoni, at Venture Literary, is an ace shepherd. In one fell swoop, he provided a rugged rudder, context that dissolved a threatening cyclone into barely a drizzle. (Frank, I hope you have indeed discovered that, in fact, the old man—his laughter and advice—is always with you.) Matt Youmans is a finer facilitator than John Stockton. How that Purdue IM hoops team failed to win the campus title with him feeding the Big Dog, I'll never fathom. This tome simply does not materialize without his key assist. I thank several insiders and experts, who chose not to talk about their gambling exploits, for indulging my repeated inquiries. To those who added insights and perspective, anonymously, you made this better. Van Smith, the opening of those private and prized records was extraordinary. *Gratias maximas*. To those who spoke for the record, I'm in your debt for your candor, and for tending to my repeated follow-up calls and emails. Too few people are as blunt as Lem Banker, as classy as Roxy Roxborough, as gracious as Jay Kornegay, as forthright as Ron Boyles, as unabashed as Kelly Stewart. Finally, to Tommy Fleetwood (18-to-1 winner in Abu Dhabi), Bubba Watson (40–1, at Riviera), and Bruce Koepka (20–1, at the PGA), my wallet thanks you for expanding it nicely-nicely in 2018.

# DIRECTORY

Optimal contacts—with Twitter handles, unless otherwise noted—and resources sure to enhance the sports-betting experience, starting points that could lead to other more nuanced or specific destinations, per taste or areas of interest.

**Andrews, Chris. @andrewssports** Veteran oddsmaker now at the South Point who imparts that wisdom to his feed and interacts, daily, with followers.

**Barton, Tom. @TomBartonSports** New York-based handicapper whose specialty, at TomBartonSports.com, is under-the-radar value, like Ivy League hoops.

**Baseball-Reference.com.** Invaluable for researching the histories of players and teams. How has Tampa starter Blake Snell fared in Yankee Stadium? It's here. How many winning streaks of at least six games did the Dodgers have in 2017? Right here. Clayton Kershaw in the last third of a game (innings seven, eight, and nine?) over his career? Yup. Here. All the major sports are under the "-reference.com" address. Vital.

**BloodHorse. @BloodHorse** Blanket coverage of the thoroughbred racing industry.

**Cokin, Dave. @davecokin** Longtime handicapper offers regular advice and opinions, and he updates his blog, at smokincokin .com, daily.

**Dewey, Todd.** **@tdewey33** *Review-Journal* betting scribe who knows the pulse of both sides of the counter, where the money is flowing, and who's profiting.

**Dye, Dave.** **@Dyedave** The former sportswriter logged time behind the counter, writing tickets, and taps that wealth of experience for *Gaming Today.*

**Everson, Patrick.** **@Covers_Vegas** Tirelessly provides a wealth of information, videos, and line movements, in real time, for Covers.com.

**Fezzik, Steve.** **@FezzikSports** An accomplished punter who can also be found on national radio spots and at pregame.com.

**Fitz, Doug.** **@fitz_doug** "The Sheriff," a retired police officer, doles out information and plays for free on Twitter and at Systemplays.com.

**FootballOutsiders.com.** A thorough compilation of unique analytics, from Bill Connelly, to analyze the best, and worst, of collegiate and professional teams.

**Fratto, Bernie.** **@BernieFratto** Concise, no-b.s. insights and suggestions laced with quality, and just as sharp with his movie reviews.

**Ginsbach, Jay.** **@FairwayJay** He writes for various publications and offers regular information on every angle of the betting scene.

**Holt, Matthew.** **@MatthewHoltVP** The Prez of U.S. Integrity, LLC, is a rich source of insights, especially on the fight games and college hoops.

**Kornegay, Jay.** **@JayKornegay** Stellar nuggets and opinions from the leader of the industry, the executive veep of the Westgate SuperBook.

**Michaels, Ralph.** **@CalSportsLV** The consistency of line information and historical context is beyond impressive for this WagerTalk.com operative.

**Miller, Tony.** **@Gollumlv** The sports-book director of the Golden Nugget is a Dallas Cowboys fan, but, please, do not hold that against him.

**OddsShark.** **@OddsShark** For trend breakdowns and tips, and a rotation of projections, at oddsshark.com, on the major games of the day.

**OSGA. @OffShoreGaming** For breaking news and betting insights, with a global view on the trends, games, and matches.

**PropSwap. @PropSwap** Ian Epstein and Luke Pergande's secondary-ticket market offers an additional hedging outlet that can lead to profits.

**Purdum, David. @DavidPurdum** ESPN's resident sports-gambling scribe covers that gamut of the business.

**Roberts, Micah. @MicahRoberts7** The former Vegas book director gives betting spins to all sports, but his forte might be NASCAR.

**Roxborough, Roxy. @RoxyLasVegas** Las Vegas royalty, who has donned every important industry hat that's possible to wear in the gambling hotbed.

**Rynning, Erin. @ersports1** The longtime bettor-handicapper is a Vegas radio regular, and those truly in the know place him in a select, respected group.

**Seeley, Nigel. @seeley_nigel** The Britain-based journo-punter offers fantastic *futebol* information, and his darts opinions are top-of-the-tree, too.

**Sevransky, Teddy. @teddy_covers** A Las Vegas radio mainstay, he's a part of the crew at sportsmemo.com and offers a wealth of information on a daily basis.

**Sherman, Jeff. @golfodds** As the moniker suggests, the Westgate SuperBook VP of risk management is a go-to source for all links-related minutiae.

**Steele, Phil. @philsteele042** Anyone who has flipped through his college football annual, THE bible of the sport, knows the importance of this follow.

**Stevens, Derek. @DerekJStevens** The rare independent hotel-casino mogul who does not shy away from publicity, or a big wager.

**Stewart, Kelly. @kellyinvegas** Parlayed a 2012 three-team money-line college pigskin parlay into fame, backs it all up at WagerTalk.com and elsewhere.

**Stone, Paul. @paulstonesports** Every college football enthusiast and punter needs to follow Stone for his even, insightful opinions.

**TeamRankings.com.** Go here for simple ATS and Totals updates on college and pro football, and other computations for other major sports. For college football, it goes back to 2003. It can be separated by conferences, and divided into specialty stats like After A Bye and As Home Underdog.

**Vaccaro, Jimmy. @JimmyVaccaro** The South Point senior lines-maker is a gem of a follow for stream-of-consciousness entertainment.

**VegasInsider.com.** Track point-spread movements, in Las Vegas and at select offshore entities. Get synopses of upcoming games and matchups, and past performances. Backtrack for quarter-by-quarter scores in collegiate and professional football.

**Veno, Rob. @robvenosports** One of several stellar handicappers to graduate, and blossom, out of former radio host Tim Trushel's "Sports Memo" family tree.

**White, Kenny. @KWhiteyVegas** His football power ratings might be tops. Whitey unearthed fixing shenanigans at Toledo in the mid-'00s.

**WhoScored.com.** A comprehensive guide for the world's top soccer leagues, Champions and Europa leagues, and World Cup. Includes live scores, statistics, comparisons and previews for upcoming matches, and news. Detailed histories show the past six matches between two sides, the best and worst aspects of each squad in the run-up to the match, and various odds and prognostications from the Bet365.com site.

**Youmans, Matt. @mattyoumans247** The VSiN writer and broadcaster is a must-follow for his deft acumen and keen vision, often weeks in advance.

# PRIMARY SOURCES

## INTERVIEWS

Lem Banker, Tom Barton, Ron Boyles, Dave Cokin, Todd Dewey, Ian Epstein, Patrick Everson, Doug Fitz, Michael Gaughan, Case Keefer, Kip Keefer, Jay Kornegay, Steve Lavin, Chris Maathuis, Vinny Magliulo, Luke Pergande, Jonathan Ribaste, Michael (Roxy) Roxborough, Nigel Seeley, Quinton Singleton, Van Smith, Steve Stallworth, Kelly Stewart, Derek Stevens, Jimmy Vaccaro, Sonny Vaccaro, Kenny White, Matt Youmans.

## PERIODICALS

*The Atlantic, Chicago Tribune, Epoca, The Financial Times, Gaming Today, The Guardian, The Independent, Lapham's Quarterly, Las Vegas Review-Journal, Las Vegas Sun, Nature, Nevada State Journal, New York Times, Omaha World-Journal, Pittsburgh Post-Gazette, Sports Illustrated, Tulsa World.*

## BOOKS

Atherton, Mike. *Gambling*. London: Hodder & Stoughton, 2006.

Banker, Lem. *Lem Banker's Book of Sports Betting*. Las Vegas: Self-published, 1986.

Charteris, Leslie. *The Saint Around the World*. Seattle: Thomas & Mercer, 2014.

Elliott, Russell, and William Rowley. *History of Nevada*. Lincoln: University of Nebraska, 2015.

Goodman, Oscar, and George Anastasia. *Being Oscar.* New York: Hachette, 2013.

Hall, William III. *Changing the Game.* Portland, Me.: Bookworm Sports, 2012.

Huff, Darrell, and Irving Geis. *How to Take a Chance.* New York: W.W. Norton & Co., 1959.

Manteris, Art. *SuperBookie.* Chicago: Contemporary Books, 1991.

McDougall, Bruce. *The Last Hockey Game.* Fredericton, New Brunswick: Goose Lane Editions, 2014.

Millman, Chad. *The Odds.* Cambridge, Ma.: Da Capo Press, 2002.

Mustain, Gene, and Jerry Capeci. *Murder Machine.* New York: Onyx, 1993.

Nelson, Warren. *Always Bet on the Butcher.* Reno: UNR, 1994.

Pileggi, Nicholas. *Casino: Love and Honor in Las Vegas.* New York: Simon & Schuster, 1995.

Sharpe, Graham. *Poker's Strangest Hands.* London: Robson Books, 2007.

———. *William Hill: The Man and His Business.* Berkshire, England: Racing Post Books, 2014.

Thompson, William. *Gambling in America.* Santa Barbara, Calif.: ABC-CLIO, Inc., 2001.

Vernetti, Michael. *Sen. Howard Cannon of Nevada.* Reno: UNR, 2008.

Winslow, Don. *Satori.* New York: Grand Central Publishing, 2011.

## WEBSITES

AmericanGaming.org, BaseballReference.com, BusinessInsider.com, BBCNews, ClarkCounty.gov, Covers.com, GangsterReport.com, Nevada.CasinoCity.com, NewsOK.com., VegasInsider.com.